—ON—
TRADITION

Scene from T. S. Eliot's *Murder in the Cathedral* at the Canterbury Festival (1935) in which the Knights confront St. Thomas Becket. Staged in the Chapter House at Canterbury Cathedral; directed by E. Martin Browne. Courtesy of the Cathedral, City, and Diocesan Record Office, Canterbury.

——ON—— TRADITION

Essays on the Use and Valuation of the Past

Clifford Davidson

AMS Press, Inc.
New York

Library of Congress Cataloging-in-Publication Data

Davidson, Clifford.
    On tradition: essays on the use and valuation of the past/
Clifford Davidson.
        (AMS studies in the Middle Ages: no. 20)
        Includes bibliographical references and index.
        ISBN 0-404-64160-1
        1. Arts—History. I. Title. II. Series.
    NX440.D38 1992
    700.9—dc20   91-57959
                                                                        CIP

All AMS books are printed on acid-free paper that meets the guidelines for performance and durability of the Committee on Production Guidelines for Book Longevity of the Council on Library Resources.

AMS PRESS
56 East 13th Street
New York, N.Y. 10003, U.S.A.

MANUFACTURED IN THE UNITED STATES OF AMERICA

Contents

Illustrations

(following page 113)

Frontispiece. Scene from T. S. Eliot's *Murder in the Cathedral.* Canterbury Festival (1935).

1. *Winter Light.* Scene from the film by Ingmar Bergman.

2. Adoration of the Magi. Painted glass, Great Malvern Priory Church.

3. Corporal Acts of Mercy. Painted glass, All Saints Church, North Street, York.

4. Placing Christ on the Cross. Woodcut, *Spiegel der mensche-liker behoudenisse*, chap. XXIII.

5. Crucifixion. Painted glass, York Minster nave.

6. Doom. Painted glass, west window, Fairford, Gloucestershire.

7. Brigittine Nativity. Painted glass, Great Malvern Priory Church.

8. The world upside down. Woodcut on title page of John Taylor, *Mad Fashions, Od Fashions, All Out of Fashions* (1642).

9. *Bonta.* Engraving from Cesare Ripa, *Iconologia* (Venice, 1669).

10. Interior of All Saints, Margaret Street. Photograph, c.1890.

11. Virgin and Child (nineteenth-century copy, altered in line with contemporary taste). Roof boss, York Minster nave.

Acknowledgments

My interest in tradition as a living dimension of Western culture—of its literature, art, theater, and music—dates from the 1960's, a time when in many circles the term 'change' was rather mindlessly adopted as a positive value at the same time that traditional elements of culture tended to be denigrated. My reaction to the turmoil of the 1960's should not be seen as hopelessly reactionary; instead, the kind of conservatism that I would espouse should be more or less consistent with the *fin de siècle* emphasis on conservation and on maintaining a world community that will preserve the earth's ecosystem. In short, my interest is in critical explorations that, on a more theoretical level, may lead to a genuinely viable preservationist aesthetic. Essential to my point of view is the principle that one must first of all have respect for the traditions on which Western culture is based before as a Westerner one can appropriately have respect for other cultures. Unfortunately, the past today seems on the whole neither valued nor respected, and the medieval traditions and accomplishments which form the foundation for the twentieth century are ignored. In academia, history prior to c.1500 is marginalized, while the Church, which boasts a continuous existence that quite literally depends on a succession of hierarchy and believers since the time of the apostles, seems to have turned its back on the practices of two millennia, in the United States often opting for "contemporary" music with mindless texts and inappropriate music incompetently performed in place of words and melodies which have sustained it for so many generations. But perhaps these comments seem too much like a jeremiad, and indeed I am anxious to present the essays in this volume in a positive light and not as merely negative reactions to the current cultural situation. There is little room, in my view, for sentimental antiquarianism if we are accurately to see how the past has been (and is) valued.

The earliest of the essays in this book was written in 1975 but has been reworked for the present volume. "Northern Spirituality and the Late Medieval Drama and Art of York" was prepared initially for a seminar in Western Spirituality sponsored by the Medieval Institute and the Institute of Cistercian Studies and subsequently published in *The Spirituality of Western Christendom*, edited by E. Rozanne Elder; I am grateful to Cistercian Publications for permission to use a revised version of that essay here. Other essays in this volume have been adapted from articles originally published in *Shakespeare Studies* ("What hempen homespuns have we swagg'ring here?"), *Papers on Language and Literature* (copyright by the Board of Trustees, Southern Illinois University) ("Jonson's *Bartholomew Fair*, Stage Plays, and Anti-Traditionalism" and "T. S. Eliot's *Murder in the Cathedral*: Reviving the Saint Play Tradition"), *Fifteenth-Century Studies* ("The Sociology of Visual Forms, Tradition, and the Late Medieval Theater"), the *George Herbert Journal* ("George Herbert and Painted Glass Windows"), and the *American Benedictine Review* (for a segment of the final chapter originally entitled "When Actors Play God"), and have been used in the present book with permission. The chapter on *King Lear* and medieval drama is the English version of an article initially published in French translation in the *Revue d'Histoire du Théâtre*.

I am also grateful for various other occasions on which I was able to present my work before academic audiences, among them the Colloquium sponsored by the International Society for the Study of Medieval Theater at Perpignan, France; the Medieval Mania: Perceptions of the Middle Ages conference sponsored by the Emory University Art Museum; and the Midwest regional meeting of the American Academy of Religion. So many individuals encouraged or criticized my work on aspects of tradition either appearing in this book or elsewhere that I could not possibly name them all, but I owe a special debt to Norman Reed Cary, Ann Eljenholm Nichols, Sidney Gottlieb, Dom Jean Leclercq, John H.

Stroupe, and those members of my Renaissance Literature course who helped me to clarify my thinking about iconoclasm and *Bartholomew Fair*. My wife Audrey has helped me to sustain my belief in the need for attention to Western tradition at the same time that she has constantly reminded me of the necessity of keeping an open mind to the non-Western world and its traditions—to the old as well as the new—and to her this book is dedicated.

Research which has informed this book either directly or indirectly has been conducted in many libraries and archives where librarians, archivists, and their assistants have been most helpful, and I am very aware of the great debt that I owe to them. In particular I am grateful to the University of Minnesota libraries, the University of Michigan libraries, the British Library, the Bodleian Library, the Warburg Institute Library, the York Minster Library, the Council for the Care of Churches, the library of the Society of Antiquaries, the National Monuments Record in London, and, last but not least, the Western Michigan University libraries. Sarah Brown and Gunilla Iversen helped me to obtain photographs included in the plates appearing in this book.

Financial assistance at various stages of the writing of this book came from grants and fellowships through the Division of Research and Sponsored Programs at Western Michigan University. The Medieval Institute gave substantial support during the period when the final version of the book was being written, and Earl Hawley assisted in the final stages of preparation of the computer copy.

1

Tradition and the Individual Scholar

There is admittedly a question implicit in the title of this introductory essay—that is, "Tradition and the Individual Scholar" may evoke the query "What has the individual scholar to do with tradition?" It is a query that does not generate an automatic answer, nor do I want to gloss over the fact that there is in the modern scholarly community a large contingent of those who are surprisingly hostile even to the idea of *tradition*, for, as Hans Robert Jauss has observed, modernity may itself be defined as "the ever renewed effort at self-definition by rejection of a past."[1] Frank Kermode may be correct when he insists that "the idea of tradition has never been so weak as it is now."[2] It is even common enough to encounter those —and this may be a peculiarity of the American scene—who are not only hostile to tradition but also to scholarship and research in themselves. When such persons appear in the university, research for them is something to be done cynically in order to achieve tenure and promotion—a pretense, if you will—and not the serious business of the committed academic. But my purpose in this essay will hardly be to analyze the sociology of American education, its successes or failures, its tendency in some areas to lose ground at the same time that it has elsewhere gained ground in the last generation—that is, in the time that I have been teaching in the university, which during some of these years, especially in the late 1960's and early 1970's, has endured periods of turmoil across the country. Nor do I wish to open up the matter of the relative value of various kinds of scholarship: everyone in the academy knows that some scholarly tasks are more valuable than others, and in some cases we have come to give undue weight to our own research and publications. But instead I want to take up a quite basic topic with regard

1

to scholarship—one aspect, at least, of what it is for: its relationship to tradition. This will be by way of providing some groundwork for subsequent chapters that will in turn largely examine instances in which traditional ideas and forms have been received into dramatic, theatrical, poetic, and artistic practice at a given historical moment.

In my view, one of the necessary functions of scholarship must be to have to do with tradition, with the cultural design of the society, with the historical as well as contemporary context in which we live, with the way in which the past *hands over to us* patterns of thought and behavior. This practice may not seem practical to some or useful to others. But must scholarship always be immediately applied if it is to have a legitimate function? I believe that we should beware of addiction to the immediately practical, the short-range goal, the kind of scholarship which we might conveniently bracket as *myopic*, and this can include the explication of texts for students as well as certain other contemporary approaches in the humanities. The American way is too often the adoption of short-range gains—and of long-term losses—a problem which academia shares with other American educational, industrial, and financial institutions in these final decades of the twentieth century. This is not to say that scholarship or research should not at any time be useful in the short run or that we should ignore practical solutions to problems which are of lesser dimensions. In this introductory essay, however, it seems appropriate to identify one role which scholarship needs to play—and in my opinion it is a vital role. Along with other functions, then, scholarship should constitute the means of discovering and hence of preserving our cultural roots, which can thus not only help us to understand modern cultural structures but also to assist us in preserving or even in "recyling" aspects of the past that seem to us to be viable. As the scholars of the Warburg Institute have taught us, then, our obligation is to provide a *cultural memory*,[3] which is the opposite of cultural amnesia or the loss of knowledge of our cultural identity. In other words, scholarship and tradition need to be seen as symbiotically linked in Western culture, though I must include here a disclaimer concerning the word 'Western' since I do not want it to be regarded as the only focus of all studies; it is merely that as Westerners we are obligated to start with our own cultural traditions, reminding ourselves that the West was insulated from other traditions to an unusual degree from the end of the fifteenth century until very recent times.

The hostility or impatience which often is so evident with regard to the idea of tradition—an attitude to which I have alluded above—is symptomatic of the persistent modernism that even dominates many of our learned societies today. Such an attitude is in part responsible for the controversy that erupted in the mid-1980's around a report on the state of the humanities by the National Endowment for the Humanities. While there is much in this report that should be questioned, and I would certainly quality the presuppositions behind its Western bias, I believe also that there is a healthiness about possessing traditional knowledge or about knowing the basis of one's still-living traditions. When we dissociate ourselves from our past, we become changed, but the change makes us like trees cut off at our roots. Such change, driven by the forces of ignorance, is loss—and, potentially, cultural death. I remember having my attention caught by a letter which appeared on the editorial page of the *New York Times* some years ago.[4] It was written by someone who had opted out from the academic scene after completing a Ph.D. and giving teaching a try. This disillusioned person, who had taught in a department of economics, charged that typical university students, so far from sharing Western cultural values, "are privy to a body of experience defined only by the perimeters of teen-age popular culture. Punk they know; history, literature, politics and the arts are beyond them." On the other hand, there is the "pressure to publish" felt by the faculty—a pressure which may issue into books and articles that illustrate how well "our trained minds have learned . . . to jump through formalist hoops," with the result that culture is left "to the sentimentalists."[5] Let us not, like the students described by this writer, disengage ourselves at our very roots culturally, nor ought we to become escapist, fleeing to discourse designed only to pose and answer questions of formalist interest only. There is also the danger that we might be tempted to become the modern equivalents of George Tesman in Henrik Ibsen's *Hedda Gabler*, an academic with the mind of a technocrat who can collect and classify but who lacks totally the creative spark.

It should be axiomatic that each age—indeed, each generation—builds on the previous one, and also that the structure of the present age is only so strong as its foundation—i.e., its past. But along the way there is of necessity a shift back and forth between health and decadence, between cultural strength and weakness. In no sense does culture automatically display a neat evolution from good to better, from lower to higher cultural forms. Instead, a generation paradoxically will need to reach back to previous history if any semblance of progress is to appear in the present. For the automobile to have been produced in the late nineteenth and early twentieth centuries, it was not only necessary to have the wheel which was invented in antiquity but also the moveable front axle that established the required technology for the four-wheeled wagon in the Middle Ages. For the modern flush toilet, we similarly seem to owe something to the Cistercian order of monks, who built their monasteries on running water so that their privies could have the natural advantage of constantly flushing water. For the computer with its word processing ability, we owe something literally to thousands of years of development, from the achievement of the new mathematics of the medieval period to moveable type to Benjamin Franklin's toying with electricity. Without a grounding in previous inventiveness, the silicon chip could hardly have been developed at all. Without its foundation in the past, the present could not stand.

Turning now to a consideration of ways in which scholarship has made contact with past traditions and has re-vivified them, I should like to point to a specific example from theater history. In recent years the thrust stage has become a popular development, even among college and university theaters. This staging configuration approximates the kind of playing area that existed prior to the triumph of the procenium arch stage with its picture frame effect, which in the presentation of English-language drama dates from 1605 when Inigo Jones borrowed the Italian innovation of perspective scenery for the *Masque of Blackness* at the English court.[6] Twentieth-century scholarship rediscovered that earlier kind of stage, which had served William Shakespeare, Christopher Marlowe, Ben Jonson, and their colleagues well. It was also, we need to remember, a stage which in turn was based on medieval vernacular traditions, on playing areas in the streets, in halls such as the great halls of the colleges at the universities, and in the outdoor theaters which we now know to have existed in Cornwall and East Anglia. Through scholarship, the thrust stage, particularly in its Renaissance manifestation, became the basis for new ideas about staging that broke down a modern innovation, the picture frame stage which held sway through the nineteenth century and into the twentieth century. The effect has been a very considerable difference in our cultural life. Except in television where we seem doomed to live with the picture frame and its attendant realism, knowledge about the early stage has been at once liberating and exhilarating. Fortunately, this kind of stage also determines that the events portrayed on it will be regarded with more seriousness—an important factor in seeing to it that the drama and stage are viewed as more than mere "entertainment."

For the Renaissance, scholarship also had learned to function as a mediating force between the past and the present. In architecture, the classic style recovered from ancient Greece and Rome tended to replace the modern or "Gothick" style. Such classicism was a counterpart of the Humanist ideology, which laid the groundwork for seeing cultural models in the past as the standard by which we might judge current accomplishments. Not only were buildings in the new antique style symmetrical and tidy in their structures, but also they conformed to the accepted forms and decorative patterns that had been laid down in classical times. In the earliest years of the nineteenth century, such taste still prevailed, even influencing domestic architecture in the American Midwest. Typical examples from the early nineteenth century are the building which became the Church of the Madeleine in Paris, the Copenhagen Cathedral (built after the British bombardment during the battle of Copenhagen had destroyed the previous cathedral in 1801), and the Church of St. Pancras in London. With the coming of the Gothic revival, however, the antique or classical style tended to be solidly rejected in favor of

what had once been the unfavored "modern" or "Gothick" style—
the style adopted for the Houses of Parliament in Westminster when
rebuilding began in 1837. It was discovered during the Gothic Revival period that this style with its flexibility meant actually a mix-
ing of once-rejected stylistic elements with new building techniques,
and that this union of old and new could produce structures which
adapted themselves to cultural functions in more satisfactory ways
than previously had been the case. There is, then, a connection between the revivification of architecture in the nineteenth century
through knowledge and use of past forms—for example, in the important Church of All Saints, Margaret Street, London, designed by
William Butterfield in 1849, which exactly suited the liturgical
functions for which it was designed[7]—and more recent architectural
successes, which likewise use light and height for good effect and
organize space for the intensification of whatever human acts are intended within the structure. The architectural precept that form
should be consistent with function is, of course, associated with the
names of the Americans Louis Sullivan and Frank Lloyd Wright.
But both men owe much more to tradition than they would have admitted. Wright's houses are, as those who have lived in them can at-
test, much more than mere "machines for living" just as Butterfield's All Saints Church is more than an acoustical and visually
oriented machine for music and liturgy. Buildings provide interior
space in which we live and act out the majority of our traditions,
and they perform their functions best when they remain in touch
with past architectural traditions though not when they are pedanti-
cally bound by conventions, as in the case of the Church of St. Pancras or the so-called ranch style house, the latter a representative of
the forms and principles of prairie style architecture in a state of
decadence.

   Can we say that there is an advantage—nay, even an obligation
—to restore the essence of the old forms, which, however, must
never be blindly replicated? Tradition, if it is to be a living principle, requires the handing over rather than the handing down of past
structures, past ideas, and past ways of acting and reacting. Thus the
Church Fathers had understood by the term a vivifying process rath-

er than a betrayal of the present to the dead letter of past usage.[8] In the history of culture, we therefore have something very different indeed from an evolutionary development from less complex to more complex forms as civilization allegedly progresses. In fact, we do not with any certainty ever experience progress as a necessary condition: regress may be no less common. Positive development, rather than decline or decadence, seems difficult to achieve without an awareness which scholarship may bring to culture. There is thus nothing inevitable at all about the evolution of culture: new standard grade American wine is not necessarily, even with the help of additives and chemicals used to achieve uniform taste, superior to a good estate-bottled wine made in the same way that wine was made five hundred years ago. Old wine-making techniques that have been handed over generation after generation, then, do have the advantage. The corollary is this: change is loss, at least potentially.

There should be general agreement, on the other hand, that to insist on the inevitable truth of the maxim "change is loss"—that is, on the radical devaluing of innovation—must be as suspect as the notion that change is by definition a positive force in society. In no way does it make sense to agree with the Emperor Julian the Apostate, who insisted: "Innovation I abominate above all things."[9] A scholar, even one who is studying traditions of the past, should be able to take advantage of such a modern innovation as the computer, which simplifies the task of writing, makes possible more complete and accessible indexing, and quite effectively reduces the cost in time and secretarial help of doing research. The computer, which is an invention of our time, however, does not restore the soul. It is a tool, as important in its way as any number of medieval innovations, including: the horse harness, which displaced less efficient oxen for farm work and hauling; the new type of plow, which, by turning over the soil rather than merely scratching it, increased agricultural productivity and helped to provide the basis for an increased population in Europe;[10] or the clock, which made possible the exact measurement of time and thus cleared the way for the chronomania of the modern factory as well as for a significant proportion of our modern science and technology. Nevertheless, when modern innovation is as unsatisfactory as the so-called electric organ—reputable organ builders rightly call them "electrones"—no addition of silicon chips or integrated circuitry can make them the equal of the mechanical-action instruments that Johann Sebastian Bach played and for which he wrote. It is scholarly knowledge of these earlier instruments, not technical gimmickry, that has revitalized modern organ building since World War II.

Musical instruments designed for orchestra or band have, as we know, become fairly standarized. Even the best eighteenth-century violins, which have not been equalled by modern makers, have been modified to alter the sound according to modern taste—a taste only recently questioned. But scholarship, including research into the iconography of musical instruments when no physical examples exist, has helped not only to rehabilitate earlier designs but also to bring back an amazing array of highly successful early instruments, the best known of which is the harpsichord, which is first recorded in iconography in a fine example on the choir screen at York Minster about 1420.[11] Usually such instruments when re-created by modern makers are called "reproductions," but there is no reason why a medieval rebec or a Renaissance viola da gamba is any more a reproduction than a recently-made violin or bassoon or piano. The model chosen for reproduction simply happens to be different from what is accepted as a so-called modern instrument, or in some instances the builder must rely almost exclusively on the study of early pictures in order to fabricate his instrument—a process that takes more imagination and skill than, say, in the instance of a modern clarinet being assembled in a factory, at least if the result is to be a viable musical instrument. By reading back into the past, modern builders and musicians have added a rich orchestra of sound to the concert hall—adding indeed the possibility of reclaiming additional centuries of our musical heritage beyond the mostly modern music of the nineteenth and twentieth centuries—which is not, of course, to undervalue such modern music. At the same time, research into instrumental and vocal styles and the preparation of playable and singable editions of early music have likewise made us all more sophisticated in our musical taste, which no longer is required by circumstances to be limited to the contemporary and near-contemporary repertoire—that is, the music of the past two centuries. Instead of having our operatic taste, for example, confined to Puccini and Verdi—or, at the earliest, Mozart—we can, as Noah Greenberg and E. Martin Browne taught us years ago, even add the medieval music-dramas—for example, the plays of *Daniel* from Beauvais Cathedral, *Herod* from the Fleury Playbook, the *Sponsus* (*The Bridegroom*) from St. Martial of Limoges, or the inspired *Ordo Virtutum*, the latter the first music-drama for which a composer is known, Hildegard of Bingen, a remarkable woman of the Middle Ages.

The studies which follow in the present book naturally cannot treat all the issues which I am raising in this introductory essay, but I shall nevertheless strive to show a few ways in which scholarship can bring understanding to traditional knowledge and forms as they occur and recur in literature, the theater, and the visual arts. But there is also a difficulty in translating the past into the present—a difficulty which is in part sociological and in part theological, especially in the case of the greatly changed middle class culture that has developed since medieval times. It seems therefore reasonable to pay full attention to the contexts in which early forms, especially theater and the visual arts, existed, for to read these like modern manifestations will only lead to a parodying of the spirit of the original examples. We may call to mind here the British National Theatre's production of *The Mysteries* which transformed the medieval mystery plays into a six-hour show complete with popular music, fork lifts, and miners' hats. The program sold at the performances cited *The Staging of Religious Drama in Europe in the Late Middle Ages*, edited by Peter Meredith and John Tailby,[12] a scholarly collection of translations of stage directions, documents, and other sources of information about medieval staging. Very possibly this book was influential when the staging plan for *The Mysteries* was being drawn up, but in no sense does its scholarship justify the parodying of medieval forms and the patronizing of early theatrical traditions present in the production. Yet Shakespeare, in *A Midsummer Night's Dream*, does in fact patronize medieval drama in a rather wonderful way. Shakespeare apparently knew the medieval civic drama and the conditions of its production from his childhood, and uses it to good purpose in the play-within-a-play presented by the "rude mechanicals" before the king. Ironically, of course, his own theater and its practices owed a great deal to the very traditions that he ridiculed in this play.

Shakespeare's debt to medieval stage traditions is indeed very great, and hence deserves careful analysis, especially since it is through his plays that most modern audiences and readers have tended to come into contact with the the ancestral voices of the medieval theater. As I have argued elsewhere, the cosmic dimension so often remarked upon in Shakespeare's plays needs to be recognized as a part of the medieval heritage which informed his theater.[13] Shakespeare's plays, particularly his tragedies, are at once treatments of cosmology, history, sociology, religiosity, and politics—and all interpenetrate. And their effect when presented on the actual stage was at once verbal *and visual*. The spectacle of this drama, though sometimes indeed savage in the manner suggested at the murder of Julius Caesar where a ritual of sacrifice has gone awry,[14] nevertheless is not disconnected from the realm of transcendence, a factor unfortunately often thoroughly denied in secular productions in our time. That which Shakespeare received from the medieval stage, therefore, we need to examine with great care, for by such a scholarly and critical route we may come to see how traditional aspects of staging, of aesthetic response, and of dramatic form have been made available to us in dramatic works of the greatest intensity.

Shakespeare's contemporary, Ben Jonson, was in spirit a classicist, much more in touch with the pre-medieval literary and dramatic traditions toward which the humanists of the Renaissance were reaching in their study. But he was also strongly enough attracted to medieval religious traditions to become for a number of years a Roman Catholic. Jonson was thus acutely aware of the resistance among certain men of his time to traditional lore, including folk customs. The anti-traditionalism of radical Puritanism, which had begun to reject the stage and which would also be at the forefront of English iconoclasm, was in Jonson's opinion a threat to good sense. His *Bartholomew Fair* may thus be read as a document opposing the anti-traditionalism of many of his contemporaries.

To turn from the Renaissance stage, especially its debt to medieval traditions, to lyric poetry, we find George Herbert, the reputed high churchman, striving deeply toward immersion in traditional liturgical forms, though these were forms which he felt required cleansing of the impurities of pre-Reformation times. The concern of Herbert and others like him in the seventeenth century was to receive and use the traditional worship of the Church for spiritual enlightenment—and such worship involved the role of the church building in a very real way. Ecclesiastical architecture is in Herbert's view the setting for some of the most profound experiences of life, and it is an architecture inherited from the Middle Ages and only slightly changed by the English Reformation except for the removal of images, wall paintings, and other accouterments of Roman Catholicism. Herbert's religion therefore was in practice a purified (but hardly a Puritan) catholicism, a recognition that worship was a poetic and traditional act of meditating and presenting oneself before the ultimate realities of the universe and before its Creator.

Just as persons in the sixteenth and seventeenth centuries were impelled to look to tradition on account of their feelings of insecurity in the face of changes that had taken place both politically and religiously to alter English life, so also in the nineteenth century when the industrial revolution, even bringing new modes of transportation to the country to link it radically together in a single network of rail travel, was threatening to overturn an entire older way of life, there would be a turning to tradition. At this historical moment the return to tradition came most significantly in the Oxford Movement and the Cambridge Camden Society, both of which were to affect the religious life of the nation and, in those days of empire, much of the rest of the English-speaking world. But there were also other effects, such as the effect on architecture already mentioned in this essay, and, though it is a subject outside the scope of this book, the medieval guild system had a profound influence on both the trade union movement and socialism, which in its non-Marxian manifestations demanded democracy and guarantees consistent with the Corporal Acts of Mercy specified mainly in the twenty-fifth chapter of St. Matthew's gospel.

The interest in medieval traditional forms evidenced in T. S. Eliot's *Murder in the Cathedral*, recognized in spite of its flaws as one of the outstanding plays of the century written in the English language, is an offshoot of scholarly investigation of medieval drama, which began to a large degree with the preparation of texts for purposes of studying the language—a study which ultimately led to the monumental *Oxford English Dictionary*. At the time this play was produced, there had been few serious revivals of medieval drama with the exception of William Poel's rather eccentric *Everyman*. Even in this case the placing of God on stage in the form of Adonai, albeit wearing a rather strange-looking costume, was controversial from a legal standpoint, and it was not until much later that we have the active revival of medieval drama in both England and America.

While the essays in this book in no sense can pretend to cover every aspect of the topic which I am introducing here, they have nevertheless been written as modest contributions to a literature of the aesthetics of tradition. It is time that the twentieth century, now in its *fin de siècle* phase, should start to come to terms with the issue of tradition, which ought to be the intellectual counterpart of the conservationist movement and the thoroughly legitimate focus on ecology. These matters are interrelated. Rachel Carson's forecast of a "silent spring" is not irrelevant to our concern with a past which provided the basis for the present. Acid rain, for example, affects stone buildings and stained glass as well as trees, and there is also another even more corrosive element—a cultural hostility—that may lead to rootlessness and social insecurity. This has happened in other cultures, sometimes through the intervention of colonialism in so-called Third World countries where now neither local and inherited traditions nor Western values are able to provide the cement needed to tie the society together in a workable way.

As no one will fail to recall, it was Henry Ford who insisted that "History is bunk." We need to take the diametrically opposite view if we are to establish a viable preservationist aesthetics. History, including the history of drama and the other arts, visual and musical, is important to us, for these things are a part of our cultural heritage. Separated from this cultural heritage—that is, from our *cultural memory*—our modern age is like the proverbial house built on sand rather than on the foundation of past traditions. It is not possible for us to live in the present alone as if our age were self-generated. Such a view is, I realize, contrary to the thinking of those who seem to believe that all past events and past forms have been used up, consumed, relegated to the "ash heap of history." This terminology, "the ash heap of history," is, I feel, extremely disconcerting; it was, if Harrison Salisbury is correct, first used by Leon Trotsky in 1917 during the Russian revolution,[15] but it was used also in recent years by none other than the Chief Executive of the United States, Ronald Reagan. There was, during Reagan's Presidency, a real danger of nuclear holocaust since the world had developed its own death machine capable of annihilating the human race. But we are now discovering that in many other ways as well this wonderful "pendant earth," of which the poets have sung and of which even astronauts in their way have waxed eloquent in their descriptions, may be threatened with apocalypse. While apocalyptic thinking was highly visible in the past—for example, among early Christians who expected the imminent arrival of the Parousia, the medieval thinkers and people who expected the end of time to come without any great delay—the end of time is now a potential reality, and it could occur quickly through a renewal of international hostilities leading to a nuclear exchange or over a longer period through ecological irresponsibility joined with other factors such as overpopulation. Both possibilities are sufficiently horrifying, it seems to me, and in the light of such eventualities we need to see our cultural traditions—and the cultural traditions of other peoples—as all the more precious and worthy of saving and improving.

Just as in the West there is a tendency to deny death—and this may be done through fantasizing of the kind that can be observed every night on television—so also there is a surprising inclination among scholars in the humanities to avoid the potential question of the demise of all traditions. If, as Seneca and Jesus insisted, we should live as men and women expecting not to live forever on this globe which is the earth, then we must also now come to terms with the larger mortality that threatens both humans and their traditions alike. The human condition, often insulated from the larger reality within the ivory tower of academia, may be best described after all by a story, retold in the *Golden Legend* (as translated by William Caxton, the first publisher-printer to set up in England); in its original form, it was a story about the Buddha from India—a story here Christianized and yet marvellously rich with Eastern wisdom.

The story is about a hermit, here called Barlaam, who speaks to a pagan king of India and tells this parable, explaining that there are those who are

> lyke to a man that fledde before an vnycorn that he shold not deuoure hym and in fleyng he fyll [fell] in a grete pyte and as he fyll he caught a braunch of a tree with his honde and sette his feet vpon a slydyng place, and thenne [saw] two myse that one whyte and that other blacke: whiche wythout cessyng gnewe[d] the rote of the tree, and hadde almost gnawen it a sonder. And he sawe in the bottom of thys pytte an horryble dragon casting fyre and hadde his mouth opene and desyred to deuoure hym. Vpon the slydyng place on whiche his feet stode he sawe the hedes of four serpentes whiche yssueden there: and thenne he lifte[d] vp his eyen and sawe a lyttyll hony that henge in the bowes of the tree: and forgat the perylle that he was in and gaue him all to the swetenesse of that little hony.[16]

The unicorn, as the *Golden Legend* explains, "is the fygure of deth whiche contynuelly foloweth man and desired to take hym." For the rest, there is no need to follow the explanation of the allegory in the *Golden Legend*; in this instance it may suffice if we should supply our own explanation of what this parable might mean to us in our own time and in times to come. In the study of cultural traditions, we might thus apply the suggestion that the honey is formalist scholarship and criticism that withdraws tradition itself from its rightful context, or it may be whatever exists in modernist culture that makes us forgetful of the slippery cliff on which we as a race seem to be stranded. There may be a deconstructionist solution to the dilemma here, but I suspect that it will not help very much.[17] If there is to be a way off that cliff, it must be by facing the specter of the unicorn, which also in medieval iconography was a symbol of salvation. In this effort, our traditions can be of the greatest help; at least they can offer hope where before there was only an avoidance of the realities of existence or, even worse, a condition which psychologists have labelled a "sense of radical futurelessness."[18]

I offer scholarship and research into past traditions not as a solution to all problems, nor as the source of pseudo-religious salvation, but as a remedy which may help us to make contact with history, to re-vivify the present, and to give us hope for the future because we have faced the unicorn of death—the unicorn which is also the symbol of life and of rescue. For we are not autonomous creatures, self-generated, existing in the moment without the necessity of being brought into being by the past. No age, no culture is an island unto itself; like the final plays in the famous civic Creation to Doom cycles on the medieval English stage, our personal experience is required to flow into general concern about the end of time itself.

But, most of all, our personal experience and concern should certainly not be disjoined from our scholarship and our research, which need to be seen as conserving forces which can join the present and past together and achieve a life-giving union of past and present—a union which can even, let us hope, affect the future. Such an endeavor becomes, if we may borrow the words of Edmund Burke, "a partnership not only between those who are living, but between those who are living, those who are dead, and those who are to be born."[19]

The endeavor to which I have addressed myself in this essay may seem to some to involve an unnecessary burden. The task is one that requires energy and hard work—and personal sacrifice—and it requires a break with the comfortable concept of the scholar as a gentleman or lady of considerable leisure. More important, because the "sense of radical futurelessness" may seem to prevail, or because the contemporary crisis of faith may appear to immobilize us, we need all the more urgently to put away our historical forgetfulness. The essays in this book are only forays into the field—mere excursions into the consideration of tradition from the standpoint of those who are living in it and creating art, and of those who look back on past traditions worthy of preservation or revival.

In the final analysis I am reminded of the priest of the Church of Sweden dramatized in Ingmar Bergman's film *Winter Light* (1961)—a man physically ill (he has the flu) and suffering even more deeply from the crisis of belief which has overtaken him and the modern world (fig. 1). Yet at the conclusion of the film where the pastor is faced with an empty church at Fröstnas where he has gone to conduct a service at sundown—both the name of the church and the time of day are important aspects of Bergman's symbolism—he signals to the organist to begin and proclaims the traditional words which open the Swedish Mass: "Helig, helig, helig är Herren Gud allsmäktig. Hela jorden är full av hans härlighet" ("Holy, holy, holy, Lord God Almighty. All the earth is full of his glory").[20] The power of this moment in the film is a reminder that the old forms retain immense energy and that they have for us a significance even in the face of our rational doubts and our cynicism. Furthermore, the old forms—ceremonies and traditions—may stand opposed to the despair imposed on our world by anti-traditionalist attitudes and ideologies which would perverely see the past as used up or as something to be tossed onto the "ash heap of history." In Bergman's film, tradition is able to heal (though only momentarily) the fractured life cut off from the past, present, and future. So it seems to me to be the obligation of the individual scholar to recognize in tradition a restorative presence and more a permanent force for continuity in a world that is broken, alienated, and isolated from its own past as it is also frightened of its future.

2

The Sociology of Visual Forms, Tradition, and the Late Medieval English Theater

A first step in any scholarly endeavor which aims to focus on traditional forms, whether theatrical or of one of the other arts, would seem to be the understanding of the social and religious context in which those forms arose and were sustained. With regard to the theater, there is indeed an urgent need to develop a sociology of visual forms as these provided the core of theatrical experience, at least in the religious stage for which we have textual evidence. (The pre-sixteenth-century English secular theater is, unfortunately, very nearly lost to us because of the absence of texts.) This sociological examination is needed because the theater's traditions cannot subsist in the actors, playwrights, and directors alone; the audience, sponsors, and patrons are also vital to the process of drama.

Drawing on the work of Hans Robert Jauss, C. Clifford Flanigan, in a paper that remains unpublished, has underlined the importance of audience expectations in the reception of drama in medieval as well as in modern times.[1] Audience expectations may, as Professor Flanigan has insisted, even determine the genre of a medieval drama—that is, the same text might be produced and received as a rite or ceremony at one time and place, and at another it might be understood as drama or play. If we are to accept the validity of this observation (as I think we must), then we will recognize that our historical scholarship requires adequate attention to the social and religious context if we are to achieve a viable approach to dramatic texts, whether the music-drama to which Professor Flanigan was referring in his paper or the vernacular drama that was increasingly popular in the Europe of the later Middle Ages. But not only does genre depend on that context, for also the function of the text in the

17

process of being produced or staged demands that it be tied to the visual scene or iconographic tableau—a scene or tableau likewise bound by the time, place, and culture in which it is displayed. The entire work, both the words spoken on the stage to be heard by the audience and the spectacle that is seen, is not in fact something autonomous, but rather is the result of a "reciprocal interaction" between text and the community which brings it into being and/or observes it in performance.[2] The *function* of a text, therefore, sometimes cannot be fully determined from internal evidence alone, but needs verification by appeal to other kinds of evidence.

Yet in the methodology involved in such study, there remains the danger of a kind of circularity which it may be wise to mention at the outset. The text is one of the sources of what we know about the community (or, in the current jargon, the "larger semiotic system") in which the play arose and received performance, and at the same time the community traditions and practices must be understood in order for the text to be explicable.[3] The external evidence which we would desire to have is not always possible to recover, and we need in these instances to beware making assumptions merely on the basis of current thought and practice. This is especially important because the community in which we now live, in spite of the fact that it is historically based on the cultural patterns of the Middle Ages, is distinctly different, for example, from either the Benedictine monastic communities of the twelfth century or the urban communities of the late Middle Ages. While the former was nourished on the traditional monastic liturgy—the Offices as well as the Mass—within the setting of contemporary monastic spirituality, the latter was characterized by civic practices and civic piety that are quite different from the forms we encounter in our own time in city or town. However, while a twentieth-century monk might be able yet, perhaps with a certain amount of difficulty, to fit himself into the monastic milieu of the twelfth century if it were possible for him to return to that earlier time, the contrast between urban culture of the fifteenth century and that of our own day is immense. The difference is first of all one of orientation in the world. Space and time were regarded in significantly different ways,[4] and the visible world itself was seen as a mask for the numinous world of transcendence rather than as a mechanical contrivance explainable by scientifically defined laws. Further, the social organization of the medieval city differs radically from that of a modern city, as urban historians such as Charles Phythian-Adams have demonstrated;[5] a modern person, either a working-class factory worker or a modern academic, would find himself or herself to be hardly at home in a tightly organized medieval city such as Coventry or York or even London. We can focus our scholarly attention on medieval cities, therefore, but it would be quite impossible to return to the exact conditions or traditions under which the plays were originally produced in their streets. Nor can we ever hope to replicate the audience response of earlier historical periods exactly, since our social and psychological and religious experiences are necessarily not the same as those of earlier members of the audiences watching these civic plays—plays which have, however, been very successfully staged on both sides of the Atlantic in recent years.

When we examine the visual expectations which a medieval audience would have had, we find that there is a degree of consistency that we can define for a given date and place. Our discoveries of such patterns in visual design are derived in part from descriptions in texts, but even more from the surviving examples of the visual arts. If we wish to achieve an understanding of the importance of the visual dimension of medieval religion and medieval art, then, it is important that we should not attempt to impose modern preconceptions on these products of earlier cultures, though they are cultures which indeed provide the historical basis for our modern culture—and we need to avoid the kind of condescension to be observed in Keith Thomas' otherwise remarkable study, *Religion and the Decline of Magic*.[6] As an initial example, let us take a negative image, one that is the reverse of the sacred but one that Thomas would surely dismiss as mere superstition. The medieval audience knew, as modern audiences usually do not, the precise form and shape of a devil—or, rather, the exact possibilities of shape and form that might be assigned to a devil either on stage or in a representation in the visual arts. Thus, while we do not have artists' sketches showing the appearance of devils in the plays of York and Coventry, the dramatic records do not contradict what we see in the visual arts in these locales:

ij garmentes for iij deuels vj deuelles faces in iij Vesernes[7]

Item for mendyng the demons Garment . . .
Item for newe ledder to the same Garment

. . .

payd for a yard of canvas for ye devylles mall & for makyng

. . .

pd for mendyng ye demens cotts & hose . . .
pd for ij pound of heare for ye Same[8]

Devils appear in hairy garments, apparently of leather, with double masks, one over the face and another elsewhere, often in the genital region; they sometimes carry clubs, which, if we may believe the Coventry records, were made of cloth, stuffed, and painted. The color associated with devils was black, not red, and the present-day stereotyped red devil with a pitchfork and forked tail would have impressed the medieval audience as a sanitized and tame creature that does not adequately signify the potential for evil inherent in the world or in the human condition. As Thomas notes, "the immediacy" of the concept of the devil in the Middle Ages has "long disappeared. The Devil . . . who appeared dramatically to snatch a poor sinner at his cups and fly off with him through the window, is difficult for us today to take seriously."[9] But for the medieval audience, devils were real—a demonic presence in one's daily life, in dreams, and in the social order. As living beings, these hellish figures were recognized as participants in life as lived in the medieval family and city—that is, as beings that might plausibly appear in York or Coventry or Chester but as aliens and not as citizens.

Devils are not only so grotesque that they are capable of inspiring laughter, but also they are dangerous and dirty. The sources of their hostility are explored in the first play of each of the English cycles or collections of plays—i.e., the York, Towneley, N-town, and Chester plays. These dramatize the Fall of Lucifer and his followers among the angels, who for their arrogance are thrust into hell where they are transformed from creatures of light into creatures of darkness who are also subjected to the filth, heat, and smoke characteristic of those lower regions of the medieval cosmos. So it is in the Barkers' play of the Fall of Lucifer from York, in which the Second Devil comments that even their food is now "filth."[10] Historically, then, in the medieval view it was the serpent which, having crawled out of this "filth," would lead mankind quickly to the fallen condition—a condition that would make him subject to suffering and death. The fallen condition, however, had been provided with a remedy in the Second Adam, the Savior whose life marked the center of history—a time when, indeed, history had been given a new beginning. The rituals of the Church as established in the parish churches of the city—churches with which the citizens identified themselves (as opposed to, say, a local cathedral, which more than likely would be looked on with distrust and even antagonism) —were designed to recall the events of the life of the Second Adam, whose acts of renewal are remembered in the Church Year and are repeated in the Mass. While frequently associated with Corpus Christi, the cycle plays' connection with this Feast was probably more historical accident than intentional choice, but yet Corpus Christi nevertheless provided an occasion for plays of this kind,[11] since on this day people were encouraged to consider the saving power of the transcendent God who had come into history to give his body and blood for the salvation of mankind—body and blood which are offered in contemporary time in the Eucharist. As the Eucharist was looked upon as a symbol of healing for the members of a parish and for humans generally,[12] so the celebration of the Feast was regarded as salutary for the civic unit, the city, which thus was brought together in unity and love on an important civic occasion. For this day the streets were cleaned, and everything was done to promote the honor of the city—an appropriate response, when we consider that the occasion was one in which the citizens, at least in York and at some other locations, would represent in plays the history of mankind ranging from the beginning to the end, when the effects of the Fall and of the salvation offered by the Savior would be seen. At this latter time, men and women would be consigned either to an eternal life of joy and purity or to a life-with-out-end of punishment among the devils in dirt, smoke, and heat. But now, at the Festival, the community is affirmed, and at the same time the community is demonstrated to be defined in terms of its opposition to all the alien powers of darkness, which are visualized by means of traditional iconography and which function as the basis of sociological principles of very great significance to the social order.

At the same time, as Mervyn James has demonstrated, the ritual and plays produced as part of the religious Festival not only function as a way of establishing a unity among the citizens of the city which thus achieves a kind of wholeness not present in the ordinary time of non-feast days, but also they serve as a means of "social differentiation"—that is, the adopting of signs of social stratification based on "segmented occupational roles in the urban community."[13] Hence it is no surprise that various kinds of social differentiation are established in the visual display of the various plays in the cycle.

It is nevertheless important to see that the devils and the alien men and women who are their followers and subjects are excluded not only from the wholeness of the community but also from the various levels of social strata of which it is composed. In other words, these are true aliens—the race of Cain and the followers of Judas. In the Towneley *Mactacio Abel*, Cain, destined to be the first permanent human resident of hell, demonstrates his lack of concern for community by his refusal to sacrifice and by his scatological remarks and gestures directed toward his brother Abel, whom in the end he kills in a scene which illustrates his isolation and his separation from whatever would be indicative of wholeness.[14] Such a person will be the recipient of God's "malison" (l. 355) just as will Judas in New Testament times. Judas—the refuser of wholeness and of salvation, like Cain an exemplar of despair—is the apostle who breaks the unity of the twelve disciples and who betrays his Master with a kiss, which ought to be a sign of love. This principle of rejection is also in medieval iconography represented in terms of the Synagogue and the Church. At York, there is extant painted glass in the York Minster Chapter House vestibule which shows the Synagogue typically as a woman blindfolded and holding a staff that is breaking in several places; in contrast, the figure representing the Church, holding a church and a cross,[15] is a sign of the vision and wholeness of the Christian community achieved through the sacrifice of the Crucifixion. The unity of the Christian community as reflected in the medieval English city, however, does not demand a totally egalitarian social order since its structure was, as noted above, based on a deliberately defined social structure which ranked the occupations in an order of prestige. In the Corpus Christi procession, therefore, the order of the occupational guilds was carefully defined in civic ordinances, with the most important coming at the end of the procession in close proximity to the Host. Hence in York in 1501, the humblest guilds led the parade, with the end being made up of the Weavers and Cordwainers side by side, the Tailors "goyng by tham self," and the mighty Mercers—the guild also responsible for the final play of the Doom in the York cycle—followed only by the aldermen and mayor.[16] In Coventry, it was the Mercers and Drapers that among the guilds had the place of precedence at the rear of the procession.[17] Such cities as York, Chester, or London thought of themselves in terms of the earthly Jerusalem (in contrast to Babylon),[18] and their understanding of the social organization of a city which also was to be identified with the City of God did not exclude the concept of hierarchy. It was, after all, the character of Satan in the civic cycle plays that, before mankind was created, had attempted to deny hierarchy and order in heaven with the consequence that he and his cohorts were consigned to permanent alien status in the lower regions of hell.

As the mayor is the chief officer and hence the embodiment of the essence of the city, so his position is the most exalted in the civic order. As Mervyn James reminds us, he gives the city its "corporate identity which, for example, enabled it to plead or be pleaded at law."[19] (In a parallel way, the parish priest represented the individual members of the parish in the realm of the spiritual, for he was the principal mediator between the individual parishioner and the deity, though he had competition from higher levels of the hierarchy and from saints whose cults were active locally.) The model is that of Christ as "head" of the Church, which is identified as a "body" with "members." Here too the head is representative of the whole and incorporates the members (see *1 Cor.* 12.12). Hence, as previously noted, the mayor's place in the Corpus Christi procession is at the rear—the place of precedence according to the biblical principle that "the last shall be first" (*Matt.* 19.30)—and his role in the social hierarchy is an exhibition of the honor of the city within the larger kingdom. It was considered important for the mayor and other officials of the city to wear proper clothing in processions and other civic functions, and generally speaking these dignitaries were chosen from the most prestigious occupations in the city.

Hierarchy is implicit in the structure defined at the creation of man, who from the first is to be regarded as differentiated from the woman that will be made of out of his rib (at Norwich, "A Rybbe colleryd Redd"[20]) and also is to be seen as in charge of the world.[21] In the plays about Noah, his wife is frequently rebellious, acting the role of the woman who does not respect her husband's place.[22] Her disobedience, however, motivated, is of a piece with the countless depictions in the visual arts, especially wood carvings such as misericords, of women who beat their husbands; at Stratford-upon-Avon, a misericord thus shows, on a supporter, a woman scratching a man's face while he grabs her hair, and another misericord illustrates a woman beating the man with a pan.[23] Such inversion of normal gender ascendancy was clearly considered comic, but more importantly it was recognized that, in terms of the established social order with its accepted patriarchal bias, this type of behavior was to be demonstrated to be perverse.[24] Children too were expected to be properly obedient and, even when grown, to show their obedience in ritualized ways (see, for example, Isaac's request for forgiveness and blessing[25] in the York play (X.251–66); in the cycle plays, such expectation, of course, even extends to Isaac's behavior when faced with his father's plan to sacrifice his only beloved son. The head of the household, like the mayor, was considered the embodiment of the social unit, in this case the family, which too was a unity at the same time that its structure involved a careful definition of roles.

But no smaller social structure, whether it be a family or a municipality, exists only unto itself, and neither the head of a household nor a mayor theoretically had the right to act tyrannically, though autocratic behavior, especially in the home, was common enough.[26] The tyrant—one, that is, who behaves as though the community has no rights—is typified in Herod, whose raging and whose acts of violence against children are well known. Herod is thus another negative example, in this instance one who fails to respect the system of laws and obligations inherent in the social system. The visual configuration normally associated with Herod is, of course, child murder, and in very well preserved painted glass of c.1500 at Fairford, Gloucestershire, he is typically shown with an infant impaled on his sword.[27] The roof bosses illustrating the life of the tyrant in Norwich Cathedral are well known and have been claimed to reflect directly the visual tableaux of the drama.[28] Not surprisingly, it is common in the visual arts to see Herod with darkened face and even wearing a devil crown.[29] A letter by John Whetley to John Paston II in May 1478 describes a contemporary nobleman, the Duke of Suffolk: "Ther was never no man that playd Herrod in Corpus Chrysty play better and more agreable to hys pageaunt then he dud."[30] Quite clearly the iconography of the tyrant, most exactly defined in the figure of Herod, could be discovered in the acts of the nobility of the time; yet such behavior was regarded as a departure from the norm and as a threat both to community and to its hierarchical structure.

Appropriate behavior for a king in the presence of the royal Child Christ is presented in another segment of the cycle, which illustrates the coming of the three Magi to Bethlehem to see the infant. Here decorum is of particular importance, and careful attention needs to be given to the iconographic tradition to see what the limits of such decorous behavior might be. At Chester in 1977, in a production of the Chester plays remarkably inattentive to the visual traditions in which this drama was embedded, each of the three kings gave a gift to the Child rather indecorously and without first removing his crown. It is, however, reasonably certain from our study of visual examples that as each king gives his gift, he should remove his head covering, usually a crown (fig. 2), and often but not necessarily this is done in the extant examples with his left hand.[31] If the medieval respect for age above youth influenced the play (as I believe it undoubtedly did), the oldest Magus would have tendered his gift to the Child first, the youngest last. The text of the Chester play indicates that each king shall approach the Child, speak a stanza of praise (the form is that of the *Hail* lyrics), give his gift, and receive the blessing of the Child. In two manuscripts of the Chester plays, the Child actually speaks to the Magi following the Third Magus' request for him to "blesse mee with thy hand."[32] We may guess that the initial approach of the Magi is accompanied by genuflection such as we find illustrated in three corbels in the north choir stalls of c.1380 in Chester Cathedral, where crowned figures that appear to be the three Magi are shown kneeling on their left knees,[33] for such signs of veneration would have been regarded in the late Middle Ages as highly appropriate to one who is both king and deity. The manner of giving gifts and of receiving the blessing of the Child is established in the visual arts, with the two gestures most conveniently shown in an alabaster in the collection of the Victoria and Albert Museum.[34]

Especially in a devotional tableau such as that which accompanied the giving of gifts by the Magi in early productions, the expectations of patrons and contemporary audiences with regard to the design of the scene would have set specific limits within which the actors were expected to realize the action and to present their speeches. Indecorous behavior by the Magi, or carelessness with regard to matters of gesture, would have been seen as violations of the integrity of the scene—in some cases violations of the same type that today are the source of humor in secular cartoons which link together the incongruous and sometimes also make a political statement. Thus in the Chester play which dramatizes the Magi's gifts, the text indicates that the Magi should point out the star in the sky over the stable (IX.25) and then the stable itself (ll. 29–30) as they approach. Both star and stable are again indicated, presumably by gestures as in the visual arts, when they come closer (ll. 124–25). When they arrive before the Child in the stable, according to the late banns, they see him "betwixte an Oxe and ane Asse."[35] He is held in the arms of his Mother, the Blessed Virgin Mary, while seated below "at hir knee" will be the "ould man" Joseph (ll. 128–29). The conclusion of the play dramatizes the warning of the angel to the Magi, who have now left the scene of the Child in the stable, and they take the advice of the heavenly messenger to travel home by another way.

The play identified in the Chester cycle as *De Oblatione Trium Regum*, called the play of the "iij kinges of Colyn" in the early banns of 1539–40, was presented by the Mercers, who were sometimes joined by the Spicers.[36] The play is, as we have seen above, instructive, appropriately functioning as speaking tableaux that will remind the audience of events which are central to the story of the Incarnation. However, there is a further level here, for the principal scene that is depicted—the actual giving of the gifts to the Child—provides a visual tableau that was frequently the object of devotion. In pre-Reformation times, the tableau when found in the visual arts functioned as an icon—that is, as an image which was believed to be a useful channel for piety, before which candles might be burned, and through which the individual worshipper might make contact with the deity.[37] Scenes of this type were often seen in alabasters, as the previously cited examples demonstrate; at Chester, there is possibly a lost wall painting which illustrated this scene in St. Peter's church.[38] Such representations in the early life of Christ certainly had great cultic importance, though after the Reformation the official attitude toward them changed; alabasters and wall paintings were brought under an official ban, while the same scenes might still be staged for some decades before the theatrical versions of the tableaux were also suppressed.[39]

For the Chester Mercers, who are described in the early banns as "worshipfful of degre," the play gave their guild an opportunity to display a splendid pageant wagon—"with sondry Cullors it shall shine/ of veluit veluit satten & damaske fyne/ Taffyta Sersnett of poppyngee"—on which the stable was placed.[40] As one of the occupational guilds, the Mercers thus were expected to "bryng forth their [play] Solemplye" for the honor of the city and for the inspiring of devotion.[41] But the guild also saw its acitivity in producing the play to be a way of establishing its own honor within the community and of expecting that community to be obligated to it on account of this service.[42] Yet, in addition to such functions, the role of the plays in the civic piety of the guild members as well as of their audiences must not be overlooked. Even if the members of the guild might be expected to benefit financially from the crowds coming to a city such as Chester or York to see the plays, the religious motive was nevertheless a deeply imbedded factor, and the plays reflect rather exactly the more or less emotional spirituality that characterized the towns and cities of northern Europe immediately prior to the Reformation and of which more will be said in the next chapter. The high value placed on such plays will be compared to the value placed on the parish churches and their fabric, upon which the parishioners spent large amounts of money up to the latter part of the reign of Henry VIII. Such spirituality may be dismissed as no more than an attempt on the part of the members of the guild to produce plays and to do other acts which will provide status within a spiritual sphere, but we need to remember that religious behavior cannot be reduced to its outward signs or sociological effects though it may have a great deal to do with how the social order functions. This chapter may be regarded to be, on the one hand, prologomena to further study in the sociology of visual forms in drama, and hence must leave aside further attention to the psychological and religious questions raised here. On the other hand, these remarks are more importantly a warning against seeing the search for tradition—especially for elements of tradition in the arts—as a simple quest. It will not do to establish a new canon of artistic works in the name of preservationist aesthetics uncritically applied.

The application of literary or artistic analysis, even analysis as sophisticated as the reception theory advocated by Jauss, should be seen as necessitating recourse to specific examination of the nature of the community and of the conditions of production of the drama which utilized a particular text. Only thus can we begin to come to terms with the alterity of such a play text, and only thus is it possible fully to understand the context of the tableaux and spectacle that accompanied the words of the dialogue. Ignorance of visual traditions and their social context would also seem to be a serious lapse in any re-creations of the medieval cycle plays on the modern stage. Traditional forms are not infinitely malleable, and their value may be diminished if they are absorbed entirely into the fabric of contemporary popular culture, as was the case in the production of *The Mysteries* at the National Theatre with its pop music, strange mixture of costumes, and Monty Python effects.[43] There are problems with seeing Pilate in a bow tie, or the Virgin Mary's wheelchair being wheeled off after her death.[44]

3

Northern Spirituality
and the Late Medieval Drama and Art of York

Critical fashions change. The evolutionary approach to drama and art so prevalent in the early part of our own century has been thoroughly discredited during the years since World War II.[1] This development has been very fortunate, since it has forced upon us the recognition that any rigidly diachronic methodology must severely limit our discussion to events and details thoroughly wrenched out of their context and hence separated from their place in tradition. If the critical process does not therefore retreat into a formalist consideration of the literary elements of a play or the technical processes of a work of art, the possibility emerges of providing a criticism which is of necessity interdisciplinary because it is synchronic and because it takes into account the larger traditional milieu.[2] The task includes the historic perspective derived from close attention to the development of ideas, attitudes, and images, but, as the previous essay indicates, it insists nevertheless upon understanding the work which is being subjected to analysis in terms of its interrelations with other factors and events simultaneously occurring in the same location. The present essay will emphasize the presence of certain cultural and religious forms and expressions which are of very great importance for the understanding of the play texts, the local visual arts at York, and their subsequent significance as examples of late medieval tradition.

The plays and the art of a city such as York during the late Middle Ages will require examination as sophisticated expressions rather than as primitive attempts aimed at crude didacticism—a didacticism that is said to have grown up in the fourteenth century. Neither the art nor the plays were in fact primitive. The amateur and

quasi-amateur status of the plays, it is true, made them less polished
than the liturgical music-dramas that were being performed in various cathedrals and monastic churches until the sixteenth century, but
they nevertheless shared traditions which assured that, on the whole,
high quality would be preserved. The fact that they were middle
class and popular should hardly prejudice us against them. The plays
and the art both express the central images and actions of the Christian story or religious myth, which we may define as matter held to
be true in a deeper than literal sense.[3] Such artistic expression par-
ticipated in the spirituality of the city during an age when public
and private piety still formed the focal point of civic life in York.

The citizens of York in the fifteenth and early sixteenth centuries did not distinguish, as we tend to do, between art and myth, or
between drama and myth. It was a less rationalistic and less skepti-
cal time. When we hear that a cross on the high altar in York Minster contained a piece of the column to which Jesus was bound
during the Flagellation,[4] we may remain unconvinced. Yet no doubt
this cross was a thoroughly fine piece of workmanship, and when
Archdeacon Stephen Scrope gave it to the Cathedral in 1418 he certainly meant to provide a gift which was at once aesthetically pleas-
ing and spiritually valuable. Both the piece of column and the cross
would have reminded those who looked at this work of art that
Christ's Passion was the central event upon which the Christian
scheme of salvation depended, and we know that for the later Middle Ages the Passion and the Crucifixion took on new importance
for their role in personal religious response among the laity, for to a
considerable extent emphasis on these events even supplanted the
early Christian stress on the fact of the Incarnation and the event of
the Resurrection. This shift was one that would survive the Reformation, and indeed helped to establish patterns of religious thought
that would eventually inform radical fundamentalism with its eccentric theology of salvation in the twentieth century.

It is not possible to gauge exactly the precise individual response on the part of spiritually inclined persons (or of less spiritually inclined persons) looking at the reliquary cross at York Minster
with devotion (or lack of devotion) and awareness of its fragment of

the column, and it is further unfortunate that the artwork on the gold cross itself has been lost since it disappeared in 1509.[5] However, art in this and other cases did provide the focus for much popular meditation, which most importantly established a closeness between viewer and the scene represented by the artist.

Even more than drama usually performed annually at Corpus Christi, therefore, the visual arts were indicative of the central experiences of the religious lives of the citizens. The period was one of tremendous expenditure for rebuilding and refurbishing churches, and even the Cathedral, which was distinct from the city and was the domain of the clergy rather than the citizens, was adorned with some painted glass given by the crafts.[6] In the instance of the bell-founders' window, given in the fourteenth century by Richard Tunnoc, the work of the guild itself is set forth by workmen shown at their tasks. But in the city churches, the men of the crafts, along with the merchants, took principal financial responsibility for adorning the windows. For example, Reginald Bawtree, a merchant, left one hundred shillings in his will in 1429 for a new window in All Saints, North Street. The moving force in providing new windows in this case was the pastor of All Saints, Father James Baguley, a rare man of learning who must have approved the iconography—in this instance, the Corporal Acts of Mercy (fig. 3)—and may have insisted that the contract be let to the very best glass painters available locally. This window, like the famous Fifteen Signs of Doomsday window in the same church, was painted in the workshop of John Thornton, previously of Coventry and made free of the city of York in 1410 after the completion of his massive East Window in the Minster.[7] The difference in style between this window and the Tunnoc window is remarkable, and a comparison of the two is indicative not only of the introduction of innovative techniques in glass painting but also of new aesthetic values and of a new mode of spirituality that became pervasive even in conservative York in the fifteenth century.

The Corporal Acts of Mercy window provides specific examples of feeding the hungry, of clothing the naked, of giving drink to the thirsty, of offering housing to the homeless, of visiting prisoners and the sick. The figure painting in this window is much more highly individualized than in the work of the previous century, for the artist here was attempting to bring the scenes to life as never before in glass painting. In contrast, the fourteenth-century bell founders' window in the Minster is formalized and abstract. It is clear that by the beginning of the fifteenth century citizens and clergy alike were coming to appreciate a new kind of art which emphasized particulars,[8] which brings to life scenes from devotional life. The new style is indicative of changing modes of religious devotion and of new ways of understanding, popularizing, and vivifying religious and artistic traditions. To be sure, conservative York was hardly the location where innovative modes of devotion and a new aesthetics could have originated, but the city, with its connections with the clerical training grounds of Oxford and Cambridge and through trade with the Low Countries, nevertheless was not immune to the new trends.

The spirituality of the late Middle Ages in York, as in the Netherlands, could clearly be very personal and often emotional. The sight of a religious painting or a pious object could be enough to release a flood of tears. The object of the continental painters from the Low Countries was to present the details of a religious scene in such detail that the imaginations of the viewers would be stimulated to the highest extent. The Northern painters were not simply formalists, rather they used their discovery of perspective as the means whereby they might all the more carefully present iconographic details laden with traditional meaning. In such a painting as the miniature illustrating the Flagellation in the courtly Hours of Catherine of Cleves, we see the carefully painted tiled floor as well as the sharply visualized details of the torturing of Christ during his Passion.[9] The attention to detail had as its purpose the establishment of credibility. The agressiveness and anger of the torturers are not only represented by their faces but also by the way in which the fist and scourge extend into the border of the miniature. In other instances, Northern painters tended to make literal much of the symbolism of the Christian story with a view toward emotional effect— an art at once realistic, symbolic, and affective. This kind of painting was scorned by Michelangelo, who sneered that "Flemish painting pleases all the devout better than Italian. The latter evokes no tears, the former makes them weep copiously. This," he asserted, "is not a result of the merits of this art; the only cause is the extreme sensibility of the devout spectators," especially women, nuns, monks, and "men of the world who are not capable of understanding true harmony."[10] If one can believe the Travel section of the *New York Times* (18 May 1975), pious tears are still evoked in Flanders by the sight of an object of piety such as the vial of Precious Blood brought to Bruges during the Second Crusade.[11] That the spectators responded similarly to the tableaux offered by the actors of the Corpus Christi plays at York and elsewhere in England is suggested by the author of *A Tretise of Miraclis Pleyinge*, a Lollard tract against the plays. This treatise takes into account the argument that plays are like paintings come to life, and curiously admits the aesthetic effectiveness of the vernacular religious drama of England; the plays inspired pious tears: "Also, ofte sythis by siche myraclis pleyinge men and wymmen, seinge the passioun of Crist and of hise seintis, ben movyd to compassion and devocion, wepinge bitere teris. . . ."[12]

The sources of the traditions of late medieval spirituality are well known:[13] St. Augustine, St. Anselm, St. Bernard of Clairvaux, St. Francis of Assisi, the *Meditations on the Life of Christ* formerly attributed to St. Bonaventura. A key figure seems to have been Anselm, whose writings figured importantly in establishing the new interest in Christ's humanity. Instead of emphasizing the divinity of Christ as the supernatural power who overcomes sin and death through the strength evidenced in the Resurrection, the late medieval Church turned to the Savior who experienced human suffering and death and brings relief to humankind in need of salvation. The shift is particularly noticeable when vernacular plays are compared with the earlier liturgical music-dramas which were presented as additions to the liturgy as early as the tenth century.[14] The liturgical plays have their roots in the earlier theology, and hence it should come as no surprise that they are at first found closely linked to the Easter ceremonies. The oldest extant example of these plays was apparently a simple dramatized ritual re-enacting the story of the three Marys at the empty tomb, where they are greeted by the angel who speaks the famous words "Quem queritis. . . ."[15] The origin of this brief play, often attached to the Easter Matins service, is not entirely clear, but its spread across most of Europe has been documented and hundreds of texts have been edited, in some cases along with extant music.[16] This dramatization, which may have been more of a ceremony than a play, focused on the event of the Resurrection, which in the earlier Middle Ages was considered the most significant event in the life of Christ. More elaborate versions of the Easter drama and utilizing the same traditions also appeared, most notably in the *Visitatio Sepulchri* from the twelfth-century Fleury Playbook where not only the race of the two disciples to the sepulcher is included but also there is added a *Hortulanus* scene in which Mary Magdalene mistakes the risen Lord for a gardener. The Fleury play does not lack emotion, but it is as stylized as the figures in eleventh- and twelfth-century art; like the miniatures and sculptures, it aims at stylized visualizing of the scene in a manner that gives very close attention to the essence of the event. As a rule, particulars are of little concern and are set aside in the interest of perfectly realized form. The form of this drama is aesthetically very sophisticated, but there is no attempt to convey the *humanity* of Christ which was demanded by the later spirituality.

When we compare such a play as the Fleury *Slaying of the Innocents*[17] with the late fifteenth- or early sixteenth-century play *Magnus Herodes* by the Wakefield Master in the Towneley manuscript, we see that we have moved into a different world from that dramatized in the stately verse and traditional music of the Fleury Playbook. In the Towneley play,[18] Herod's anger is much more genuinely unrestrained, though his raging in early productions of the play in Yorkshire may have been a little less restrained than in the case of the Coventry play where the stage directions insist that he should rage both *"in the pagond and in the strete also."*[19] When the Towneley Herod learns that the Magi have gone back to their lands by "Anothere way," he shouts: "Why, and ar thay past me by? We! outt! for teyn I brast!/ We! fy!/ Fy on the dewill!" (ll. 147–50). He attempts to beat his knights, and then announces that he is so angry that he is about to "yelde my gast" (l. 155). And he really does not settle down until, after he has heard the prophecies that enrage him further, one of his counsellors suggests that slaughter might be a good way to handle the problem; the infant Jesus is to be put to death "on a spere" (l. 252). As noted in the previous chapter, Herod's role becomes that of child-killer—a distinguishing mark which identifies him in late medieval iconography. The entire *Magnus Herodes* develops at considerable length the futile attempt of a mad earthly king to destroy the human Child who is also divine. Particular details are used to underline the nature of evil which will seem to triumph at the Crucifixion, when paradoxically the victim will become the victor. In the *Magnus Herodes* the soldiers, who later figure in the story of the Passion, are brutal and abusive (they call the mothers names, e.g., "hoore," l. 340); furthermore, they are ultimately cowards, though not so cowardly as the base messenger named Watkin in the *Massacre of the Innocents* in the Digby manuscript.[20] Watkin asks Herod "for Mahoundes sake" to make him a knight as a reward for his valor in infanticide (l. 136), yet he quakes when he envisions the mothers: "Though the moder be angry, the child shalbe slayn!/ But yitt I drede no thyng more thanne a woman with a rokke" (ll. 158–59). He is in fact eventually beaten by them, and is only rescued by the knights. Two examples of painted glass in the choir of York Minster witness to the popularity of the theme of the Killing of the Innocents. In the glass in the south choir clerestory, Herod himself reaches out and stabs a child—a detail reminiscent of the Fairford glass cited in the previous chapter. In the *Magnus Herodes*, the soldiers who return to their king brag that they have murdered "Many thowsandys" of children (ll. 418–19). For their exploits, Herod offers them ladies, castles, and towers, and then launches into his last speech in which he boasts for approximately fifty lines. "I lagh that I whese!" he exclaims (l. 472), and finally he concludes with this absolutely incoherent advice to the audience: "Syrs, this is my counsell:/ Bese not to cruell./ Bot adew!—to the deuyll!/ I can [speak] no more Franch" (ll. 510–13). Obviously the children whom he has killed are identified very closely with Christ himself, and these scenes from Christ's infancy look forward to the scenes between his Betrayal and death as Savior. Then again the threat to Christ's life will be made manifest when he is betrayed on a very human level by a follower who feels aggrieved and cheated. The multiplication of particulars in the *Magnus Herodes* underlines threats to Christ's humanity—a humanity that must suffer for the rest of humanity on account of the weakness inherited from our first ancestors. Even such a lively play as this must be seen as pointing to the human nature of Christ which figured so largely in the spirituality of the late Middle Ages.

Devotion to the humanity of Christ was central to the spirituality of St. Bernard, whose Cistercian principles seem to have directed him away from visualizing any images in his meditations. Dom Cuthbert Butler points out that Bernard's "contemplation" involved "no framing of images of the scenes of the Passion, nor any portrait presented to the mind of Our Lord's human form."[21] Yet Bernard's regard for the Infancy and Passion of Christ had an immense influence on the spirituality of the period between his own lifetime and the Council of Trent. Though Cistercian monasteries such as those which took root in Yorkshire at Fountains and Rievaulx would not allow the relevant scenes from Christ's life to be shown in their art, elsewhere representations seem strongly affected by the emphasis found in Bernard's spiritual writings. In English wall paintings as early as the thirteenth century, Christ's life is normally presented in two series of paintings, one of which represents the Infancy and the other the Passion.[22] Significantly, the Passion in the later Middle Ages becomes the more important of these series, and the rood with the crucified Christ flanked by Mary and (usually) John became the obligatory focal point in English churches since the carving was placed over the chancel arch. Removed by the iconoclasm of the reigns of Henry VIII and Edward VI, the rood was clearly considered among the most urgent items ordered replaced in churches in the time of Queen Mary (1553–58) when England was being steered away from the Protestantism of her father and brother.[23] Indeed, for the late Middle Ages the Passion was generally considered to be the most significant segment of Christ's life; by this period it had supplanted the Resurrection as the crucial occurrence in the life of Jesus for the devotional experience of the Church.

The Franciscans, especially through such works as the *Meditations on the Life of Christ*, carried devotion to the Infancy and Passion of Christ one step further: they brought back the images as agents of meditation, and insisted that Christians attempt actively to imagine and visualize the events of sacred history as if they were present at the very places.[24] For instance, in its account of the Crucifixion, the *Meditations* advise:

> Here pay diligent attention to the manner of the Crucifixion. Two ladders are set in place, one behind at the right arm, another at the left arm, which the evil-doers ascend holding nails and hammers. Another ladder is placed in front, reaching to the place where the feet are to be affixed.[25]

The account continues to describe in minute detail the appearance of the Crucifixion, always with the implicit invitation to the reader to visualize the scene with as much particularity as possible. Christ's right hand is first fixed to the cross, then the left. Nevertheless, in spite of all the apparent certainty, the *Meditations* admit that Christ may have been crucified another way, with the cross on the ground. "If this suits you better, think how they take Him contemptuously, like the vilest wretch, and furiously cast Him onto the cross on the ground, taking His arms, violently extending them, and most cruelly fixing them to the cross. Similarly, consider His feet, which they dragged down as violently as they could."[26]

This second way of visualizing the Crucifixion (*jacente cruce* instead of *erecto cruce*) suited the writers of the plays in the York cycle and the Towneley manuscript, and it is the way in which Christ is placed on the cross in the late fourteenth-century glass formerly in St. Saviour's, York, and now in the west window of All Saints, Pavement.[27] The visualizing of the scene in devotion and in the visual arts also leaves open possibilities for greater "realism" in the treatment of particulars in drama. In the York play,[28] the soldiers discover that the holes are drilled too far apart, so before they drive the nails they must stretch Christ's body with ropes until it fits the cross. "It failis a foote and more," the Third Soldier complains, and the Second Soldier comments: "Than muste he bide in bittir bale" (ll. 107, 110). They try to stretch him, and fail. The First Soldier, responding like a workman with a problem, takes up a rope and suggests a solution: "Why carpe ye so? faste on a corde/ And tugge hym to, by toppe and taile" (ll. 113–14). After some difficulty, the soldiers, who are almost unconscious of their sadism ("It is no force howe felle he feele," the First Soldier says, l. 136), are able to stretch the body to the point that "all his synnous go asoundre" (l. 132) in order to be able to hammer the nails into place. The intense suffering of Christ is underlined in a most graphic and kinetic manner: "Yaa, assoundir are bothe synnous and veynis/ On ilke a side, so haue we soughte" (ll. 147–48). It is quite clear that this play of the Crucifixion, which particularly dwells on the human agony of Christ, was intended to bring forth pious tears in the audience among people who felt sympathy for the sufferings of their Savior.

Yet the rationale for the brutal and realistic nailing of Christ to the cross in the York play is not merely sadistic effect. F. P. Pickering has forcefully demonstrated that here the medieval writers and visual artists were giving a literal depiction of the symbolism of the Crucifixion as it was prophesied in Psalm 21 (22), which along with Psalm 68 (69) determined the particulars of Christ's death.[29] In the twenty-first psalm, the psalmist writes: "They have numbered all my bones" (17). The sadistically extended placing of Christ on the cross which is suggested by this passage was new to Western art about 1400, and is utilized in the *Speculum humanae salvationis* (fig. 4) and in the painting *The Nailing of Christ to the Cross* by Gerard David in the National Gallery, London;[30] in the East this symbolism was noted in the Byzantine *Painter's Manual*.[31]

Christ on the cross also has his sinews stretched like the strings of a harp in the York play;[32] after all, he is, as the Flemish music theorist Tinctoris insisted, the "greatest of musicians" because he brought God and man into harmony.[33] Since late medieval spirituality placed very great emphasis upon the act of atonement—the Crucifixion itself—this act was also deliberately presented in art in the most sensational ways possible. While early Anglo-Saxon Crucifixions had represented Christ in a more or less formalized manner against the cross, by c.1338–39 when the aisle window in the West end of York Minster was painted by Thomas de Bovesdun[34] his arms had become stretched out at a painful angle and his suffering had become the emotional focus of the composition. In English wall painting, the middle of the thirteenth century marked the change in the presentation of the crucified Christ; after this time, as E. W. Tristram notes, the artists "stressed the pain and pity of the theme."[35] In the continental illumination which shows the Crucifixion in the Hours of Catherine of Cleves,[36] Christ's suffering humanity becomes particularly evident, and similar treatment may be observed in other manuscript illuminations. Finally, careful examination of the crucified Christ in the Isenheim Altarpiece of Matthias Grünewald exhibits the beaten and bruised body stretched out with all the sensationalism that a visual artist could utilize.

Good Friday, which commemorates the atonement of Christ for the sins of men and women and which serves as a reminder that a second Adam has suffered in exchange for the lapse of the first Adam and his companion Eve, became the center of the liturgical year. The victory over sin is achieved here rather than on the Sunday following, when the Resurrection is commemorated. Within the Mass itself in the late Middle Ages, the elements of bread and wine were connected very clearly with the events on the cross.[37] In the York rite, the celebrant at the crucial point in the canon of the Mass "spreadeth his arms after the manner of a cross." As a manuscript of the *Lay Folks Mass Book* from the Cistercian monastery of Rievaulx indicates, "When the preste the eleuacyon has made,/ He wille sprede his armes on-brade. . . ."[38]

A great concern with the Passion as a focus for the spiritual life and as a subject for meditative images in art and drama marks the period following the appearance of the Black Death in Europe in 1348–49. Students of the art of the period have almost invariably commented upon the preoccupation with death and mortality, and have commonly identified the age as morbid. Those who have studied the population of medieval England have found themselves surprised to discover that the population had already leveled off around 1300 and that the great decline in population after the plague may have had other causes in addition to disease and pestilence.[39] People, passing through a phase of supreme pessimism, may not have married as often or as early, and they may not have been as willing to bring children into the world as formerly. In any case, the population of England fell to approximately half of what it had been in 1300. The later portion of the Middle Ages in England, from 1349 to the reign of Henry VIII, was also a period of almost frenetic church building. At York, almost every extant church building was either rebuilt or remodeled during this period, with St. Michael le Belfrey being the last church to be completed before the coming of Protestantism—a period when ecclesiastical building schemes for practical purposes stopped during the remainder of the sixteenth century. In the fifteenth century guilds had thrived, especially with regard to their religious functions.[40] This was the heyday of the Corpus Christi procession, which was under the sponsorship of the prestigious Corpus Christi Guild after 1408. During the celebration of Corpus Christi and deriving from the spirituality prevalent in such cities as York in the late Middle Ages came the cycle (or Corpus Christi) plays which were staged by the guildsmen.

Perhaps the very greatest concern of all for the citizens of York was for the health of the soul after death. On the institutional level, not only the parish churches but also the chantry chapels were of vital interest; Maud Sellers, who edited the *York Memorandum Book A/Y*, was even convinced that "the real link between municipality and church was the chantry priest; in the chantries the mayor and his brethren had a personal, a vivid interest."[41] She cites the mayor as declaring "that all the chantries of this city have been and are founded by the citizens and notabilities of this city; therefore, both the priests of this city and suburbs having chantries, and stipendiary priests not having chantries, are the special officials 'oratores' of the citizens, their patrons and masters."[42] In January 1424, in the third year of the reign of Henry VI, Nicholas Blackburn, Sr., "alderman of the cytye of Yorke," founded the chantry chapel of St. Anne on Foss Bridge. The stated purpose of the chapel was for the use of a priest who would "syng wythyn the sayd chappell for the sowle of the sayd founder and all Crysten sowles . . . betwene the howers of xj and xij before none, and nowe alteryd [at a later date] by th' advyce of the parochiners there, as well as for ther commodytye as travelynge people, between iiij and v in the mornyng."[43] In his will, probated in 1432, he left liturgical vestments, a missal, and a chalice to his chantry devoted to St. Anne on Foss Bridge.[44]

The affluent Nicholas Blackburn, Sr., was also the patron of four other chantry chapels in the city. His portrait, along with that of his wife Margaret, appears in a window which he gave to All Saints, North Street, before his death. A leading citizen and alder-man who served twice as mayor, Blackburn was concerned with much more than amassing wealth. As a merchant, he moved easily among the ruling oligarchy, which was composed of people whom Eileen Power has identified as "the representatives of capitalism in a pre-capitalistic age."[45] It may be tempting to try to understand such men in terms of modern businessmen, but clearly Nicholas exempli-fies traditions of piety that we need to distinguish from the devout-ness normally found in the modern business profession. Words at the bottom of the donor panel in the window in All Saints, North Street, once asked worshippers to "pray for the souls of Nicholas Blackburn, Sr., *quondam* Mayor of York, and of Margaret his wife, and of all the faithful departed."[46] On the book held by Margaret Blackburn are written the words from Psalm 50 (51): "O Lord, thou wilt open my lips: and my mouth shall declare thy praise."[47] Other donors who appear in windows of the same church are his son Nicholas Blackburn, Jr., and his wife, also named Margaret, and possible members of the Wiloby and Hessle families as well as oth-ers. Such people as these not only rebuilt, remodeled, and decorated churches where the traditional worship of the Office and Mass was continually celebrated, but also, as we have seen, provided for the future of their own souls and the souls of others through the endow-ment of chantry chapels which were expected to function "for ev-er."[48] They were supporters of the ecclesiastical arts and, perhaps fully as importantly, they gave staunch backing to the plays which presented he the traditional story of the Christian way of salvation on the streets of York in almost every year.

The plays in Middle English at York probably had their origin in the second half of the fourteenth century (the earliest record is dated 1376[49]), and by 1399 they were being presented processionally at twelve stations through the city along a route[50] that can still traced today. In 1415 when Roger Burton, the town clerk, copied an Ordo describing the pageants, the Creation to Doom structure for the day's theatrical presentation had been firmly established[51] and was not to be altered in any major way until the suppression of the mysteries at York in the reign of Queen Elizabeth. The Ordo of 1415 specified the plays be presented only "at the places that is assigned therfore and nowere elles," and "that euery player that shall play be redy in his pagiaunt at convenyant tyme that is to say at the mydhowre betwix iiij[th] & v[th] of the cloke in the mornyng & then all other pageantes fast folowyng ilkon after other as ther course is without Tarieng. . . ."[52] Further, the Ordo insisted that the actors be "good players well arayed & openly spekyng"[53]—a sign that there was concern at this date that these pageants, already regarded as traditional, be fully worthy of the honor of the city, able to benefit the citizens, and reflecting the reverence demanded by God.

Early on the morning of the Feast of Corpus Christi, the pageant wagons were brought around early in the morning and began serving as platforms for the plays at the gates of Holy Trinity Priory near Micklegate Bar, not far from the assembly point on Toft Green and where the wagons had been stored when not in use. They passed along the strcct, past the end of North Street and across Ouse Bridge, then up Low Ousegate, which is today much wider than it was in the fifteenth and sixteenth centuries. Edwin Benson aptly describes the streets at that time as "mere alleys, passages between houses and groups of buildings"; he continues: "They were narrow and often the sky could hardly be seen from them because of the overhanging upper storeys of the buildings along each side."[54]

The whole affair must have had all the trappings of a major event—a medieval Church festival with both procession through the streets and colorful plays being presented throughout the day. The streets, not noted in York in ordinary times for their cleanliness, would be cleaned, and banners were hung along the route at the various stations where the pageants were to be played.[55] The crowds on this day apparently ranged from a rowdy minority to those who found themselves edified and deeply affected by the plays. In 1426, A Franciscan friar, William Melton, argued in a series of sermons for the separation of the Corpus Christi procession and the plays, since attendance at the latter had been leading some people to miss the service at the Cathedral and hence to lose the indulgences promised to them; at the same time he praised the Corpus Christi cycle as "good in itself and most laudable" in spite of some disorderliness—"feastings, drunkenness, clamours, gossipings, and other wantonness"—which took place on the day of performance.[56] The Corporation, which sponsored and controlled the plays, was obviously very much concerned that everything should be done decently and in good order. In 1476, the House Books record an ordinance stating that all the plays to be presented by the various craft guilds were to be inspected and incompetent actors barred from appearing:

> yerely in the tyme of lentyn there shall be called afore the Maire for the tyme beyng iiij of the moste Connyng discrete and able playeres within this Citie to serche here and examen all the plaiers and plaies and pagentes thrughoute all the articiferes belonging to corpus christi Plaie And all suche as thay shall fynde sufficiant in personne and Connyng to the honour of the Citie and Worship of the saide Craftes for to admitte and able and all other insufficiant personnes either in Connyng voice or personne to discharge ammove and avoide.[57]

In the sixteenth century, the City Clerk was even on hand with the Register or complete manuscript containing the play texts at the first station early in the morning to see that each play was being presented properly.[58]

The first pageant in the York cycle dramatized the Creation and Fall of Lucifer, for which the text has been attributed to the York Realist, the master of alliterative verse who also contributed in a major way to the central plays on the Passion. The opening play was the responsibility of the Barkers, who were closely associated with the Tanners. (Indeed, in the Ordo of 1415 the Tanners are listed as the responsible guild, though a second list drawn up by the town clerk in c.1422 gives the pageant to the Barkers.) These guilds, though because of the nature of their craft rather lacking in prestige, had been very important in the life of the city in the early fourteenth century before the wool trade had become dominant.[59]

The York cycle continued in subsequent pageants through the Creation and the fall of Adam and Eve, through certain other Old Testament stories, and through the life of Christ from the Annunciation to the Ascension and the final scenes of the life of Mary before concluding at last with a spectacular Doomsday pageant presented by the prestigious Mercers. The pageant and properties for this pageant are described in an indenture dated 1433 which includes puppets representing angels and an elaborate mechanism for Christ, who wears "a Sirke Wounded," to descend upon at the Judgment, whereupon he will sit upon a "Rainbow of tymber" as he sits as Judge.[60] The scene must not have been too different from the well-known restored Last Judgment wall painting in the Church of St. Thomas of Canterbury, Salisbury.[61] A lost fourteenth-century window in the Bedern Chapel at York had illustrated the Last Judgment which, like the York play, had included angels with the signs of the Passion (one held a cross, and another a crown of thorns) as well as figures rising from their graves below.[62] An illumination in the early fifteenth-century Bolton Hours (York Minster Library, MS. Add. 2, fol. 208), a book copied by a scribe named John in or near York in c.1420, shows Christ's wounds profusely bleeding, as he sits on a rainbow with clouds folded underneath; he also is flanked by two angels blowing trumpets.[63] In spite of the stylized and even crude figure drawing in the lower part of the illumination, terror and joy are nevertheless present among those who rise from their graves with the expectation of salvation (represented by the presence of St. Peter) or damnation (to which hell mouth opens).

In the scene of the Last Judgment in the York play, the tableau is much more complex emotionally than any such simple issuing forth into joy as might have been expected if the drama had been primarily dependent upon the Corpus Christi liturgy rather than on scenes commonly depicted in art. Here the end of the world comes, bringing home to the viewer a strong element of fear, for who knows how he will fare on that "dredful" Last Day? Significantly, the Last Judgment as set forth in the drama, unlike the Apocalypse scenes in the East Window of York Minster, draws mainly on the account in *Matthew* 25 rather than on the *Apocalypse*; Christ, when he turns to saints and sinners who are arrayed at his right and at his left, stresses the Corporal Acts of Mercy—a topic which forms the basis for a window in All Saints, North Street. On the Last Day, all souls will be raised from the grave and will look forward to an eternity of either bliss or torture. Those who have lived wicked lives, even if they had been ecclesiastics of high rank, will be forcibly taken off to hell by demons; such is the case in a fifteenth-century alabaster at the British Museum which shows the damned entering into hell. On the other hand, another alabaster shows those who, however, have respected the work of salvation wrought by Christ; these will receive a much happier reward—everlasting bliss—after being welcomed into Paradise by St. Peter.

In some cases the visual traditions drawn upon by the York Mercers in their pageant are not easy to establish. For example, the nine puppet angels "payntid rede to renne aboute in the heauen"[64] were apparently moved by mechanical means, but we can only surmise that they circled around Christ, clockwise, as in the original glass in the West Window at Fairford, where the Judge was encircled by flamelike red angels which we must identify as seraphim (fig. 6).[65] (The present glass in this part of the West Window is a nineteenth-century "restoration" by Chance Bros. & Co. of Smethwick.) The musical effects into which the play dissolves at the end are perhaps no less difficult to ascertain. The Judge indicates that "Nowe is fulfillid all my forthoght" (l. 373) to signify the completion of all his work as Creator; following the final line of the play, angels will continue to sing as they cross from place to place: "*Et sic facit finem, cum melodia angelorum transiens a loco ad loco*" (l. 380*sd*). Though the dramatic records do not indicate the nature of the singers employed for such angel roles, a reasonable conjecture would point to singing men and boys from one of the ecclesiastical foundations of York, perhaps from the Cathedral itself.

The Doomsday play is a powerful reminder of the *terminus* of earthly life for the individual man or woman, and it is particularly suited to the emphasis on last things which appears in fifteenth-century art. The painting of the Last Judgment at St. Thomas, Salisbury, is over the chancel arch, and hence will be immediately noticed by anyone who steps into the nave of the church. Tristram notes that by the fifteenth century the "normal position" for the Last Judgment "was above the chancel arch, since it symbolized the division between this world and the next."[66] The nave itself had come to represent life in this world, beginning from the West, a direction associated with evil and death, and moving toward the high altar in the East, the direction associated with heaven and ultimately the Second Coming, for which reason prayers were always directed in an easterly direction.[67] The crossing between the nave and chancel was held to symbolize the entry from earthly life into heaven. The sanctuary, where the sacred rite of the Eucharist was performed daily for the salvation of the living and the dead and where the Sacrament was reserved at the high altar, was distinguished by the real presence of God. When a citizen or anyone else worshipped in the nave of the parish church, he was conscious that he was within that portion which symbolically represented his current location in the scheme of things; it was appropriate that the upkeep of the nave of the church was normally the responsibility of the parishioners while the upkeep of the chancel was the duty of the clergy. When a person stepped forward to receive Communion at the high altar on the most solemn festival of the year, at Easter, he was offered a fore-taste of heavenly bliss, and attendance at Mass on other days normally meant looking intently and devoutly at the consecrated Host held up by the priest for all to venerate as the body of Christ.[68] The sufferings of Christ, who was *human* as well as divine, were being made real for the worshipper within the structure of the rite, and everything was directed toward his ultimate salvation. Because of the rite, he might hope to enter into the final rest of heaven after Judgment Day. But the painting of the Doom over the chancel arch would remind him that the final salvation of heaven could only be reached by passing the ordeal of God's judgment, both in the Particular Judgment immediately following death and the Last Judgment at the end of history.

The Christ who returns in Judgment is, however, not merely a figure to be feared. The tableau which was offered to audiences at the end of the York cycle was also a dramatized version of an important devotional image. Very prominent in the late medieval representations of the Last Judgment are, as we have seen, those wounds which had been inflicted on Christ in his Passion and Crucifixion. Likewise, the symbols of his Passion also frequently appear, often held by angels.[69] On the roof bosses of the choir of Winchester Cathedral are representations of an unusually large number of symbols associated with the Passion, including the ewer and basin which Pilate used when he washed his hands and the lantern dropped by Malchus when St. Peter cut off his ear. One of these bosses also contains the wounds in Christ's hands, feet, and heart;[70] we see merely the parts of the body afflicted in sculpture that today might remind us of work by René Magritte. To a fifteenth-century viewer, however, the design of this boss would have had a devotional purpose which it shared with the representations of the instruments of the Passion. Badges worn by participants in the Pilgrimage of Grace included a similar design.[71] So also the text of the York Mercers' play announces that the people on the final day of history shall "see the woundes fyve" suffered by Christ (l. 71). The Mercers' Indenture of 1433 calls specifically for "vij grete Aungels halding the passion of god" and "iiij smaler Aungels gilted holding the passion."[72] The play itself seems to demand a minimum of four signs of the Passion: a crown of thorns, a scourge, a cross, and a spear which "vnto [Christ's] side was sette" (ll. 253–64).

Elsewhere in painted glass and other art, angels appear separately, holding the spear which pieced Christ's side, the scourge used for the Flagellation, the nails pounded into his hands and feet, the sponge which was put to his mouth, and so forth. All of these are brought together in the arms of Christ, the *Arma Christi*, as in painted glass formerly in St. Saviour's, York, and on a devotional woodcut now attached to a book of hours from York (York Minster Library, MS. XVI.K.6, fol. 44^v).[73]

The emphasis on the Passion even in representations of the Doom is reminiscent of the handling of the Image of Pity, in which

Christ appears above the tomb with the object of showing his wounds. The Image of Pity, which has been discussed by J. W. Robinson, combines the Resurrection theme—Christ rising above the tomb—with the soteriological work that he accomplished on the cross.[74] The focus of the practice of piety among clergy and citizens alike at York was often these five wounds, each of which might provide a meditative "place" successively. The number five itself becomes of supreme significance, and Sir Martin Bowes, for example, founded an Obit which covered the cost of distributing five penny loaves of bread "every sonday in the yeare for evermore within the . . . churche" of St. Cuthbert, Peasholm Green, "to v severall poore householders be it men or women of the said paryshe . . . in the honour of the v woundes of our Lord Jesus Chryst. . . ."[75] The wounds of Christ are hence connected not only with the Mass and its commemoration of the Crucifixion, but also with the works of mercy. Good deeds, then, will help to weight the balance against the Seven Deadly Sins at the Last Day, when the Archangel Michael performs the active task of separating the good and bad souls—a task he is doing in fifteenth-century painted glass at St. Mary Bishophill Junior, York, where he is using a scales to determine the worthiness of souls.[76]

In an interesting variant of the Christ showing his wounds and surrounded by the instruments of the Passion, the so-called "Christ of the Trades," found only in the West and South of England, connects the work of good deeds with the work actually performed daily by the crafts.[77] An example of a wall painting completed c.1490 at Breage, Cornwall, shows Christ crowned, with the wounds of the Scourging. He wears only the loincloth that we associate with the Crucifixion so that his bruised body may be shown off to the greatest extent, and he reaches up with his right hand to point out the wound in his side. His other hand is open to show the wound in his left palm. Around him is an aureole-shaped display of the tools of many trades, including a rake, shears, a saw, a trowel, etc. He stands upon a wheel.[78] These instruments of the trades substitute both for the symbols of the Passion and for the aureole which might be expected to surround the body of Christ. Such "paintings of

Christ in the apotheosis of manual work," writes O. Elfrida Saunders, "seem to reflect the new social ideas of the time."[79] But the paintings go much further, for they identify work as the appropriate offering of workmen to a Savior whose wounds provide a means of salvation and a devotional center for their lives. It is no accident that the York plays seem also to glorify work, with the good workmen pictured as pious craftsmen who understand fully the Christian story; bad workmen, on the other hand, are like the men who nail Christ to the cross: "What thei wirke wotte thai noght," Jesus says (*Crucifixio Cristi*, l. 261).

Also important in this regard was the identification of the craftsmen of York with the Infancy story, which was, along with the Passion, the part of the life of Christ most commonly illustrated in the visual arts. Joseph was, after all, a carpenter, whose status in life might cause Satan to sneer, in the York *Harrowing of Hell*, that Jesus' "fadir . . . was a write his mette to wynne" (ll. 229–30), but whose occupation was responsible for staging the very next play in the cycle, the *Resurrection*. The first announcement of the birth of the Savior, after all, had been to the humblest of men, shepherds watching their sheep on the hillside. In the York play dramatizing the annunciation to the shepherds, the shepherds, who were traditionally musicians who played instruments and sang as they tended their flocks, begin immediately after seeing the angel to attempt to imitate the angelic song (ll. 60–64, and *sd* at l. 64). Then they offer gifts, which are no less in value because they are humble than the gifts that will be presented to the Child by the Magi. The offerings of the crafts themselves must not be less worthy than the gifts of the greatest men in the realm. What emerges here is a civic piety that is democratic even within the socially stratified structure of a city dominated by the more affluent citizens, who controlled the corporation and from whose ranks the mayor was selected.

The society of York in the late Middle Ages was tradition-bound and conservative, obstructing change even at the price of declining as a commercial force in the region. Local religious preferences appear to have been thoroughly orthodox, though resistance to the ravages of Protestantism, which dissolved guilds and confiscated property within the city, would be slow to materialize before the ill-fated Pilgrimage of Grace—an act of rebellion that the city supported.[80] In Queen Elizabeth's reign, the citizens tended to cling to the older spirituality, which for many years included the presentation of the cycle plays or other dramas such as the Creed or Pater Noster[81] plays during the early summer each year. Archbishop Edmond Grindal, who played a role in the suppression of the plays, complained shortly after his arrival in the North in 1570:

> For the little experience I have of this people, methinks I see in them three evil qualities; which are, great ignorance, much dulness to conceive better instruction, and great stiffness to retain their wonted errors. I will labour as much as I can to cure every of these, committing the success to God.[82]

Ideas which seemed alien and aliens themselves were never very welcome in York, and among aliens were numbered men from other parts of England, especially the South. In 1578, the Minstels' Guild, which in the twilight of the civic plays had been assigned the pageant of Herod formerly "brought forth at the cherges of the lait masons of this Cittie," drew up ordinances that absolutely forbid any "forreyner" from "singinge or plainge vpon anie instrument within anie parishe within this Cittie. . . ." But the traditionalism in York did not mean that her citizens could not change their taste in art or in civic expression, yet conventional forms sometimes carried great weight with regard to iconography or other aspects of artistic presentation. In the text of the Ordo of 1415, the Nativity play is said to have included midwives—marking a traditional way of presenting the events of Christ's birth which had pertained in the earlier liturgical dramas such as the *Officium Pastorum* from Rouen.[83] Excellent fourteenth-century glass in York Minster shows the scene after the birth of the Child, with Joseph on the right and the Virgin reclining in bed, with the Infant in a manger overhead, and for midwives in the vernacular drama we need only consult the N-town Nativity, in which Salome attempts a gynecological examination of Mary that results in the withering of her hand.[84] But the text of the Nativity play in the York Register demands something quite different, with the need for the midwives totally eliminated and with the scene entirely changed.

The play exemplifies a treatment of the iconography of the Nativity influenced by the *Revelations* of St. Bridget of Sweden who, during a visit to Jerusalem near the end of the third quarter of the fourteenth century, had a vision in which she saw Christ's birth. Her description of the event is as follows:

> When all was prepared, the Virgin knelt down with great veneration in an attitude of prayer. . . . Thus, with her hands extended and her eyes fixed on the sky, she was rapt as in ecstasy, lost in contemplation, in a rapture of divine sweetness. And while she was engaged thus in prayer, I saw the child in her womb move, and suddenly in a moment she gave birth to her son, from whom radiated such an ineffable light and splendor that the sun was not comparable to it. . . . [A]ll of a sudden I saw the glorious infant lying on the ground naked and shining. . . . Then I heard also the singing of angels, which was of miraculous sweetness and great beauty.[85]

In painted glass at Fairford and Great Malvern (fig. 7), the Child, who is shivering with cold, extends "His hands in expectation of being clasped to His mother's breast,"[86] and in the York play the Virgin takes up the Child and prepares to dress him in whatever clothing happens to be available. Thereupon the play reintroduces Joseph, who, as in a portion of the Fairford window, returns on this cold evening with a candle and is struck by the greater light radiating from the Child. In this new way of setting forth the Nativity, the scene has been made specifically devoid of "cloth" and "bedde" (1. 24), an aspect which underlines the poverty of the place of Christ's birth—a theme which had been much emphasized in such Franciscan works as the *Meditations on the Life of Christ*. Joseph must be gone on an errand when Mary kneels to pray for grace, experiences "grete ioie" in her soul (1. 50), and recognizes that she has painlessly given birth to a Son who is at once God and man. It is characteristic of this new representation of the Nativity that the Child should miraculously appear on the ground before the Virgin; in drama at York he was probably represented by a doll placed in the center of a radiant mandorla, but the local dramatic records are silent about such details.

The York Nativity play simply carries one step further the devotional attitude which was normally directed at sacred images, both those imagined and those present in art or drama. Mary reacts to her divine Child in a way consistent with Northern spirituality, in which men and women responded emotionally to the event depicted. The scene takes on a life of its own as the action is generated by the image of the Infant Christ on the ground. The play is dependent not only upon the iconography found in St. Bridget's *Revelations* as filtered through the visual arts, but also upon the emotional aesthetic of religious art which arose in the Low Countries and spread to York and other parts of England. The stage at York was simply not innovative with regard to iconographic details, but depended on other traditions for the receipt of its visual tableaux. It hence seems not credible that the stage was iconographically innovative or that it was a major influence on the painting of scenes in art, the carving of alabasters, or the production of illuminated manuscripts.[87] On the other hand, the presentations on pageant wagons and on fixed stages in York, Chester, Coventry, East Anglia, and elsewhere in England were likely to have been deeply influenced by forms present in the visual arts. Painters and other artists, after all, were retained to work on the pageants to prepare them for the productions, and when a new Mercers' pageant was required in the early sixteenth century the task was done by Thomas Drawswerd and his workshop, normally workers in alabaster but also skilled painters.

Oddly, however, the record in the Ordo of 1415 seems actually to represent a later practice, and involves an alteration in the entry in the *York Memorandum Book*, which hence designates a later version—presumably written after the copying of the plays in the Register in c.1470—that seems to have replaced the Brigittine-influenced play.[88] Thus, during the final decades in which the Nativity play was presented at Corpus Christi as part of the York cycle, there seems to have been a return to the old iconography and to the inclusion of midwives, who would certify the virginity of Mary and help to dispel disbelief. Also, judging from the incomplete evidence in the visual arts, the Brigittine iconography for the Nativity never actually became popular in York, for the only extant examples of this type are contained in woodcuts in service books printed on the continent for York use in the early years of the sixteenth century.[89]

The rather mechanistic examination of the visual arts for evidence of the stage hence would appear to be a highly speculative endeavor, but on the other hand if both stage and the visual arts are together seen as evidence of traditional forms, traditional spirituality, and a common context for artistic expression, then the range of what we can discover will be potentially very broad in scope. Respect for the traditions which underlie the art and drama—and which historically in many cases underlie modern attitudes and social structures—would, however, seem to be absolutely necessary if we are to succeed in allowing the drama and the art to illuminate the past and to allow us to find the ways in which we are connected to that past. York in the fifteenth and early sixteenth centuries may seem to us to be very foreign, but the middle class culture that was engendered in that city and in so many other cities in late medieval Europe was ultimately critical for the rise of those cultural patterns which would enable Western culture to achieve modernity. And if modernity rejects its roots in the past, such a turning away from its debt to its dead forebears—and to the images and dramatic scenes that nourished them—would seem to be an ultimate form of denial, a process that is analogous to the denial in which an alcoholic engages when he or she insists that "there is no problem."

To understand the past is not to sentimentalize it. But if the York of the period under discussion has nothing more to teach us, it nevertheless will show us how important the *visual* deserves to be in our lives. The religious theater in the streets of York and of other cities was a visible sign of unseen realities—and an imaginative display designed for the religious feast of Corpus Christi. So too the visual arts were regarded as central to the cognitive experience of the citizens. Both stand in contrast to the popular arts of our day which, in the guise of commercial television, for example, may function as a true opiate of the people as the Corpus Christi plays or religious images in the fifteenth and early sixteenth centuries never did. York's history is not a story of repression but of the achievement of a social balance, and its adopting of the spirituality common across Northern Europe liberated its creative forces so that it could sustain a popular civic theater—and a very expensive theater indeed—for two centuries. When under Protestantism the religious images were destroyed, hidden away, or sold on the continent, and when the plays were suppressed, the visual imagination found itself under attack—and in the England of the middle of the seventeenth century that attack would seem to have been successful. The pageant houses which had housed the pageant wagons at York and Coventry by then were no longer in use—a sign that the wagons themselves had been disposed of—and when James Torre wrote his descriptions of the painted glass of York Minster and the city churches, he often could not recognize the most common iconography[90]—a sign that the understanding of visual traditions had been successfully undermined even as the Protestant clergy claimed to have improved the quality of religious education, now an exercise dependent entirely on language rather than images.[91]

4

"What hempen home-spuns have we swagg'ring here?"

By the last third of the sixteenth century, there was a tendency in England to be very selective about the choice of traditional practices and values to preserve. Iconoclasm had swept away much of the imagery of the medieval Church, in the case of the Guild Chapel at Stratford-upon-Avon involving Shakespeare's father in the vandalizing of the building's Catholic iconography in the months before the birth of the future dramatist in 1564.[1] At the same time, as every reader of Edmund Spenser's *Faerie Queene* will recognize, much traditional iconography was retained. For example, the figure of the Red Crosse Knight in Book I is adapted from St. George, whose role as the patron saint of England was reinforced rather than obliterated under the Protestant Queen Elizabeth I.[2] In the visual arts, there was also a curious return to the flat surfaces and symbolic designs but without the Catholic religious content of medieval times. Nevertheless, the official attitude toward the popular religious arts—and also the popular religious theater with its Catholic iconography—tended more and more to be condescending.

In his *Defense of Poesie*, the most important critical work of the period, Sir Philip Sidney had complained about the persistence of allegedly decadent traditional forms (he sees them as "gross absurdities") in the London theaters, which staged plays that did not conform to the classical models and, significantly, failed to maintain the pure genres established in antiquity.[3] The appeal to classical standards was the outgrowth of the Protestant variety of humanism which Sidney shared with a large segment of educated persons in England. It was probably not only the Catholicism of the York Creed Play, therefore, that informed the reaction of Dean Matthew

56

Hutton in 1568 when he objected to the performance of this play as an alternative to the Creation to Doom cycle. Dean Hutton, upon examination of the playbook, saw much that was not allowable because it was inconsistent with the "the senceritie of the gospell" to a degree which could not be remedied; though the "ignorant sort" would like the play, and though it would have been satisfactory in the 1530's, it now needed in his view to be regarded as obsolete, barbarous, and seditious: "I knowe the learned will mislike it. . . ."[4]

Shakespeare, who was to become the principal playwright of his age, may be said to be both a product of the theatrical traditions that grew out of the Middle Ages—traditions which determined the configuration of the stage and even denied that stage to women actors[5]—and, in typical Renaissance fashion, consciously unsympathetic to the theatrical forms of the popular medieval stage as he himself must have encountered it as a young man. Such earlier popular drama is parodied by Shakespeare in Act V of *A Midsummer Night's Dream* in the play-within-a-play, which adapts a debased classical plot to amateur theatricals.

The play-within-a-play in Act V, entitled *The Most Lamentable Comedy and Most Cruel Death of Pyramus and Thisby* (I.ii.11–12),[6] is a skit which, according to Shakespeare's text, will be acted at court by a group of amusing "handicraft" men of ancient Athens (see IV.ii.10). Puck, when he sees these amateur actors in rehearsal in Act III, exclaims:

> What hempen home-spuns have we swagg'ring here,
> So near the cradle of the Fairy Queen?
> What, a play toward? . . . (III.i.77–79)

Clearly Puck represents the view of one who is sophisticated and who can recognize citizens of a provincial town when he sees them. Visualized in terms of craftsmen—like Shakespeare's own father, a glover, such men were potentially of some standing and political power in provincial cities of his own time—Bottom the weaver and his companions are not intended to flatter the pretensions of civic pride among this category of men outside of London. For his portrait of these amateur actors, Shakespeare seems deeply indebted to the theatrical practices in the time of his childhood. Of course, such craftsmen-actors are hardly imitated in *A Midsummer Night's Dream* without distortion or caricature. Ultimately Shakespeare's amateurs are transformed into players who present a broadly comic travesty of a mythological tragedy before a courtly audience.

The purpose of this play-within-a-play seems to be at least threefold:

1. To exploit questions of imagination and stage reality as they are established in the main action and the themes of *A Midsummer Night's Dream*.

2. To burlesque the older dramatic styles (including especially, of course, the theatrical styles of the public theaters fashionable before c.1585) with their tendency toward bombastic language and clumsy use of mythological subjects.

3. Further to link this burlesque with the acting of craftsmen amateurs, which Shakespeare in any case would have regarded as inadequate in comparison with the kind of highly professional work that was being done at the time by the dramatist's own company.

The confusion which exists in the minds of the craftsmen-actors between reality and illusion, between the actual and the imaginary,[7] thus not only serves to achieve the impression of the *primitive* but also reflects the traditional theatrical practices of those members of the craft guilds in England who formerly presented stories from the Christian myths to audiences of their peers and, upon occasion, to royal audiences.

The "hempen home-spuns" thus represent the parodying of a tradition of acting with which Shakespeare as a child could hardly have avoided contact in Stratford-upon-Avon, a town dominated by tradesmen among whom his own father, John Shakespeare, served as a chamberlain and eventually, in 1568–69, as bailiff or chief officer of the Corporation.[8] In Stratford, it is inconceivable that a boy who later joined a professional acting company would not have seen all types of theatrical presentations, including the productions of plays by amateurs from the same social class as his father, whose trade as a glover included business interests that extended to other kinds of transactions such as dealings in the wool trade.

As is well known, Shakespeare very likely as a boy attended one of the most extensive and highly honored amateur presentations in the England of his time in nearby Coventry—the Coventry Corpus Christi plays on biblical topics ranging from at least the Nativity to the terminus of history on Doomsday.[9] Shakespeare's acquaintance with these plays may be surmised by Hamlet's reference to a ranting player (comparable perhaps to the "tyrant" roles in which Bottom claims to specialize) as one who "out-Herods Herod" (*Hamlet* III.ii.14). Such an acting technique, characterized by noise and exaggerated action that tips over into comedy, was precisely what was achieved in the presentation of the tyrant Herod in the Coventry Shearmen and Taylors' Pageant, where, as we have seen above in the previous chapter, this figure demonstrates his anger in wild ways, culminating in the raging described in the stage direction which reports his antics both *in the pagond and in the strete.*[10]

That Shakespeare later in his career recollected such characters as Herod that he had seen in his boyhood while attending the plays at Coventry was suggested more than a century ago by Halliwell-Phillipps,[11] who also noted Dugdale's comment in the seventeenth century on the former popularity of these plays: "I myselfe have spoke with some old people who had in their younger yeares bin eye-witnesses of these pageants soe acted, from whome I have bin tolde that the yearly confluence of people *from farr and neare* to see that shew was extraordinary great, and which yielded noe small advantage to this citty."[12] The possible influence of these plays on the presentation of the "hempen home-spuns" in *A Midsummer Night's Dream* had been further claimed by Howard Staunton: "in the rude dramatic performance of these handicraftsmen of Athens, Shakespeare was referring to the plays and pageants exhibited by the trading companies of Coventry, which were celebrated down to his own time, and which he might very probably have witnessed."[13] It is unwise to follow the nineteenth-century critics in too great a precision in treating the question of this background in traditional civic drama for the "rude mechanicals" of *A Midsummer Night's Dream*; nevertheless, we would be advised to look more closely at the amateur craftsman traditions of the city with which Shakespeare would have been most familiar—a city which in many ways may be regarded as typical of the late medieval stage.

The Coventry plays, which according to the city annals cited by Thomas Sharp were "invented" in 1416[14] though an earlier date is more likely,[15] cannot not be entirely documented: with the exception of the Shearmen and Taylors' Pageant of the Nativity and the Weavers' pageant of the Purification and Christ in the Temple at Age Twelve that were preserved in sixteenth-century copies,[16] the remainder of the cycle is lost. However, extensive records do exist for the Smiths' play which treated the central Passion scenes, the Cappers' (Cardmakers' prior to 1531) play of the Harrowing and Resurrection, and the Drapers' Doomsday play.[17] These plays were scheduled for production each year at Corpus Christi time[18] as part of the festivities associated with the Great or Corpus Christi Fair, a major event in the economic life of the city. Even Lollardy among the citizens and, later, Protestantism[19] seem not to have affected zeal for the production of this drama, though economic decline in the city clearly had an effect on its staging. In 1539 Mayor Coton had appealed on economic grounds to Thomas Cromwell for relief from the expenses of the plays: "at Corpus christi tide/ the poore Comeners be at suche charges with ther playes and pagyontes/ that thei fare the worse all the yeire after. . . ."[20] The plays themselves were, however, apparently regarded very highly in the sixteenth century among both Catholics and Protestants, suggesting that certain Catholic devotional elements may have been purged in the course of the period between the 1530's and their suppression in 1579, when official Protestantism was indeed coming down more strongly on the side of the abolition of the mysteries.[21] Nevertheless, it is reported that in Queen Mary's time a weaver, John Careles, whose Protestant piety was intense enough to earn him imprisonment and a place in John Foxe's *Acts and Monuments*,[22] "was let out to play in the Pageant about the City with his companions. And that done, keeping touch with his keeper, he returned agayne into prison at his houre appointed."[23]

Royal spectators came to Coventry upon occasion to see the plays, which were regarded as an appropriate offering for such distinguished visitors. In 1456, for example, Queen Margaret came to see the plays, which were acted before her with the exception of the Doomsday play that was not staged due to the lateness of the hour.[24] Another royal visitor who came to see the plays was King Richard III in 1485,[25] but such honored guests of the city when visiting at other times than Corpus Christi would even then be treated to pageants, using the wagons owned by the craft guilds, at various stations throughout the city. Hence for Queen Elizabeth's visit to Coventry in 1566 the pageants of the Tanners, Weavers, Drapers, and Smiths were utilized.[26] The craft guilds at Coventry were thus accustomed to present pageants and plays before the most distinguished visitors the city might entertain. It would appear from the records that the choice of pageants might be made by the Corporation and that to be chosen for such presentation was considered to be an honor for the craft involved.[27]

Further, as Furness had suspected, there is also an implied relationship between Shakespeare's play and the Midsummer watch or Midsummer show.[28] Sharp quoted a manuscript copy of Coventry Annals which under the date of August 1628 cited "the Pageants playing here in this Cytty, and Midsummer watch, which said Pageants and watch have bine put downe many yeares since. . . ."[29] Unfortunately, the extant documents from Coventry tell us little about the content of entertainments for Midsummer, a festival which (as in modern Sweden) was traditionally associated with the Feast of St. John the Baptist.[30] Nevertheless, the participation of the pageants at least upon occasion is indicated by an entry of c.1541–43 in the undated Cappers' accounts: "It[em] for the pagant that was gyven to maister merre on mydsomer night off ye Crafte" at the cost of twenty-six shillings and eightpence.[31] But in May 1591, the commons requested that John Smith's play on the subject of the *Destruction of Jerusalem*, which had been first staged in 1584, be revived for presentation on "Midsomer daye."[32] The council further in the same entry, however, proceeded to legislate that "all the mey poles that nowe are standing in this Cittie shalbe taken downe before whitsonday next, non hereafter to be sett vpp in this Cittie."[33] The *Destruction of Jerusalem* may have been "preferr'd" this year and thus staged—it was one of three possible choices—though the short time allowed for preparation of the play possibly proved inadequate for the revival of a spectacular production such as that originally staged in 1584.[34] The evidence for dramatic involvement in the festivities of Midsummer at Coventry is murky; nevertheless, the documentation is sufficient to suggest the appropriateness of civic drama on such an occasion—an occasion which, to be sure, largely informs the spirit of *A Midsummer Night's Dream*.[35]

In the case of *The Most Lamentable Comedy and Most Cruel Death of Pyramus and Thisby*, production by a group of craftsmen begins with a meeting to cast the play—a procedure not so different from what took place in Coventry and elsewhere. Those present—a carpenter and joiner,[36] a weaver and a bellowsmender, a tinker and a tailor—have their names listed on a scroll as those regarded as most "fit, through all Athens, to play in our enterlude before the Duke and the Duchess, on his wedding-day at night" (I.ii.5–7). Such a list of Coventry men, drawn from the Cappers' records, is available for 1566, when it would appear, however, that their pageant was not one of those "preferr'd." The list, which contains the names of two dozen amateur players, is headed with the statement: "The names of them that be agrayd to playe our pagyand and tobe at commandement to that we shall be laydto atthe quenes."[37] That such guilds also did not choose all their actors from their own numbers is indicated by other records from Coventry—e.g., in 1550 Hugh Heynes, a capper, played the role of Anna in the Weavers' *Purification*.[38]

In charge of casting *Pyramus and Thisby* is Quince, the carpenter, who functions as director. Evidence for pageant masters in charge of individual plays in the Coventry cycle is fragmentary at best,[39] but in the Smiths' accounts for 1453 Thomas Colclow, a skinner, is appointed to "have the Rewle of the pajaunt unto the end of xij yers next folowing he for to find the pleyers and all that longeth therto all the seide terme. . . ."[40] Colclow was not an author of the Smiths' play, nor should we assume that Quince, because he provides a prologue for the production and oversees changes in the play prepared for Act V of *A Midsummer Night's Dream*,[41] is the original author of the play script of the play of *Pyramus and Thisby*.

This play, like the plays in the craft cycle of Coventry suppressed only slightly more than a decade and a half prior to *A Midsummer Night's Dream*, does not avoid female roles, though the amateur actors assembled in Act I, Scene ii, are all male. Such a practice of assigning male actors to female roles, as noted above, also reflects the usage on the Elizabethan professional stage. The role of Thisby is to be played by Flute, the bellows mender, who objects that he has "a beard coming" (I.ii.48)—an indication that the role is to be taken by a youth whose voice may be beyond the breaking stage—while Robin Starveling, a tailor, will play Thisby's mother. (The latter role, of course, is eliminated in the actual play in Act V.) Female roles at Coventry had also apparently been handled traditionally by an all-male cast. For example, in addition to the example of Hugh Heynes cited above, the role of Anna in the Weavers' play was taken in 1524 by Thomas Sogdyn and in 1544 by Richard, Borsley's man, while in 1524 the Virgin Mary in the same play was played by Richard Bryskow.[42] In 1496, Procula, Pilate's wife, was played by Ryngold's man, Thomas, and in 1499 the role was also taken by a man.[43] Unquestionably male actors playing such roles would have spoken "small," indeed quite appropriately affecting "a monstrous little voice," as Bottom labels it (I.ii.52). The term 'small' in connection with voice indicates "Gentle, low, soft; of little power or strength; not loud, harsh, or rough" (*OED*). Surely *falsetto* would seem to be indicated for the actor playing Flute when he takes on the role of Thisby. To allay his embarrassment, Flute is further told that he will be allowed to wear a mask that will provide additional disguise to hide his true identity (I.ii.49). Animal disguise will also need to be provided for Snug the joiner, who will play the lion.

Once the roles have been assigned, Quince will hand out the "parts" containing the actors' lines and their cues. Further evidence of the contents of the texts distributed to the actors is contained in the rehearsal in Act III, Scene i, when Bottom insists on speaking "all [his] part at once, cues and all" (III.i.99–101). These parts are then to be learned quickly—"con them by tomorrow night" (I.ii.100–01)—prior to the rehearsal which is being called "in the palace wood, a mile without the town," where they will rehearse "by moonlight" (I.ii.101–02).[44] In Coventry, rehearsals were recorded to have been held indoors in St. Mary's Hall but also outdoors in a park, the latter outside the city walls south of the city.[45] The location of *A Midsummer Night's Dream* is thus unusual, but in the context of the play the rural setting is necessary to connect the amateur players with other elements of the action of Shakespeare's drama.

During the time between the casting of the play and the rehearsal, Quince will take it upon himself to "draw a bill of properties, such as our play wants" (I.ii.105–06). Presumably this "bill," or list, was an inventory which would include not only the necessary props—e.g., the fatal "dagger" which will cause the deaths of the hero and heroine of the play-within-a-play—but also the essential costumes, beards, wigs, and masks. Such inventories are present for the Coventry plays as they are for other similar cycles of plays in the Middle Ages.[46] Hence in 1591 the Coventry Cappers' accounts list, among "the Implments of the company," those items that belonged to their Corpus Christi play, which to be sure had been "laid down" and not performed since 1579. Included are "one play boke," costumes such as a doublet for Pilate and a gown for Mary Magdalene, a spade and distaff for Adam and Eve (after the Fall), a hell mouth, streamers, masks, and/or wigs (e.g., "pylates heade fyve maries heades," "godes head the spirites heade"), beards, armor and weapons such as a sword and dagger, etc.[47] Of particular interest here may be the head-pieces for the Marys, who will appear in the scene of the holy women at the empty tomb where they will encounter the angel that will inform them about the Resurrection. But others will also appear to have worn masks and/or wigs—i.e., Pilate, Jesus, and the Anima Christi who harrows hell.

The mask which is promised to Flute thus may be a reflection not of any practice in antiquity but rather of a traditional practice of the popular (and perhaps folk) theater. If such a disguise were actually used in early productions of the play-within-a-play in *A Midsummer Night's Dream*, the disguise would have set off the amateur actor very distinctly from the professionals in Shakespeare's company playing the roles of aristocratic men and women of Athens. It is remarkable perhaps that the reference to a dramatic presentation staging the Resurrection at Beverley as early as c.1220 includes mention of masks, which are worn by actors "as usual."[48] Caution may, however, be in order. The use of masks in the medieval drama has recently been surveyed by Meg Twycross and Sarah Carpenter,[49] who have provided a reliable guide to this traditional aspect of the medieval theater for the first time. In examining the earlier Coventry Cappers' inventory for 1567, they suggest that the reference there to "heds" was most likely to *wigs*.[50] Such items of attire indeed would have been necessary not only for men playing, for example, the three holy women at Coventry, but also for Flute in Shakespeare's play. The mask to be worn by Flute therefore turns out to be ambiguous, though minimally we can assume that it included a wig and also perhaps involved some kind of face covering as well.

We are on safer ground when we turn to the facial disguise mentioned for the character of Pyramus: "I will discharge [the role] in either your straw-color beard, your orange-tawny beard, your purple-in-grain beard, or your French-crown-color beard, your perfit yellow," Bottom insists (I.ii.93–96). Admittedly, some of these options seem bizarre enough, but the use of an easily attached beard itself involved a disguise that was standard practice in the amateur theater. Three beards remained in the Cappers' inventory in 1591,[51] whereas in 1579 and earlier years two beards were supplied for the Weavers' play, a drama that included only two mature male roles, Symeon and Joseph, with speaking parts.[52] From the Weavers' accounts of 1572, we learn that these beards were at that time rented from a man named Harry Benete.[53] May we not assume that the kinds of beards listed as options by Bottom might have been available for loan or hire in the imaginary ancient Athens of Shakespeare just as perhaps they might have been in a contemporary English city?

The animal mask and further disguise demanded by the role of Lion in the play-within-a-play bring us to the complicated question of animal disguise, which has been observed in folk tradition as a strong convention throughout England at least since the sixteenth century.[54] Actors disguised as lions, however, appear to have been used much earlier in the medieval Latin music-dramas on the subject of Daniel; these theatrical beasts must have had elaborate mouths that were large enough to open and "swallow" human beings.[55] Other kinds of animal disguise associated with the theater and entertainment are illustrated by Twycross and Carpenter—e.g., the mummers with animal heads in Bodley MS. 264, fol. 181[v], from the middle of the fourteenth century, and a lion parade helmet dated c.1460 from Aragon.[56] The use of lion disguise in the play-within-a-play in *A Midsummer Night's Dream* may also have provided a hint to Shakespeare concerning the transformation of Bottom, who is fixed with an ass' head—one of the disguises shown in the miniature in Bodley MS. 264 noted above.[57]

In the rehearsal which will be interrupted by Puck in Act III, Scene i, the actors meet on a "green plot [which] shall be our stage, this hawthorn brake our tiring-house" (ll. 3–5). The staging envisioned here is hardly that of the civic mysteries of the streets of Coventry, where pageant wagons were utilized to give flexibility and visibility to portions of the action, which would be augmented by the use of the place, or *platea*. The idea of the stage thus seems purely Elizabethan. During the rehearsal, Bottom in his humorously obnoxious way continues to give advice concerning the production and encourages Quince to "Write me a prologue" (III.i.17ff), a task which of course will be carried out prior to the performance. Quince, as the person who holds the book containing the text of the play, also is responsible for seeing that the agreed-upon changes are made in the play-text. There is also some radical alteration of the casting, with one actor re-assigned to be the Man in the Moon and another to be the wall that separates the two lovers. The representation of the parents seems to be dropped in the curious interest of a comic attempt at achieving verisimilitude with actors personifying the moon and the wall! Needless to say, contrary to the general practice of the Coventry amateur actors as documented in the Coventry records, which suggest either two or three rehearsals,[58] this is the only rehearsal that the rude mechanicals will have before their presentation before the Duke and the court.

The production is only saved from cancellation by the reappearance of Bottom, who ought, if Flute is correct in his judgment, to be given payment of sixpence per day for life hereafter for playing Pyramus (IV.ii.21–24): "Sixpence a day in Pyramus, or nothing." It is unfortunate that instead the playwright does not give the amount of payment expected for playing in this particular production. Payments to individual actors in the Weavers' accounts for 1579 range between fourpence each for angels and the infant in arms (for the Child Jesus) to three shillings fourpence for Symeon, though there were other expenses which would tend to suggest fringe benefits, probably in the form of refreshments, during the rehearsals.[59]

In Act IV, Scene ii, the actors must collect their costumes, see that their beards have "good strings," attach "new ribands to [their] pumps," and look over their parts. The show will go on. Bottom's final advice concerns Thisby's need for "clean linen," the lion's need for long fingernails ("for they shall hang out for the lion's claws"), and all the actors' requirement that they should not eat anything that might give them bad breath during their staging of the comic tragedy which they have attempted to patch together. We next see the actors in their appropriate disguises entering the hall before the Duke and the court, who have chosen the "tedious brief scene of young Pyramus/ And his love Thisby; very tragical mirth" for their entertainment—a play to be presented by "Hard-handed men that work in Athens here,/ Which never labor'd in their minds till now" (V.i.56–57, 72–73).

The prologue and the play itself will begin with trumpet flourishes,[60] thus utilizing an instrument that was widely used in the civic drama in Coventry and elsewhere. In 1571, the Coventry drapers paid the trumpeter twenty pence for his services in their play,[61] while the Mercers' accounts for their participation in the new *Destruction of Jerusalem* in 1584 provide a direct comparison between the cost of the trumpeter (3s 4d) and the rest of the musicians (5s

4d). In the same year, the Smiths hired a flute player for two shillings and sixpence, other musicians for five shillings, two drummers for fivepence each, and "Cocckam in earnest for to playe on his bagpypes, iiij d."[62] If, according to one plan for the conclusion of the play-within-a-play, the ending was to be a song or "ballet" (IV.i.214–19), very possibly some kind of accompaniment would have been envisioned. Musicians nevertheless were required for the Bergomask which does in fact stand at the end of the play of *Pyramus and Thisby* (see V.i.361). Such framing by music would have been most appropriate for this play, which, as Theseus invites us to recognize, provides us with sport at what the actors mistake (see V.i.90).

The "enterlude" of the "hempen home-spuns" thus serves by its burlesque of amateur actors to set apart their play-within-a-play from the main actions of *A Midsummer Night's Dream* and hence to provide a comment on the role of imagination itself—a theater which Shakespeare's company represented at its professional best. Shakespeare's use of representations of such amateur actors drawn from the tradesmen's guilds functions as parody of the practices of those whose abilities and theories were less than professional. It is likely, therefore, that Shakespeare was indeed in part thinking of the kind of acting that he had presumably seen as a child in Coventry and also perhaps elsewhere in the Midlands. But his burlesque of such actors and their theatrical practices could surely as well have been directed at the pretensions of volunteer thespians at any number of English towns and cities throughout most of the sixteenth century. Nevertheless, it should be countered that Shakespeare's negative view of such plays and players in provincial cities and towns is probably misleading in the extreme, for the spectacles that cities like Coventry were able to mount were surely not so rough and amateurish as we might imagine. Coventry spent a surprisingly large amount of money on the plays each year when they were presented, and indeed it would seem that civic honor hinged on the excellence of the plays, which functioned like a magnet to bring visitors to the city. Even Henry VII, upon visiting Coventry to see the plays in 1493, "much commended them."[63] In other words, the quality of the production was surely much, much higher than Shakespeare's play-within-a-play in *A Midsummer Night's Dream* would seem to suggest.

The play-within-a-play therefore utilizes traditional drama as a way of patronizing the past for the achievement of a specific dramatic purpose in the context of comedy; Shakespeare's debt to the earlier dramatic traditions of England in the play which is perhaps his greatest tragedy will be explored in the next chapter.

5

The Phenomenology of Suffering, Medieval Drama, and *King Lear*

The skepticism which recent scholars have directed toward the formerly neat explanations about the supposed origin of Elizabethan and Jacobean tragedy, said to have been located in the early morality tradition, has paradoxically revealed even closer connections between the theater of Shakespeare and his contemporaries, on one hand, and the medieval stage, on the other, than had previously been suspected. For example, John Wasson, noting that there is a total lack of reference to morality plays in dramatic records in England before the sixteenth century, has produced a highly convincing theory that finds one aspect of Renaissance tragedy already present in the medieval saint play with its potential death or martyrdom of the hero (e.g., St. Thomas Becket).[1] Thus too, as this chapter will suggest, certain elements of the medieval cycle drama that often staged the whole history of the world (with emphasis, of course, on the Nativity and Passion) likewise share something with the tragic spectacles of Shakespeare's time.

Connections of the sort that I shall trace in this chapter further are best examined by putting aside the critical methodology of pure literary criticism and by adopting a stance that is capable of probing the contours of dramatic and theatrical structures in their appropriate social, psychological, and historical contexts. Thus the attempt will be to expand somewhat the methodology utilized in Chapter 2 in the interest of allowing the data to emerge from the analysis of the play, which needs to be referred not merely back on itself but rather outward to the complex and historically distant context in which the writer, the actors, and the audience all lived and moved and had their existence. It will not serve merely to find political tensions in the drama (tensions which assuredly are there, though they may ultimately have a different signification than many literary critics with amateur historian status might imagine),[2] and instead I shall focus here on one aspect only—sorrow and *suffering*—as background to a single Jacobean play, *King Lear*.

As implied in Chapter 2, drama and the theater are not self-contained units capable of analysis only when they are regarded apart from their cultural and historical milieu. Plays as presented on stage unite words with visible images and actions, and when the latter are removed we indeed have but half the performance—a remnant only of the spectacle which has impressed itself upon an audience and moved it to laughter and tears. Nor will the audience have been a passively mechanical observer of all that has been heard or seen on the stage. Each viewer of the play joins what he or she sees on stage—the gestures, the postures, the scenery, the costumes—with the functioning of his or her own mind; that is, the action is *internalized* and hence is transformed into something unique for each individual. The intent of the playwright or of the actors was to plunge the viewers into an experience where they might be inspired to devotion, entertained, integrated further into the social order, or taunted with visions of suffering and sorrow that touch the sensitive places in their hearts. The latter, as it emerges in English dramatic traditions and extends into an early seventeenth-century play, provides the focus for this chapter.

Needless to say, the phenomenology of suffering is no simple matter. Suffering, as distinguished from the simple feeling of pain, requires human rational powers superior to the functions of the lower animals, and it necessitates a world-view that is inherently dualistic. Perhaps it is even possible to claim that suffering is not possible in any broader sense in a world that is not balanced between good and evil, between the power of deity and the antagonistic powers of darkness, between man's capability for harmony and love as opposed to his capacity for disharmony and hatred. If this is so, a world controlled absolutely by fate rules out the possibility of true suffering, for in such a world things are precisely as they are without choice. And without choice, there may be pain but, at least in the larger sense, no suffering. Further, suffering is a response to loss, a condition that implies change from a more desirable state to a less desirable one. When presented on stage, suffering will further result in a particular kind of audience response: i.e., members of the audience will share in the suffering and will experience *sorrow* concerning its ultimate termination, as in the death of a hero and/or heroine such as King Lear and his daughter Cordelia.

In the Middle Ages and Early Modern period, people tended to view evil as something outside themselves and yet also as residing within.[3] Suffering in medieval theology was the consequence of estrangement from God, the source of all good, while reconciliation was regarded as the route to healing the wounds of mental and physical anguish and suffering. *Suffering* indeed was widely regarded as the sign of man's humanity; to come to terms with the human condition was to accept suffering, which was man's heritage following the Fall and the Expulsion from the Garden of Eden. Eden, often represented in art as round or even womb-like—e.g., in the *Très riches Heures* of the Duke of Berry[4]—was the location in time and space for which the concepts of suffering and sorrow could as yet have no relevance. Hence, contemplation of Eden must inevitably have impressed on mankind his or her loss in terms both spatial and temporal. For a medieval audience, the presentation of the Creation with its setting forth of the Garden in the mystery cycles would have elicited nostalgia for the lost perfection represented by Adam and Eve before their Fall. Therefore it is not surprising also that Dante should have placed the Earthly Paradise atop the mount of Purgatory—i.e., at the last step of his pilgrimage before reaching his heavenly goal as it would be described in the *Paradiso*. The route to the redemption of eternity must thus lie through the geography of Eden, for which its circularity and perfection can no longer be discovered in the normal realm of Becoming disconnected from true Being. But to know about the perfect state, or to wish to reach it, must be the source of anguish among imperfect men. Suffering is therefore inevitable for anyone recognizing his or her true spiritual state, which cannot be truly measured or weighed until the Last Judgment when, as represented in the iconography of the *psychostasis*, the archangel Michael will test one's spiritual worth in the eternal scales. The springs of this suffering, then, are two-fold: inward and outward, through the demonic tempting which is exterior, and through the inward heredity which in spite of the real effects of baptism nevertheless determines a person's weakness and makes him or her liable to repeat the Fall daily in his or her life. The dialectic of inward and outward provides the substance of a surprisingly high percentage of the medieval dramas with its tension pushed in upon its characters often to the point of anguish. From the standpoint of audience response, the subjects displayed on stage function further to touch sensitive points in men's and women's psyches and to accentuate their discomfort.

The medieval plays of the Fall, therefore, function to provide the groundwork for the understanding of the human condition in all its fragility. According to tradition, the Fall may have been disconcertingly rapid, occurring at noon of the first day of the creation of Adam and Eve. With the beginning of the sun's descent toward the West, the first parents of the race also began the descent toward hell —a descent that, for them, was ultimately to be reversed at the time of the Harrowing. The West—i.e., the *occident* which by false etymology was associated with the Latin word *occidere*, 'to kill'—is, of course, identified metonymically with demons and hell. It is quite appropriate, therefore, that at noon external temptation should come to Eve, who should then communicate to her husband the disease (or, to be sure, her 'dis-ease,' leading to later suffering) of her submission to the Evil One. With the decline of Adam and Eve from true uprightness—symbolically, a decline from upright posture in the 'Fall'[5]—in the Garden, the race's troubles and its suffering must begin.

The traditional medieval understanding of the Fall is quite clear: without temptation from without, Adam and Eve would not thus have condemned all their descendants to such an unhappy history; only through the assistance of exterior temptation were they tempted to gluttony and pride, which caused the first anguish of mind in the world. The primordial fall had, after all, been Lucifer's along with his cohorts, a fall frequently enough represented in the visual arts in specimens such as the early fifteenth-century glass in the East Window of York Minster which shows two transformed and ugly demons (one of them is very fragmentary) falling across the firmament.[6] Lucifer's pretensions toward godlike power had, of course, preceded those of the first parents, and for his pride Lucifer had lost his brightness. The conflict in heaven as shown in such plays as the York *Creation of Heaven and Earth* (or, *Fall of Lucifer*) is, however, a political struggle in which the disobedient angels express their utter foolishness in opposing the source of all power; as they establish their role as the unhappy antagonists of all that is good, their only anguish is their selfish response at being hurled into the outer darkness within the hell mouth that is physically present on the set—a location where all is dirty and unpleasant. The model as herein established therefore does not include the introspective suffering that we would expect of human beings, for the fallen angels, unlike men and women, do not have the choice of ever returning to their original level. Men and women will be judged at the Last Day and divided into two groups (exemplified in the earliest times by the figures of Cain and Abel), but the fallen angels always will remain alienated from their source in their Maker. Devils thus exemplify the submission to evil that men and women must necessarily overcome if they are to transcend the appearances of mundane experience. As abstract model, however, the devils are also characterized by concreteness: fallen angels play a role in the lives of actual medieval men and women, including the saints who, like St. Anthony, were not always safe from the temptations of the fiercest demons.

The moral and spiritual collapse of the race when left to its own devices (and, of course, when subjected to the expected temptations of the regions of darkness) is suggested in the English cycle plays by the story of Noah, who is commanded to build the ark which will save him and his family from the destruction that the rest of the world's population merits at that time. The plays' presentation of this segment of biblical history has direct bearing on the anguish of the human condition, which can only be fully understood by one who sees his life in terms of pilgrimage and alienation from the world. Noah is required to build the ark, normally presented in the visual arts as a three-tiered vessel symbolic of the Church which must save God's chosen ones at the Last Day.[7] Noah must take his family aboard the ship along with representative animals of all species, which thereby are saved from destruction. Those who fail to understand the necessity of taking refuge in the ark before the rising of the waters, except for Noah's sometimes recalcitrant wife, are subject to the anguish of the despairing. Noah's wife, however, may illustrate the manner in which human nature resists the means of salvation in the interest of bodily pleasure or some other value; as a second mother of the race, she surely must be seen as illustrating human weakness in the direction of lapsarian habits of thought and action.[8] Through the Church as represented typologically by the ark, however, those aboard are usually able to achieve a calm which reflects the more perfect calm of paradise. It is a calm which has its source in Being rather than Becoming, yet of course in actual practice the Christian life cannot cut itself off from anxiety, suffering, sorrow. Indeed, for the late Middle Ages such conflicts of the heart have been converted into the means of salvation, for, according to the affective piety current during that time in history, only through participating in the anxiety, suffering, and sorrow of the Passion was a person able to draw upon Christ's saving power.[9]

The fallen state is associated with work—something of which the devils in hell are not capable—but such activity is metonymically related to the potential for salvation as well as to the agony of existence in a world balanced between the power of light and the powers of darkness. As Adam must dig in the dark soil in order to stimulate the creative forces of the earth, so also must he confront the darker recesses of his own spirit if he is to avoid the darkness hereafter. But for woman, the suffering as spelled out in the biblical account of the origins of the race is explicit in another and analogous direction: she must bring forth her children from her womb in suffering and pain in atonement for her misdeed in the Garden. In Christian Europe during the medieval period, childbearing meant a period of uncleanness between the time of the child's birth and the mother's "churching," which returned her to the community and the favor of the cult.[10] As a sign of suffering humanity, therefore, a feminine example was to be regarded as more appropriate than a male, and for this reason the holy women, especially the Virgin Mary who to be sure was believed to have uniquely brought forth her son without the usual taint, are the chief mourners at the cross of Christ. Indeed, much attention is given to Mary's *sorrows*, and in Dominican tradition the sword of her suffering during her Son's Passion is made literal in representations in the visual arts: her breast is in fact shown as pierced by the sword of her sorrow.[11]

When we keep in mind the ambivalent treatment of femininity in Lear's daughters in the later drama, some further observations on the medieval dramatic tradition may be in order. Noah's wife, as noted above, is in some medieval plays the paradigm of a perverse principle within the race, though not a principle that is incapable of being overcome or subdued. C. G. Jung would have explained her perversity in terms of the *anima*, man's shadow or feminine side which is in fact his point of greatest weakness.[12] In the Towneley play of *Processus Noe cum filius*, Uxor, left to her own devices, would have perished in the Flood. But she is not by any means here given over wholly to pleasure; her shrewishness is at the service of her compulsion to spin—the traditional occupation of Eve and the task asserted also by Uxor as symbolic of a second mother of the race. The Chester play presents her short-sightedness in wishing to stay with her "gossips everyechone" if she cannot have them with her.[13] In the York play, she later laments the loss of her friends whom she has left behind—friends who represent the allurements of this world from which she necessarily detached herself when she entered the ark, the symbol of the Church. "Christ be the Shaper of this Ship," responds the Noah of the Newcastle play.[14] In contrast to the perversity of Noah's wife, however, Shakespeare's Goneril and Regan represent perverse femininity that will *never* come aboard the ship of the Church, but rather will die without repenting in the deluge at the tragic end of the play.

The traditional view was that women are more easily captivated by earthly existence and more easily overcome by temptation to evil. Hence the Newcastle play shows the wife of Noah approached (as Eve was) by the devil, who encourages her recalcitrance and suggests that she prepare "a Drink" (l. 132). This is also the opinion that informed such Early Modern plays as *Hamlet*, which contains two tragically weak feminine figures—Gertrude and Ophelia—and Middleton's *Women Beware Women* or his collaboration with William Rowley, *The Changeling*. No doubt by way of example we should recall further the much earlier medieval prejudice against women's songs or *Frauenlieder*, which commonly treated human passion. The frequently held attitude toward such songs was rooted in the belief that the erotic and self-centered were more characteristic of females than of males.[15] Goneril and Regan, dominated by their passions and their selfishness, therefore are to be regarded as created by Shakespeare thoroughly according to this traditional medieval pattern.

Women, however, stand for both weakness and creative suffering in medieval tradition, and of course the one—weakness—is paradoxically related to the other. Just as there was the first Eve who fatally gave Adam the apple to eat, so also the Christian dialectic insisted upon discovering the second Eve, Mary, who was the Mother of God and the source through which the Divine was able to take on the human form necessary for his saving acts in the world. Typically, as the remarkable York *Nativity* makes clear, Christ's birth was miraculously painless since the Savior was born without sin. Following, as we have seen above in an earlier chapter, the account of the Nativity derived from St. Bridget of Sweden's *Revelations*, this play produced on stage a scene familiar to us from various examples in the visual arts such as the painted glass at Fairford and Great Malvern Priory (fig. 7). In the play, the miraculous appearance of the Child in an almond-shaped aureole at Mary's feet, where she will adore him, signifies an instance in which the usual suffering has been canceled out and replaced by unadulterated joy. Such joy becomes the pattern for the natural disposition evidenced by Cordelia, whose joy must likewise be exchanged for undeserved suffering and sorrow—a daughter whose character stands at the opposite extreme from her sisters, who are incapable of such redemptive suffering and sorrow.

For at the Passion Mary exchanged her Joys for her Sorrows, which also, as is well known, were presented frequently in the visual arts. In such scenes physical weakness—a weakness very different, of course, from Eve's (or from the much more pernicious weakness of Goneril and Regan)—becomes the sign of creative suffering, since a stoic Mary would not have been able to set a pattern for all men to follow. Just as Mary became a participant in her Son's suffering, so also should contemporary men and women do likewise—and to do so is the most important task of the religious person. Hence Julian of Norwich had wished first to have a proper understanding of the Passion, and then to suffer herself *physically* and also to obtain three wounds as a gift from God.[16] The plays of the Passion in the English cycles have as their goal the presentation of the scenes from the Passion in such a way that audiences will respond devotionally to the pain and anguish of Christ. The pain and anguish must be shared if the plays are to achieve what they set out to accomplish dramatically. The people who watched were expected to receive indeed an existential understanding of the Passion, which could make them weep or otherwise feel the most sincere sorrow without which they would lack spiritual health. Sorrow and suffering were clearly regarded as *dilating the soul*, which thereby was opened to charity and works of love toward other human beings, particularly those who themselves were sufferers. Unlike the harshness of Aristotle who believed that some men were born to be slaves and that charity was not desirable, the late medieval impetus toward charity helped to broaden the basis in society for values which continued to be asserted through the Reformation period.[17] Such values appear dramatized, of course, especially in Early Modern (or "Renaissance") tragedies—plays that emphasized suffering humanity with which the audience was invited to empathize. Though, as has commonly been observed, no medieval tradition of tragic drama *per se* could be established, this period in history nevertheless provided the groundwork for those later dramatizations of suffering for which *King Lear* may stand as a representative example. Indeed, plays of this type of necessity make extensive use of the quality of suffering, which informs the emotional structure of the drama. This fact is surely of greater importance than many other kinds of continuity which critics have attempted to trace beteen the medieval stage and Renaissance tragedy.

To be sure, in its maturity English drama in the Early Modern period was very often alert to the historical traditions which made suffering a viable theatrical experience to be entered into both on stage and within the emotions of the audience. Unlike the Passion story which was regarded as *true* in its essentials, a history play such as Shakespeare's *Richard II* could not actually provide precise replication of historical events. If even the late medieval vernacular plays of necessity utilized imagination as a valid way of bringing spectators into the events depicted, however, so also on a much more imaginative level did the Elizabethan or Jacobean play function to cast the spell of its action over those sitting (or standing) and watching in the theater. Validity could be given to secular events by drawing implicit and explicit comparisons between secular events and sacred story, as in *Richard II* when the king in the deposition scene loses his crown and compares himself to Christ—a comparison that remains important for the remainder of the play, a drama which could be labeled the "Passion of King Richard." In his suffering, this character, in spite of his mixed background and former criminal pride, becomes Christlike though not in any theological sense. The murder of Duncan in *Macbeth* likewise echoes biblical events, with Macbeth's "If it were done, when 'tis done, then 'twere well/ It were done quickly" speech (I.vii.1ff) echoing the exchange between Judas and Christ in preparation for the betrayal.[18] In this instance, the suffering is at least temporarily transferred to Macbeth, who is drawn as if by mysterious external forces toward the cruel crime which is an affront to all the rules of statesmanship, hospitality, and piety. The painful event is, of course, the supplanting of the genuinely Christlike Duncan by the Luciferian Macbeth, the usurper who at the end will have lost all feeling in his hysterical attempt to retain control of Scotland. As in the Passion story, however, there is hope, and in Shakespeare's play Duncan's son comes back from England and the court of the holy Edward the Confessor to resurrect the rightful monarchy at the conclusion of the drama. Only then will the unusually terrible suffering of the Scottish people come to an end with the reinstatement of harmony and peace. In the land, a topsy-turvy political order is thus at last replaced by a king who is properly oriented toward the values of good, of reconciliation, of truth and justice.

In *King Lear*, the theatrical spectacle throughout most of the play is illustrative likewise of a topsy-turvy world—indeed, of a *world upside down*.[19] The use of this *topos* as a basic structural element in the play is crucial to its presentation of theatrical suffering, which in particular afflicts the old king whose very appearance inspires Edgar's revealing comment "O thou side-piercing sight" (IV.vi.85), an allusion to the Crucifixion—a scene which had, of course, provided the central tableau for the mystery cycles. Like Richard II, the king bears some responsibility for bringing suffering upon himself, but then in becoming "More sinn'd against than sinning" (III.ii.60) he takes upon himself the pain and anguish that are echoed in the breasts of his audience. It was, we might add, an appropriate action to mirror forth the concerns and anxieties of the early Jacobean era, particularly in the year of the Gunpowder Plot when the play was perhaps first performed at the Globe Theater. The historical anxieties were to have deep social consequences, leading ultimately to the civil wars of the 1640's but more immediately to general disillusionment and despair, with these reflected even in the population statistics during the first half of the seventeenth century.[20]

The *topos* of the *world upside down* is, of course, medieval in origin and well described by Ernst Curtius in his *European Literature and the Latin Middle Ages*. Curtius provides the example of the poem *Florebat olim studium* from the *Carmina Burana* or Benediktbeuern Manuscript, and in essence the technique utilized by this poem is "stringing together impossibilities," or, as it was known in antiquity, *impossibilia*.[21] The poem is wonderfully satiric. Curtius summarizes: "the ass plays the lute; oxen dance. . . . The [Church] Fathers . . . are to be found in the alehouse, in court, or in the meat market. . . . Cato haunts the stews, Lucretia has turned whore. What was once outlawed is now praised. Everything is out of joint."[22] This *topos* quite understandably survived into the seventeenth century when it was utilized by John Taylor in the year 1642, a time of very severe political chaos in England, as the basis for two pam-

phlets.[23] One of these pamphlets contains a woodcut on its title page
(fig. 8) that depicts a scene "like this Kingdome": the central figure
wears a "doublet on his lower body," gloves on his feet, shoes on
his hands, breeches over his arms. At the top of the woodcut, fish
fly, a church (or a castle?) is turned upside down, a candle burns
downward. At the bottom, a cat is chased by a mouse, and a hare
chases a dog. On the side a wheelbarrow pushes a man, and a cart is
pulling a horse (i.e., the proverbial "cart before the horse"). The
woodcut illustrates how "All things are turn'd the Cleane contrary
way." Thus, too, in the inverted order of the iconography of *King
Lear*, a bedlam beggar is, for example, called "this philosopher" and
"this same learned Theban" (III.iv.154, 157). But the world-upside-
down *topos* is implicit already in the first act of the play when Kent
exclaims: "Kill thy physician, and [the] fee bestow/ Upon the foul
disease" (I.i.163–64). Furthermore, at I.iv.223–24, the dramatist
gives us precisely one of the details illustrated in the woodcut on
the title page of Taylor's pamphlet: "May not an ass know when the
cart draws the horse?" In power and authority, the young seem to
have exchanged places with their own elders, with disastrous results:
Lear becomes "this child-changed father" (IV.vii.16).

Having initially reversed the order of things in England, Lear is
now surprised when his daughters, between whom he has divided
the power of the realm, expect him to be "an obedient father"
(I.iv.235). Edgar, legitimate and loyal, too must now disguise himself as a madman who possesses only a blanket to cover his naked-
ness, while Edmund rises in power and glory, in influence and
wealth. "Everything is out of joint." Such chaos could only be successfully communicated in the drama visually and by means of the
storm which Gloucester describes in terms of one of the traditional
signs of Doomsday: "The sea, with such a storm as [Lear's] bare
head/ In hell-black night endur'd, would have buoyed up/ And
quenched the stelled fires" (III.vii.59–61).

The difference between *King Lear* and the mere stringing together of impossibilities ought now to be obvious. Shakespeare has
turned the traditional *topos* of the *world upside down* to a use not
foreseen by the medieval and ancient writers. When *impossible*

things happen—i.e., when the world is torn by outrage more violent than that symbolized by the mouse chasing the cat or the cart pulling the horse—the result is suffering and sorrow, which echo the terrible deed of the Crucifixion and the normal human response to this deed. When the sycophant steward, Oswald, tells the "chang'd" Albany of "Gloucester's treachery,/ And of the loyal service of his son [Edmund]," Goneril's husband reacts by telling him that he "had *turn'd the wrong side out*" (IV.ii.6–9; italics mine). Unquestionably, the dramatist intends everyone to see that with Lear's evil daughters and Gloucester's bastard son in the ascendant, all positive values have been reversed: treachery is now "loyal service," and good service is "treachery." In such a world where the dualities of good and evil are reversed, "Truth's a dog must to kennel, he must be whipt out, when the Lady Brach may stand by th' fire and stink" (I.iv.111–13). The play was one that, as is well known, repelled the age of Dryden, when Nahum Tate provided the bastardized adaptation that played through the Age of Enlightenment and into the nineteenth century. The objection had been, of course, that the play violated poetic justice, and even Dr. Johnson reported that "I was many years ago so shocked by Cordelia's death, that I know not whether I ever endured to read again the last scenes of the play till I undertook to revise them as an editor."[24] Nevertheless, the same critic admitted that this drama is perhaps more intense than any other, and that also more than any other it "agitates our passions and interests our curiosity."[25]

The outrageousness of the spectacle presented in *King Lear* inverts wisdom and foolishness. The fool is given a role of more significance perhaps than in any other play, and he represents the *seriousness* of mental play. Painfully, the king has put aside his wisdom and taken up folly; he has failed to follow Kent's advice to "see better" (I.i.158). The Fool, however, comments accurately that Lear has in fact lost his substance and has become mere "shadow." Alas "That such a king should play bo-peep,/ And go the [fools] among" (I.iv.177–78). All law and even reasonable behavior have been banished from the land, leaving the lawless and brutal acts of evil progeny to rule Britain. Ultimately these acts will be seen as transcendentally foolish just as foolishness itself takes on a surprising value. So too are the acts of Christ's tormentors in the mystery cycles transcendentally foolish, while Christ's foolishness in dying is paradoxically presented as the greatest wisdom.

The most painful realization that is brought home to the audience is that Lear's "flesh begot/ Those pelican daughters" (III.iv.74–75). Herein Shakespeare inverts the iconographic meaning of the pelican, for in the old chronicle play of *Leir* the king had described himself "as kind as is the Pellican,/ That kils it selfe, to save her young ones lives."[26] Though the medieval *Physiologus* had also allowed for the predatory nature of the pelican's offspring,[27] in late medieval and Early Modern art this bird had become an almost universal emblem of the Atonement—on misericords, in painted glass, etc.[28] Thus Cesare Ripa illustrates Compassion (*Bonta*) with a representation of the pelican (fig. 9); this bird "is a true Emblem of *Compassion*, for she never stirs from her young, and where Nourishment fails, she feeds them with her own Blood. . . ."[29]   But the world of *King Lear* is topsy-turvy, and hence the evil children become themselves the aggressors, hitting at the one who was willing to give them "all." As vicious feminine figures, they not only deny the supremely feminine virtue of compassion but also serve to illustrate the terrible effects of the Fall upon their heredity, which they are unable and/or unwilling to overcome.

Compassion is, however, not lacking in the play in spite of its absence from the ethic of certain of the characters, whose hearts are described accurately as "hard" (III.vi.78). Writing in an age less compassionate than the late Middle Ages,[30] Shakespeare nevertheless allows the temporal movement of the play to reveal the true nature of such hard hearts: "Time" in the end has unfolded "what plighted cunning hides" (I.i.280–81). On the other hand, those who possess feeling hearts complete the vision which the playwright intends us to see: the Corporal Acts of Mercy have a validity that tanscends all selfishness, and even in the face of suffering and death these acts have a permanence that defies the logic and rationalizations of characters such as Goneril, Regan, and Edmund.

For the Corporal Acts of Mercy, which we will recall are illustrated allegorically by the "seuen Bead-men" at a crucial point in the education of the Red Crosse Knight in Spenser's *Faerie Queene* (I.x.36–43), are still the core of Christian life in Protestant England, and Shakespeare's *King Lear* indeed very carefully is organized around these Acts which have played such a large role in late medieval piety. The play shows specific violations of *all* the seven Corporal Acts of Mercy, even the seventh, which is derived from the book of *Tobit*: the Duke of Cornwall refuses to give proper burial to the servant whom he has killed in Act III. Shelter is denied, prisoners and the sick are mistreated and even killed, strangers are attacked, sustenance is refused. These reversals of merciful deeds are omens of Doomsday, when Christ as Judge will return as in the final pageants in the Middle English cycle plays to regard those who have done or have failed to do the Corporal Acts of Mercy. And the conclusion of Shakespeare's drama, with its tableau of woe, will also be a judgment scene when good is separated from evil and harmony is restored, though of course the final harmony which can be achieved in this world can only be a pale imitation of the permanent state of harmony to be instituted at the Last Day of history.

In the final analysis, the world-upside-down *topos* thus enables Shakespeare to develop fully the affects of *woe* and *wonder*—terms which describe the expected reaction of the audience sitting at the play.[31] The emotions of the actors are, of course, feigned in the manner suggested by Hamlet in his response to the speech of the player:

> Is it not monstrous that this player here,
> But in a *fiction*, in a *dream* of passion,
> Could force his soul so to his own conceit. . . .
>   (*Hamlet* II.ii.551–53; italics mine)

The player's "whole function" suits "With forms to his conceit," and it is "all for nothing" (II.ii.556–57).[32] Yet the play, like a game into which the players enter, does in some fashion "Hold as 'twere the mirror up to nature" (III.ii.22), and in the end of *Hamlet* when Fortinbras comes upon the scene of carnage, Horatio's words to him are critically significant: "What is it you would see?/ If aught of woe or wonder, cease your search" (V.ii.362–63). *Wonder* and *woe* are, of course, the dramatist's equivalents of Sir Philip Sidney's "admiration and commiseration," terms which in turn are derived ultimately from Aristotle's "fear" and "pity" through the writings of Donatus.[33] While criticism in Shakespeare's time may have failed to work out the full implications of this terminology or the phenomenology of suffering which underlies it, these affects in his most effective tragedies will result for the audience in a purging of the emotions. Purging of the emotions of the spectator, it should be admitted, will actually provide a secular and psychological parallel to the effect of the action in a drama such as *Everyman*, in which the audience is invited to participate imaginatively in the sacramental acts that will insure the hero's safe journey through the land of the dead (though it is not a journey to be undertaken without considerable suffering and anguish of mind). Though Shakespeare may indeed have thought more in terms of *praxis* than *gnosis* as the result of the dramatic and theatrical experience he is offering (and in this we have some corroboration from Hamlet's speech to the players), his work on stage must nevertheless have functioned to provide for members of the audience a surrogate religious experience in their response to the actions shown—actions which, unlike the *things done* before the altar in ritual,[34] display an *as if* quality precisely as does game.

In the late medieval Passion sequences in the great civic cycles of England, audiences were encouraged to participate in imagination with Christ in his suffering in order to bring themselves into contact with his humanity and hence with the redeeming power of his grace. In Early Modern tragedy and in related forms, spectators are liable to see the suffering characters on stage and to discover that the *sight* has a therapeutic effect on the soul. No doubt the play itself is but a shadow of human actions in the realm of Becoming, but shadows nevertheless are extremely significant in their dramatic function particularly as they stimulate our feelings and bring us to a deeper consciousness of our humanity.

The establishment of models of suffering in the medieval theater thus served in very important ways to supply the tragic plays of Shakespeare and his contemporaries with an emotional power that could not otherwise have been made available. Shakespeare's debt to the drama of medieval England—the civic plays of Coventry near his boyhood home at Stratford-upon-Avon and also the saint plays which staged the stories of the suffering of martyrs and other wonders—thus was far more than would appear to be the case when we examine his patronizing attitude toward it in *A Midsummer Night's Dream*. In such plays as *King Lear*, his attitude toward suffering was far more sophisticated than anything that he could have derived from the classical dramas of antiquity with which he was familiar, and instead he necessarily and fortunately drew upon theatrical traditions which affected the very core of his work. Ben Jonson, in attempting to write tragedies that in their classicism would set aside the medieval model (though it was a model that he could not escape entirely), was a failure in the crafting of tragic forms in his own time. It was only in comedy that Jonson could be fully successful, and in such a play as *Bartholomew Fair* he delightfully achieved success by drawing upon popular and traditional forms.

6

Jonson's *Bartholomew Fair*, Stage Plays, and Anti-Traditionalism

Ben Jonson, though an avowed classicist[1] who, even in commendatory verses in the First Folio, could accuse Shakespeare of having "small *Latine*, and lesse *Greeke*," nevertheless was capable of showing genuine respect for English traditions, as evidenced in his poem "To Penshurst," which celebrates a medieval building, "an ancient pile" that is appropriately "reverenc'd."[2] In contrast to modern buildings in the classical style, Penshurst, constructed in the fourteenth century, is seen by the poet as naturally placed in the landscape and as possessing an attractive architectural humility—in contrast to "Those proude, ambitious heaps" which mechanically imitate antique buildings and at the same time display the latest architectural fashions.

Jonson's comparison between Penshurst and modern imitations of classical architecture will bear some resemblance to his attack on Inigo Jones, whose work in staging masques he will see as ephemeral in comparison to their true soul, which is resident in their text.[3] Jonson insists in his preface to *Hymenaei* that the mere imitation of classical forms is only an appeal to "outward celebration, or shew," while traditional knowledge, communicated through the ideas and language as these are rooted in tradition extending back to antiquity, will necessarily be needed if the meaning of the masque is to function in the deconcealment of truth.[4] Caught up as Jonson was in fascination for the classical and iconographic traditions which claimed a heritage (sometimes spuriously) derived from the Greece and Rome of antiquity, he focused his drama in a play such as *Bartholomew Fair* on the tension between the traditional and the ideological. He understood comedy as a reflection of the social milieu, apparently keeping in mind Sidney's insistence "that the comedy is an imitation of the common errors of our life, which he representeth in the

87

most ridiculous and scornful sort that may be. . . ."[5] The play is not
a simple handling of traditional values and practices *vs.* innovation
—such simplicity would have been uncharacteristic of Jonson—but
by the conclusion of the play the playwright has unmasked the hypocrisy of anti-theatricalism and of Puritan iconoclasm, both symptoms of the fashionable anti-traditionalism that at this time was
building in strength, especially in London and the other cities of the
realm.

Writing a play which would be given its premier on 31 October, Halloween, in 1614, Jonson set out to establish a social milieu
on the stage that would reflect the disordered world of one of the
London fairs, Bartholmew Fair, held annually on 24 August (and
continuing for the next two days) in West Smithfield. If he was reacting to the unfavorable public response to his last venture for the
stage, the tragedy *Catiline*, Jonson may have had theatrical judgment
in mind—and he may have set out deliberately to deflect criticism
of his new play, which very significantly gives no comfort to those
who would judge harshly in other ways, especially in matters of religion where the innovative radicals were wont to clash strongly
with tradition. The clue here is contained in the Induction, through
which the playwright extends a mock invitation in the "ARTICLES
of Agreement, indented, between the *Spectators*, and *Hearers* . . .
And the *Author of Bartholmew Fayre*" that will allow the audience
to judge the play critically. However, careful examination of the
play will demonstrate that Jonson's purpose was hardly to achieve a
democratic art or to surrender entirely to "that strumpet the Stage."[6]
And if, as Jackson Cope has suggested from a somewhat different
perspective, one of the principal themes of *Bartholomew Fair* is
judgment *too rigorously pursued*,[7] then the Smithfield setting, where
normal rules seem not to apply, would appear to be appropriate with
regard to the playwright's purpose of castigating those who are self-
righteous, inflexible, and rigid in their beliefs or practices, particularly as these imply a bias against values which have been handed
over from the past to the present generation by tradition.

The unspoken standard expressed in the play thus is related to
the moderation so carefully set forth by Richard Hooker in his clas-

sic delineation of Anglicanism in *Of the Laws of Ecclesiastical Polity*. Such a standard is consistent with acceptance of the stage when it is conceived as a servant of traditional morality and truth rather than as a purveyor of illusion conveyed by means of empty spectacle, and through such qualified acceptance drama might, in Jonson's view, even be able to thrive and to achieve its proper function.[8] In *Bartholomew Fair*, therefore, the playwright was responding to his "Daintie age [which]/ Cannot bear reproof," and yet was acting as the *inventor* of drama that in its intent still remains relatively "high and aloof."[9]

If the playwright takes a somewhat detached stance with regard to his play, *Bartholomew Fair* itself is like a canvas filled with figures that seem very much absorbed in the bizarre world of the fair, itself an inheritance from medieval times. In a sense, the presiding deity of the fair is the goddess of discord, who appears disguised as Ursula, the grossly overweight vendor of roast pork at the very center of the fair. In Act II, Scene v, in which Ursula scalds her leg, she had emerged with a firebrand in her hand when a confrontation had developed at her booth. In Jackson Cope's view she is reminiscent of the figure of Ate as understood by Renaissance iconographers such as Cesare Ripa and Vicenzo Cartari—a lame figure commonly portrayed holding a firebrand and legal papers in her hands, while clouds encircle her feet, to show that she is the goddess of irascible passions and of litigiousness.[10] She is, therefore, an appropriate figure to preside over the fair.

The disorder inherent in the fair draws on the traditional iconography of the world turned upside down but in a very different way than in Shakespeare's *King Lear*. The world-upside-down *topos* as related to the matter of justice is expressed through the figure of Overdo, who in his zeal for ferreting out the abuses of the fair loses all perspective and fails utterly in his goal of cleansing the event of all corruption. In his disguise as Mad Arthur of Bradley he further has abdicated his judicial duty for the entire first day of the fair, since his normal role would have him presiding over the summary court of Pie-powders (*pied-poudreux*) which was responsible for adjudicating disputes between sellers and buyers. Believing that he has a sacred mission to impose justice—a justice which he sees as divinely derived—on the fair, he not only botches the task but also is himself accused of crime and is placed in the stocks. However inefficient his traditional means of functioning to keep order at the fair, Justice Overdo's innovations may be counted a thorough failure —in no way an improvement.

However, suffering the punishment for his alleged crime, he takes on the emblematic meaning of a personified virtue placed in the stocks—a meaning that had been established in both art and drama. For example, earlier in the sixteenth century Albrecht Dürer, in a design for a tapestry, had placed Justice and other virtues in the stocks, while the device had appeared not only in earlier Tudor drama but also in *King Lear*, which included the scene in which the Earl of Kent is thus mistreated in the course of his service to the old monarch.[11] However, unlike the instance in Shakespeare's drama, the placing of the figure of justice—in this case literally a justice of the peace—in the stocks is done presumably to the audience's delight. In the world of the fair, even the audience's sympathies are intentionally inverted. It is tempting to suggest that in this Halloween play we are in the presence of a Rabelaisian carnival that would be susceptible to analysis *à la* Bakhtin, but such an approach would likely be misleading in the light of Jonson's humanism with its concern for decorum, right behavior, and the application of good sense.

As indicated in the previous chapter, the world-upside-down *topos* had a long and distinguished history as an emblematic literary device prior to Jonson's time. In addition to examples cited above, the fourteenth-century *Land of Cokayne* may also be particularly relevant in this instance; in this legendary land, gluttons are rewarded not with wallowing in the mire in a circle of hell but with a paradise that gives them everything they might have wanted in superfluity.[12] Such a reward is ironic, for it expresses the impossible— reward for indulgence in one of the Deadly Sins—and it exactly reverses the order of things. So too does Jonson's world in *Bartholomew Fair*, for it seems in the service of irony to erase moral boundaries and to reward vice and virtue without distinction, but such must be the case if the playwright is to defend moderation as opposed to the harsh justice implied by the unimaginative and unpoetic Overdo—a justice characterized in intent by a total lack of tolerance but in practice terribly awry—or the precisionism of the radical Puritans, represented here by Zeal-of-the-Land Busy.

But the levels of irony run even more deeply in Jonson's play, for its scene is a fair which is set at a location which was historically associated with harsh justice against religious non-conformists of both the Catholic and Protestant parties and also with iconoclasm directed against the images associated in tradition with worship or devotion—iconoclasm that Busy would extend even further. Bartholomew Fair was centered in West Smithfield, an open area of approximately three acres,[13] near the Priory Church of St. Bartholomew the Great, a church which would survive the Great Fire of 1666 and is extant today. Etymologically 'Smithfield' is derived from *Smethefelde* (i.e., *Smoothfield*), and the place was for centuries a horse market located immediately outside the medieval city walls. It was here in 1537 that the friar John Forest was burned "for heresie and treason," while simultaneously, as a sermon was being preached by Hugh Latimer, there was also burned the wooden image (Wriothesley calls it "an idoll") of Darvel (or David) Gatheren from Llandervel, Wales.[14] Forest was not the last martyr to be executed at Smithfield under Henry VIII, but the location was to be made even more famous by the Tudor chroniclers because of the scores of Protestant martyrs who were executed in Smithfield under Queen Mary.[15] The "fires of Smithfield" were proverbial.

The last person to be executed at Smithfield was the radical separatist Bartholomew Legate, who was burned in 1611 for his refusal to give up his heretical beliefs.[16] Perhaps it was Jonson's memory of this last Bartholomew to be executed at Smithfield that led him to give the following words to his Bartholomew Cokes, who thinks he has been cheated in the fair: *"Bartholmew-fayre*, quoth he; an' euer any *Bartholmew* had that lucke in't, that I haue had, I'le be martyr'd for him, and in *Smithfield*, too"* (IV.ii.71-74). So too Jonson's placement of the scene of the play on the Feast of St. Bartholomew is redolent with irony, for this day also had deep associations with religious intolerance and acts of martyrdom. After the accession of Queen Elizabeth the day was chosen as a time to burn remaining religious images that were believed to be associated with Roman Catholic practice. This act of iconoclasm seems not unconnected with Bartholomew Fair, which the Lord Mayor of London had attended in 1559 to see the sports and wrestling; as he returned from the fair, he found bonfires in Cheapside destroying "roods and images of Mary and John and the other saints . . . with great wonder of the people."[17] However, though the selection of 24 August for the destruction of images in 1559 was certainly significant, another event on this day on the continent would be even more significant. In 1572, the day was chosen for the St. Bartholomew Massacre in which large numbers of French Huguenots were martyred. This event remained vivid in English memory as an example of Catholic intolerance, and indelibly marked this day in the calendar as the bloodiest since the Massacre of the Innocents by Herod. As Overdo shouts amid the confusion when Wasp begins to beat him at the end of Act II, "Hold thy hand, childe of wrath, and heyre of anger, make it not Childermasse day in thy fury, or the feast of the French *Bartholmew*, Parent of the Massacre" (II.vi.146-51).

Jonson, who had been a Roman Catholic convert for more than a decade and who had returned to Anglicanism only a few years before writing *Bartholomew Fair*, might well also have remembered that the saint who gave his name to the fair was a victim of intolerance and harsh judgment. St. Bartholomew the apostle had been flayed alive and hence is usually depicted with the symbol of his martyrdom, a knife. But this saint's feast day, representing the day on which he ended his earthly life, was also an important one in the Calendar of the Church of England, and had been preceded by a fast day in the Prayer Book in the time of Queen Elizabeth[18]—the Prayer Book still in use in 1614.

Prior to the Reformation, Bartholomew's image and an altar dedicated to him had stood in St. Bartholomew the Great,[19] and almost certainly the church would have possessed relics of the saint, though no inventory of relics survives for this location. In the Reformation, however, English churches had been quite thoroughly "cleansed" of "abused" images and relics.[20] Nevertheless, it seems that the memory of the traditional imagery of the church did in fact live on in the gingerbread figures of Jane Trash which, in spite of their indigestible ingredients (if we may believe Leatherhead), took the shape of saints such as St. Bartholomew. The remnants of the Old Religion in gingerbread explain the violence of Busy's iconoclastic efforts against them and his insistence that her stall is a "shop of reliques" (III.vi.96). Her wares are, according to him, a "basket of Popery," a "nest of Images: and whole legend of gingerworke" (III.vi.73-74). The reference is to the *Golden Legend*, the most popular collection of saints' legends, which had been translated by William Caxton. As he overturns Trash's "ware," the zeal-filled Busy identifies it also as "this Idolatrous Groue of Images, this flasket of Idols!" (III.vi.99-100).

The harshness and stupidity of Busy's judgment is emphasized as he is about to be arrested for his iconoclastic action against the gingerbread saints. "Pray you lay hold on his zeale," Leatherhead tells the officers; "wee cannot sell a whistle, for him, in tune" (III.vi.102-03). Busy has made "a loud and most strong" and "sanctified noise" against "the prophane enemy" (III.vi.104-06), by which he means objects with sacred associations in the traditional religion of pre-Reformation times. Thus he has also demonstrated a characteristic of speech among intolerant Puritans—i.e., a loud nasal tone of voice that subsequently became known as the Puritan "twang."[21] The voice of elder Busy is self-righteous, harshly judgmental, and hypocritical, but the attack on Trash's "ware" indicates the lengths to which ideological Calvinists would in fact go toward the destruction of things perceived as traditional religious imagery or as smacking of relics. When the commissioner William Dowsing in the 1640's travelled about East Anglia and Cambridgeshire "like a Bedlam, breaking glosse windowes,"[22] he was even known to order the removal of the name of Jesus painted in capitals on the ceiling of a church.[23] From the standpoint of the playwright's psychology of humors, such a mad urge to destroy and tear down as a result of men's judgments—judgments that Jonson would have found faulty in the extreme—could only be attributed to vapors oppressing the brain. And indeed, as James Robinson has demonstrated, *vapors* function as a major theme in Jonson's *Bartholomew Fair*.[24] Busy's iconoclasm as well as his tone of voice, both of which on stage are intended to parody actual characteristics of men, thus result from mental imbalance and are to be regarded as symptoms of madness.

In an early reference to the play, John Selden suggested that Jonson "satirically expressed the vain disputes of divines by Rabbi Busy disputing with a puppet in his Bartholomew fair. It is so: it is not so: it is so: it is not so; crying thus one to another a quarter of an hour together."[25] As we have seen, Jonson's aversion to a bigoted and harsh religiosity that denies its debt to tradition seems to have been a basic element in *Bartholomew Fair*—an element involving much more than merely the ridiculing of such attitudes and opinions in the final act which dramatizes the matter of the puppet play. In the puppet play, however, he has given attention very specifically to what was for many a focal point—the rigidity of radical Protestantism and its fundamentalist insistence on the text of Holy Writ against tradition or even good sense. Further, the drama now directs its audience to examine the process of criticism directed against what in this case is a thoroughly bad production based on an abominable script by the appropriately named Littlewit—a case in which the criticism is in many ways as inane as the play itself.

Just as Busy, motivated by his "most *lunatique* conscience, and splene" (I.iii.138-39), has parodied iconoclastic activity against religious art objects and relics at the Fair earlier, so now he parodies dramatic criticism as expounded by the left-wing Puritans.[26] However, the effect of Jonson's satire in this case at first appears to be two-edged, at once damaging to the thing criticized and to the character type doing the criticizing. Littlewit's foolish and rude "motion," which is believed actually to be related to a puppet play written by Jonson himself earlier in his career,[27] rewrites mythological characters in terms of London low life. Damon and Pythias echo the vapors exhibited by Knockem and his cohorts in Act IV, Scene iv; further, as Leatherhead explains, "*They are Whore-masters both, Sir, that's a plaine case*" (V.iv.242-43). Likewise the story of Hero and Leander is certainly not played "according to the printed booke"

(V.iii.106-07) by Christopher Marlowe, for the heroine in the puppet drama is a Southwark prostitute and the hero is a the son of "*a Dyer at* Puddle *wharfe*" (V.iv.119). As Jonas Barish has indicated, "The puppet play itself, written in the jog-trot couplets of the old interludes . . . , shrinks literature as well as life into the tiny compass of a peep show, and decomposes it into the grossness of its baser elements."[28] Elsewhere Barish notes that in this puppet production the "two great themes of Renaissance literature, love and friendship, are thus debased, along with everything else in the play, to the level of mere vapors"[29]—or, we might add, to the level of drunkenness and wantonness, precisely the characteristics of the stage to which the most rigid of the Church Fathers had objected in antiquity.[30] Surely the entire puppet play is to be seen as the kind of topsy-turvy production that would be proclaimed to be entirely without artistic or social value if it were not part of the masterful synthesis achieved by the conclusion of Jonson's play.

We can be sure that, in spite of possible side-glances at Inigo Jones in the figure of Leatherhead,[31] the satire is directed at the quality of puppet plays such as those associated with public fairs of the type that historically existed at Smithfield on St. Bartholomew's day. The actual evidence for such puppet drama at Bartholomew Fair is later than Jonson's play, however, and even the pamphlet *Bartholomew Faire, or Variety of fancies where you may find a faire of wares, and all to please your mind* (1641), which tells of "a Knave in a fooles coate, with a trumpet sounding, or on a drumme beating, [who] invites you and would faine perswade you to see his puppets,"[32] is so dependent upon the drama that it gives no firm evidence for this kind of entertainment. In 1648, however, a scurrilous broadside ballad entitled *The Dagonizing of Bartholomew Fayre* makes reference to the suppression of puppet plays at Bartholomew Fair by the Lord Mayor in that year.[33] Another ballad from the interregnum reprinted by Henry Morley in his *Memoirs of Bartholomew Fair* also notes "puppet-plays,"[34] and he further cites a ballad of 1655 entitled "*An Ancient Song of* Bartholomew-Fair" from D'Urfey's *Wit and Mirth, or Pills to Cure Melancholy* which reveals that at this time "For a penny you may zee a fine puppet play."[35] The subjects which are dramatized are given as the story of "patient Grisel" and "the History of Susanna." There are also ample references to this kind of popular drama at the fair after the Restoration. Pepys verifies both the puppet drama and its potentially obscene content at Bartholomew Fair in his day.[36] Hence, though Frances Teague is probably correct in seeing Smithfield as "One of the puppeteers' chief venues, from medieval days,"[37] we do not as yet have solid evidence to prove her assertion.

It is the introduction of a puppet playing the tyrant Dionysius of Syracuse, reduced in Littlewit's play to a schoolmaster and scrivener wearing a furred gown, that signals Busy's explosion of anti-theatrical prejudice. As he enters, Busy exclaims, "Downe with *Dagon*, downe with *Dagon*" (V.v.1). A sophisticated viewer would see the character's name as reminiscent of the Greek god who was so closely associated with the production of Greek drama, but this puppet is so reduced in stature from the original role of his namesake that Busy's denunciation of him as Dagon is utterly ridiculous. The puppet is hardly an "*Idoll*," nor does it seem a likely figure to "plead for *Baal*" (V.v.4, 22). Thus Busy's ranting is quite aptly characterized by Knockem as "Good *Banbury-vapours*" (V.v.26)—a reminder of Busy's status as a former baker of Banbury, a radical Puritan stronghold in Oxfordshire.

When the Puritan and the puppet formally begin their disputation, Busy's first charge, grounded in the Calvinist insistence on the necessity of a vocation, is that the puppet-actor has "no *Calling*" (V.v.52). To be an actor or an "*Idoll*" is to have "no present lawfull *Calling*" (V.v.56-57),[38] and Busy attempts to prove his point against the puppet by repetition and the force of his loud voice. To see a puppet in terms of a traditional religious image, however, involves more than merely a mental short circuit since puppets were indeed at one time frequently used as part of religious displays for important festivals such as Christmas and Easter—puppets certainly seen as idolatrous or at least as "abused" by many Protestant clergy and laymen. For example, at Witney in Oxfordshire a puppet show for Easter morning had shown "the hole Action of the Resurrection, the Preistes [having] garnished out certein smalle Puppets, representinge

the Parsons of *Christe*, the Watchmen, *Marie*, and others, amongest
the which one bare the Parte of a wakinge Watcheman, who
(espiinge *Christ* to arise) made a continual Noyce, like to the Sound
that is caused by the Metinge of two Styckes, and was therof
comonly called *Jack Snacker of Wytney*."[39] The reporter of this
puppet show, William Lambarde (1536-1601), believed it to be an
example of inauthentic "Popish Maumetrie" which, like certain other
Roman Catholic ceremonies for major festivals of the Church year,
reflected "Shadowe" instead of "Bodye"—i.e., substance—and, examined from another perspective, jesting rather than serious proclamation of religious truths.[40] Busy, like many another Protestant
iconoclast, goes but one step further and, as we have seen, proclaims the puppet to be an "*Idoll*," though in the context of *Bartholomew Fair* the charge is particularly ludicrous since Dionysius
pretends not at all to be sacred but rather is in fact incredibly profane. Hence, in spite of the traditional use of puppets in religious
shows in the past in England, Busy's claim that the puppet Dionysius' "Profession is prophane" (V.v.67-68) is at once accurate and
utterly foolish.

Having placed Busy on the defensive by enlisting the charge of
hypocrisy against Puritans, Dionysius has pre-empted the usual argument against players—i.e., that they are hypocrites. Thus Prynne,
basing his assertion on his examination of entries in various Renaissance dictionaries, would proclaim that the word "hypocrite" might
be traced to the Greek word for stage player—and that both were
"*one and the same thing in substance: there being nothing more familiar with them, then to describe an hypocrite by a Stage-player;
and a Stage-player by an hypocrite.*"[41] For Prynne, "*God requires
truth in the inward parts*; in the soule, the affections; yea, in the
habit, speeches, gestures, in the whole intire man"; on the other
hand, acting "transforms the Actors into what they are not. . . ."[42]
Jonson himself felt some anxiety about disguise and about the pretense that must be involved when the actor takes on the role of a
particular character,[43] but in *Bartholomew Fair* the playwright in his
aloofness is displaying no sign of any reservations about theatrical
practice in this regard. Instead it is the anti-authoritarian Busy, the

hypocritical representative of extreme Puritanism (which Ernst Cassirer has called "a fighting, a thoroughly quarrelsome and quarrel-seeking religion"[44]), who vents his anti-theatrical judgment against a costumed piece of wood created by a maker of toys.

Busy's final argument, which he apparently expects to be decisive, is that the puppet as an actor is "an *abomination*: for the Male, among you, putteth on the apparell of the *Female*, and the *Female* of the *Male*" (V.v.99-100). This argument is ultimately derived from the Church Fathers, in particular from the literal-minded Tertullian who based his objection to cross-dressing[45] on the prohibition in *Deuteronomy* 22.5: "The woman shall not wear that which pertaineth unto a man, neither shall a man put on a woman's garment: for all that do so are abomination unto the Lord thy God." To the biblical literalists among Jonson's contemporaries (as also to Stephen Gosson in his *Playes Confuted* of 1582[46]) the prohibition seemed to apply directly to the contemporary stage with its actors who played the roles of women—a practice that to them appeared to merit the condemnation specified in the passage in *Deuteronomy*. Prynne was to devote a bulky chapter to this question in his *Histrio-Mastix*, and his arguments concerning "Men putting on Womens Habits" and about plays being "abominable" were to be cited in his trial when he appeared before the Star Chamber to answer charges with regard to the publication of this book.[47]

The concern of left-wing Protestantism with defilement was in fact a major issue. For Busy, even the very names of traditional Catholic saints imply pollution (I.iii.129-33, I.vi.54-56). Incorrect worship, especially idolatry, was one of the central points of attack for Calvin and many of his followers both on the continent and in England. Calvin himself had written:

> So innate in us is superstition, that the least occasion will infect us with contagion. Dry wood will not so easily burn when coals are put under it, as idolatry will seize and occupy the minds of men, when the opportunity presents itself to them. And who does not see that images are sparks? What! sparks do I say? nay, rather torches, which are sufficient to set the whole world on fire.[48]

Calvin's emphasis on the danger of such pollution was extremely influential in England, and after the accession of Elizabeth I his *Inventory of Relics* had been translated into English in order to support the iconoclastic program that was proceeding under the Queen. In this treatise, Calvin insisted upon the imperative to detach visual signs from sacred signification and by implication to substitute the mediation of words.[49] Pollution is something absolute; if some relics (or images) are inauthentic, then all must be done away with because of the alleged danger that is involved. As Mary Douglas has indicated, pollution or defilement exists only when there is "a systematic ordering of ideas"—ideas which establish certain objects, persons, or behavior as dangerous in the extreme. Further, a person or image that is the source of pollution can never be worthy of approval.[50] In his invective against the puppet-actor, therefore, Busy, whose world-view is fixed in rigid Calvinistic theology imperfectly understood, quite simply assumes that his antagonist, whom he takes to be a block of wood rather than Leatherhead who makes it to move and speak, is guilty of defilement and of all the sins that have been claimed for human actors in addition to that of being an idolatrous image.

Busy, however, has made a serious tactical mistake, since his opponent has a very obvious way of refuting the harsh judgment of his antagonist. "*It is your old stale argument against the Players,*" says Dionysius, "*but it will not hold against the Puppets; for we haue neyther* Male *nor* Female *amongst vs. And that thou may'st see, if thou wilt, like a malicious purblinde zeale as thou art!*" (V.v.103-05). At this point he "*takes vp his garment*" and gives Busy ocular proof of his sexlessness. And having lost the argument, Busy will now be "*conuerted*" and will become a "beholder" (V.v.115, 117) with the others who have come to see Littlewit's puppet play.

Jonson's attitude toward the traditional theatrical practice of cross-dressing (or *transvestism*, as Meg Twycross has called it[51]), is nevertheless much more complex than would seem to be suggested by the conclusion of *Bartholomew Fair*. He apparently subsequently requested the opinion of his friend John Selden about this matter, and Selden's response, written on 28 February 1615, learnedly re-

futes the application of the verse from *Deuteronomy* to actors and
stage-playing.[52] Nevertheless, Twycross has outlined the nature of
anxiety stimulated by cross-dressing and playing, and sensibly calls
attention to the the sensitivity of an anti-theatrical writer such as
John Rainolds, the author of *Th' Overthrow of Stage-Playes* (1599),
toward the sexual implications of this practice.[53] Rainolds once himself as a boy at Christ Church, Oxford, had played "a womans parte,
the part of *Hippolyta*" in *Palamon and Arcite*, before Queen Elizabeth in 1566, and found himself everlastingly upset about the "ama-
torie pangs" stimulated by the play.[54] Rainolds was to serve as one
of Prynne's sources in his *Histrio-Mastix*, a work not noted for po-
liteness in its attack on the "putting on of womans array (especially
to act a lascivious, amorous, whorish, Love-sicke Play upon the
Stage, must needs be sinfull, yea abominable; *because it not onely
excites many adulterous filthy lusts, both in the Actors and Spectators . . .*) which is evill; but likewise *instigates them to selfe-pollu-
tion, . . .* which is worse."[55] Nevertheless, in spite of the violent
rhetoric, Prynne's objections summarized a radical Puritan position
with regard to the playing of women's roles by men and boys that
had at least caused Jonson to worry about the ethics of the practice,
which had been inherited from the medieval stage.

In the puppet show in *Bartholomew Fair*, therefore, he may
well have been working out some of his own anxieties at the same
time that he was deflecting the arguments of those who would judge
such practice harshly. That he was not entirely satisfied with the answers provided in the play explains the letter to Selden, and it perhaps also suggests something about his own general dissatisfaction
with the play, which was not included by him in his folio of 1616.
In a sense, then, *Bartholomew Fair* raises questions which have
more often than not been avoided in modern criticism—questions
concerning the kinds of erotic fantasies which are inspired by boys
and men playing female roles both of comedy and of high seriousness. We are not likely to respond with the harsh judgment of a
Prynne, but surely we need to consider the implications of a traditional practice that seriously helped to undermine the stage in the
period prior to the interregnum. But Jonson, in spite of his anxiety
in this matter, stood his ground in defense of a theater about which

he had serious reservations. That he stood his ground in ridiculing those who see defilement everywhere, including in gingerbread saints, should earn him our everlasting praise. *Bartholomew Fair* may be considered an important document in opposition to iconoclasm, anti-theatricalism, and rigid judgment based on either ideology or ethical and cultural myopia. By representing the world-upside-down of the fair, Jonson is able to make himself "Safe from the wolves black jaw, and the dull/ Asses hoofe"[56] at the same time that he achieves a drama that delights as it teaches the value of moderation.

Jonson's impatience with extreme anti-traditionalism, especially as found in Puritanism with its emphasis on the biblical *text* over against religious tradition toward which it was so severely prejudiced, is indicative of resistance to the radicalism of the early seventeenth century—a radicalism that would emphasize a legalistic explanation of the individual's role in his or her own salvation. His stance was also in opposition to a view which denigrated the visual experiences of the Old Religion and which extended its anti-visual prejudice even to the theatrical scene. While as a humanist and classicist Jonson was hardly among those who would turn to the Middle Ages with nostalgia, he nevertheless represents an important voice of moderation speaking out against those who wished to deny the connection between the present and the immediate past, especially the pre-Reformation spirituality which in fact through its own success, in particular among the middle class, had prepared the way for its own overthrow by Protestantism. While himself disturbed about some of the ethical implications of play-acting, Jonson nevertheless staunchly came down on the side of those who accepted theatrical illusion as useful to the revelation of truth for audiences. In this his aesthetic was perhaps indirectly related to the Franciscan Passion-aesthetics of the Middle Ages which held that the imagination and its role in stirring the emotions were principal factors in the renewal of the individual hoping for salvation. Drama should in Jonson's view be ethical in intent and illuminating in its intellectual content, both values deeply imbedded in the theatrical tradition of England.

7

George Herbert and Painted Glass Windows

Like so many others who lived during the decades leading up to the Civil War of the 1640's, George Herbert was concerned about the passage of time, the fragility of human achievements, and the nearness of death. In his poem "Life" he suggests that a "posie" which "wither'd in [his] hand" even before noon may be seen as analogous to fragile human existence on this earth—"Times gentle admonition."[1] His own frail health was a factor that informed his sensitivity in this matter,[2] but we may surmise that there was also here a background of societal dislocation and threat to those traditions which were most important to him.

Margaret Aston has surveyed how the devastating destruction of the religious institutions of the past in the sixteenth century—in the name of the Reformation and in many cases the service of greed by "cruel cormorants," as Thomas Fuller called them, "with their barbarous beaks and greedy claws"—inspired in many a sense of intense loss which led to strong preservationist feelings that expressed themselves in antiquarian activity and historical writing;[3] it may also be suggested that among many of those who accepted the change of religion as genuine and adequate reformation, the religious ceremonials which were retained came to be regarded as an incredibly precious heritage. In contrast to the radical element in the English Church, there were many who agreed with Richard Hooker that "the long continued practice of the whole Church" established the past as an arbiter for the present in ceremonial. From such practice, Hooker said, it ought not "unnecessarily to swerve," and indeed "experience hath never as yet found it safe" to do so.[4]

That there continued often to be strong feeling concerning Church ceremonial, even nostalgia for the worship practiced in pre-

Reformation times, is obliquely suggested by Shakespeare's Sonnet 73 with its reference to "Bare ruin'd choirs, where late the sweet birds sang." The ritual of the English Church was also defended by theological argument; Jeremy Taylor, for example, would refer to St. Gregory to demonstrate the metonymic relationship between worship in the earthly church structure and in Paradise:

> But when I consider the saying of S. *Gregory*, That the Church is Heaven within the Tabernacle, Heaven dwelling among the sonnes of men, and remember that GOD hath studded all the Firmament, and paved it with starres, because he loves to have his house beauteous, and highly representative of his Glory, I see no reason we should not do as *Apollinaris* sayes GOD does, *In earth do the works of heaven*. For he is the GOD of beauties, and perfections. . . .[5]

The point is one that will be proven relevant to Herbert's attitude toward ceremonial which is grounded in past tradition and handed over to worshippers in the present so that they might glorify the Creator and Savior.

Following the publication of Joseph Summers' *George Herbert: His Religion and Art* in 1954, considerable interest has been shown in the exact nature of Herbert's theological opinions, his churchmanship, and his place in the history of seventeenth-century Anglicanism. The point of departure for such discussion inevitably is his well-known poem "The British Church," which equates the Church of England with the Middle Way between the naked worship of Geneva (she "nothing wears") and the alleged gaudiness of Rome, represented by a woman with painted face and wanton look. In contrast, the British Church in her beauty possesses "perfect lineaments and hue/ Both sweet and bright" (ll. 2–3). If we may assume that the poem's reference is to the garment of worship as expressed within the church building through the liturgy, this poem must reflect exactly the stance of the man who also assigned the title "Mattens" to a poem about the morning, while to another, about evening, he gave the title "Even-song." Even more important than his framing of the daily hours within a liturgical structure is the fact that the entire collection of poems in *The Church*, the central section of *The*

Temple, concludes with "Love (III)," a celebration of the unity of earthly liturgical acts and eschatological reality.[6] For Herbert, in other words, liturgy was immediately associated with the existential realities of life.

The discovery that Herbert cannot be seen as a Laudian High Churchman in theology does not mean, therefore, that any affinities he might have had with Calvinism would have been at the heart of his religious practice. Herbert was not in fact anti-ritualist in spite of his acceptance of such Reformed doctrines as "covenant theology"[7] or his rejection of the Catholic practice of the invocation of saints.[8] In *A Priest to the Temple* he insisted upon the need for order and neatness in the church building, especially in the furniture associated with the sacramental functions of the parish—the font and communion table, and also the pulpit and lectern, all of which are valued "for those great duties that are performed in them." It was especially important for Herbert "that all things be in good repair; as walls plaistered, windows glazed, floore paved, seats whole, firm, and uniform."[9] He even recommended the use of incense "at great festivals."[10] His objection to carelessness or "slovenlinesse"[11] would have extended to vestments worn by the priest whose liturgical garments should be determined by his sense of decorum. In this regard, he should be "well drest" (see "Aaron," l. 15), as is appropriate for one whose role is to be an example in "Doctrine and life" ("The Windows," l. 11). Thus, like Bishop Joseph Hall, he objected to those "who place a kind of holiness, in a slovenly neglect; and so order themselves, as if they thought a nasty carelessness in God's services were most acceptable to him. . . . Hence it is, that their dresses make no difference of festivals; all stuffs, all colours are alike to them, in all sacred solemnities: hence, that they stumble into God's house, without all care or show of reverence; and sit them down at his table, like his fellows, with their hats on their heads."[12] In "The British Church," Herbert saw proper attention to the furnishings of the church in terms of what he elsewhere calls "the middle way between superstition, and slovenliness."[13] He had, after all, been ordained as a deacon by Bishop John Williams of Lincoln, who was described as a "punctual observer of the ancient Church

Orders, holding to it, that what was long in use, if it were not best, it was fittest for the People."[14] So too Richard Hooker had written that "there is a cause why we should be slow and unwilling to change, without very urgent necessity, the ancient ordinances, rites, and long approved customs, of our venerable predecessors."[15]

In its liturgical function, music for Herbert had a far richer use than among the adherents of classical Calvinism who on the whole would restrict its use to congregational singing of psalms and would prohibit instruments.[16] The singing of the Anglican liturgy was thus anathema to more rigid Puritans such as Peter Smart, who had preached a sermon on 7 July 1628 that attacked the cathedral liturgical practice at Durham. Smart sneered at "such a dainty service of heavenly Harmony" as that established in this cathedral, and complained about the "delicate noise of singers, with Shakebuts, and Cornets, and Organs, and if it were possible, all kinde of Musicke, vsed at the dedication of *Nabuchodonosors* golden Image."[17] The preference of this Puritan was quite typically for congregational singing rather than anthems—"so many Anthems to be sung, which none of the people vnderstand, nor all the singers themselues." According to his account, not only the way of singing but also even the manner of saying the liturgy at Durham meant that the words were lost to the hearers.[18] Herbert's attitude toward the liturgy and its music was thus very different indeed from this restrictive view of the role of music, for he not only found himself very much affected by the cathedral music at Salisbury Cathedral where the organ, sackbutts, and cornets were used, but also was said himself to have composed anthems and hymns. Aubrey reported that when he died the full Anglican burial service was sung for him at Bemerton by the singing men of Salisbury Cathedral[19]—an appropriate tribute to a lover of church music whose idea of harmony also expressed his highest spiritual aspirations. "But if I travell in your companie," he had written in "Church-musick," "You know the way to heavens doore" (ll. 11–12). As *The Temple* in its entirety seems to demonstrate, the liturgy as prayer, proclamation, and harmony is the safe way to salvation.

While to be sure Puritan objections to Anglicanism such as

Herbert's would involve a considerable range in the period before the Civil War, there are numerous details in the poems which indicate what we would designate as High as opposed to Low Anglicanism. As opposed to Smart's denunciation of even the very name of 'priest' in his controversial sermon at Durham in 1628,[20] Herbert's understanding of the priesthood is that it is a "Blest Order" which has been given the power of the keys inherited from St. Peter as well as the duty to distribute the sacraments as defined by the Thirty-Nine Articles ("The Priesthood," 11. 1–2, 25–30). In "Prayer (I)," acts of praying are said to be analogous to church bells—in this case bells "beyond the starres heard" (l. 13). Baptism is "a narrow way and little gate" through which one must pass on the way to salvation ("H. Baptisme [II]," l. 2), and the Eucharist likewise seems much more than a mere Zwinglian sign but rather "becomes a wing" to lift one and to assist one to "flie/ To the skie" ("The Banquet," 11. 42–44). In "The H. Communion" in the Williams manuscript—a poem not included in the collection published as *The Temple*—Herbert seems even indifferent with regard to the doctrine of transubstantiation, though he in fact in the end affirms the traditional Anglican view.

Herbert also does not reject either ecclesiastical or secular hierarchy, both of which are affirmed in "Antiphon (I)": "Let all the world in ev'ry corner sing,/ *My God and King.*" In keeping with Queen Elizabeth's proclamation forbidding the defacing of memorials in churches,[21] Church monuments receive his respect though he makes a strong point that they are not worthy of idolatry.[22] His sense of hierarchy is affirmed in "The Church-floore": "The gentle rising, which on either hand/ Leads to the Quire above,/ Is *Confidence*" (ll. 7–9). The raised choir was a feature of the Caroline church that was misliked of many Puritans,[23] and in the diaries of an iconoclast such as William Dowsing during the 1640's attention is given to leveling chancels that are deemed too high.[24]

In "The Windows" Herbert posits an analogy between painted glass windows and the priest in his preaching.[25]

Lord, how can man preach thy eternall word?

He is a brittle crazie glasse:
Yet in thy temple thou dost him afford
This glorious and transcendent place,
To be a window, through thy grace.
(ll. 1–5)

In this poem, Herbert turns to a part of the church fabric that had become most significant in the later Middle Ages when buildings of stone *and glass* became the location for worship which at once appealed to the visual and auditory senses. Joined to the Gregorian idea of visual art which would provide books for the unlearned and which would thus teach the biblical stories to the people, the great expanses of glass in Gothic churches and cathedrals also expressed the theology of light as it was formulated by Suger at St.-Denis and by various subsequent students of liturgy.[26] In glass, the stories became especially radiant—precisely the effect that takes place in the priest in his sermonizing when he has become a vehicle for the divine illumination of the Word, which is made effective by grace.[27]

But when thou dost anneal in glasse thy storie,
Making thy life to shine within
The holy Preachers; then the light and glorie
More rev'rend grows, and more doth win:
Which else shows watrish, bleak, and thin.
(ll. 6–10)

On the other hand, therefore, when the illumination is lacking, the effect is disastrous—indeed, in either glass or preacher "watrish, bleak, and thin." Lacking light from the sun, painted glass loses its ability to communicate the sacred stories visually, though the patterns are still present in the darkened glass. Presumably both glass and the priest proclaiming the Word will inspire attention and awe in spite of the brittleness of glass and the ephemeral nature of speech:

Doctrine and life, colours and light, in one
When they combine and mingle, bring
A strong regard and aw: but speech alone

Doth vanish like a flaring thing,
And in the eare, not conscience ring.
(ll. 11–15)

It is very curious, therefore, that Richard Strier should have suggested that "The Windows" is a poem which "could have been written by an iconoclast."[28] Herbert, a restorer of churches and one who had a particular respect for the fabric of the building, had little in common with an iconophobe such as Dowsing who would search out the most minute details of imagery in churches in order to destroy them in the 1640's. But, as the poem itself when accurately read should indicate, Herbert's analogy is designed to show respect for "brittle crazie glasse" through which light shines into the sacred space of the church and by means of which the biblical story might be told.[29] (Staunch Puritanism such as that entrenched at Merton College, Oxford, on the other hand, had the glass of the college chapel whitewashed over in order to cover the imagery, presumably regarded as dangerous, as early as King Edward's reign.[30]) Herbert's respect for painted glass may also be seen against the background of an iconoclastic act of approximately the same date as his Bemerton period and involving a parish in nearby Salisbury. It was an act that demonstrates the wide gulf separating Herbert from the attitudes espoused by the iconoclast, who as the recorder of Salisbury was a person of considerable local prestige.

The iconoclast, Henry Sherfield of the parish of St. Edmund in Salisbury, demonstrated indeed how "brittle" glass can be when, having gained entrance to the church with the help of the sexton's wife, he smashed a painted glass window with a pike staff in October 1630. In January of this year, the vestry of St. Edmund's, a Puritan stronghold, had voted its objection to this painted glass window of the Creation since it was said to be in poor condition and since, being "very darksome," those who "sit near the same cannot see to read in their books."[31] Nothing was said at first about the contents of the window, but the vestry order, proposed by Sherfield,[32] called for replacement "with white glass." Two members of the vestry objected and insisted upon informing the bishop. Bishop

John Davenant, Herbert's bishop who had installed him at Bemerton (on 26 April) and ordained him as priest (on 19 September) in the same year, ordered that the window should not be destroyed, but Sherfield's vandalism nevertheless accomplished the aim of severely damaging the glass, which is now unfortunately entirely lost. Sherfield's offense became a celebrated case that was tried in the Star Chamber less than a month before Herbert's death. Among those who spoke for the prosecution was William Laud, who appeared before the court on 8 February 1633. In his defense, Sherfield argued that the scene in the glass was inaccurate, with God being offensively presented "in the forms of diverse little old men, barefooted, and clothed in long blue coats."[33] Laud did not try to defend the imagery—and indeed he indicated his dislike of images of God the Father—but instead he argued the case on the basis of the ecclesiastical authority of the Bishop of Salisbury.[34] In the end, Herbert's bishop was upheld, and Sherfield was forced to submit.[35]

If Herbert was no iconoclast, so also we must not pretend that he was an iconodule, and very likely he thought of himself as conforming to the precepts set forth in the Elizabethan "Homilie agaynst perill of Idolatry and superstitious deckyng of Churches,"[36] which contains strictures that he would have regarded as less than universal and as directed not at all images but only at "abused" images. Certain images in painted glass would have been for him "things indifferent"—that is, things not specifically necessary to salvation though potentially useful, at least to some, particularly the unlearned. Such images, assuming that they are not regarded as devotional objects and that they do not promote "superstitious" stories (in these cases Herbert would be classified as an iconomach, though even here iconoclasm does not at all necessarily follow), have for him a certain usefulness, though in significance they cannot be compared to the Holy Scriptures themselves which are the fount of transcendent knowledge.[37] Painted glass, like the human being (and including the priest), is fragile, and hence church windows with their imagery are symbolic of the transitory nature of life in this world. Yet glass points out how a fragile being nevertheless may serve as a source of illumination to parishioners. This is not the opinion of Sherfield, who was said to have objected to the content of the Creation window at St. Edmund's for twenty years.[38]

"The Windows" does not appear in the Williams manuscript, and hence may be among Herbert's later poems. While we cannot assume that it was written at Bemerton, the poem nevertheless was retained in the final version of his collection of poems at the end of his life. This was a time, as we have seen, when in the diocese of Salisbury one of the most celebrated cases concerning a challenge to ecclesiastical authority over the matter of church windows was brought to trial in the highest court of the land. Further, at the end of his life Herbert committed the final version of *The Temple* to Nicholas Ferrar, his friend at Little Gidding, whose liturgical practices aroused very strong Puritan reactions—reactions as extreme as those directed against painted glass windows such as the one illustrating the Creation at St. Edmund's in Salisbury. The author of the Puritan pamphlet *The Arminian Nunnery, or A Brief Description and Relation of the late Erected Monastical Place called 'The Arminian Nunnery' at Little Gidding in Huntingdonshire* thus objected very strongly to the way that Ferrar intoned the litany and collects of the *Book of Common Prayer* as well as to the use of catholic gestures and candles.[39] A person such as Ferrar, who like Herbert was not of the Laudian party, would nevertheless on account of his sensitivity to the inner life of the spirit and its metonymic relation to the practice of worship in the church be an ideal executor of the poet's wish to see his book of poetry published.

For extreme Puritans such as Sherfield, painted glass in the windows of the church building are primarily darksome, idolatrous, and totally without value to the worshipper—a hindrance to the Word. Herbert's "The Windows," which depends for its meaning on accepting the value of painted glass containing scenes from sacred stories, suggests, in Judy Z. Kronenfeld's words, "a religious use of stained-glass as something more than a sensuously effective devotional aid."[40]

"The Windows" is not, however, a self-contained unit of poetry that will stand alone as indicative of Herbert's opinion of painted glass in all its nuances, but when seen in the context of his religious practice—and of his concern for the analogies which exist between the structure of the church building and the spiritual life—the poem serves to illustrate an important aspect of the poet's stance. For Herbert, his parish church is a "place, where I might sing,/ And serve thee"—and it is a place where he might use his wealth and assistance from his family "To set thy honour up" ("The Crosse," ll. 3–6). So he had laid plans while a deacon to renovate the dilapidated church at Leighton Bromswold, which unlike tiny Bemerton was in fact a cruciform church.[41] And thus also would he put his energy into the renovation of the church at Bemerton when he was appointed to that parish. While today no original Bemerton glass remains, nor is there very much medieval glass remaining in Salisbury Cathedral, we may be certain that Herbert was solicitous of any remaining in his own parish and appreciative of that which was present in the cathedral. Though Bishop John Jewel was said to have removed "superstitious" scenes in Salisbury glass in 1567, much must nevertheless have remained in Herbert's time. Furthermore, three windows in the cathedral had been newly glazed in 1620 with representations of the story of St. Paul.[42]

In a sense, therefore, "The Windows" may be regarded as a crucial poem in *The Temple*, since the analogy between certain physical attributes of the church building and personal experience with its need for illumination in order to achieve direction in one's pilgrimage of life is herein utilized in such an important way. The church is itself the center of one's spiritual life, and it is a building that in England is almost always oriented toward the east—the direction of the Second Coming, the Last Judgment, and the life of the righteous in eternity. Rigid Calvinists attempted to break down that orientation of the church building, and to some extent they succeeded in the time of Queen Elizabeth when certain liturgical innovations were temporarily accepted. These innovations had involved the replacement of the altar by a communion table and the rearrangement of the seating in the building. But for Herbert, the connection between architecture, psychology, and cosmology was unbroken. For medieval men such as St. Bernard, the monastery with its church "was ideally an image and foretaste of paradise";[43] so too for Herbert, writing in a less catholic age to be sure, the church was a location where the heavenly harmonies of music might resonate and where the illumination of divine knowledge might filter through both the windows of painted glass and the mouth of the priest. The church is a place where one might on earth "*do the works of heaven*," for such in Herbert's view were the acts performed in the liturgy which had been made available to the Church in the present by its past.

If Herbert shared with Protestantism a reverence for the sacred text and for the means of its explication in sermons, he insisted that greater value resided in prayer, especially of a communal sort—"the Churches banquet," he calls it in "Prayer (I)" (l. 1). His principal emphasis was on the worship that had been the Church's traditional role from antiquity. In the church building, according to Herbert, "God is more there, then thou" ("The Church-Porch," l. 404). Participation in the rituals which tradition has handed over to the present time allows men and women to "approach, and taste/ The churches mysticall repast" ("Superliminare," ll. 3–4) which in his understanding of the Church had sustained people since the first century, for the Church is a communion of the living and those who, though dead, are alive in Christ.

For the poet, the task of the priest as head of his parish is a demanding one and a source of anxiety; the fragility of the individual's nature nevertheless in his view can be overcome through acceptance of his traditional role as a window through which the sacred story and the light of grace and faith may be communicated. But the window to which the priest in his function as a homilist compares himself is not the white or clear glass preferred by the radical Puritans: instead, it is the painted glass inherited from medieval times. Hope comes to the individual through a collaboration between past and present, not through a denial of the past.

In a revealing passage in a chapter entitled "*The Parson Blessing*" in *The Country Parson*, Herbert comments that "In the time of Popery, the Priests *Benedicite*, and his holy water were over highly valued; and now we are fallen to the clean contrary, even from superstition to coldnes, and Atheism."[44] His understanding of tradition is not that it is a law that must establish present rules of behavior if in the past it has been faulty. Tradition, blindly followed, may even be demonic. But, like Hooker, he affirms the necessity of respecting traditional forms, practices, and artifacts, especially as these assist in the overcoming of the alienation which naturally tends to draw men and women away from community with those who are reconciled to the Creation and to its Creator.

1. *Winter Light*. Scene from the film by Ingmar Bergman. Courtesy of the Swedish Film Institute.

2. Adoration of the Magi. Painted glass, Great Malvern Priory Church, north nave aisle. By permission of the Royal Commission on the Historical Monuments of England.

3. Corporal Acts of Mercy. Painted glass, All Saints Church, North Street, York. By permission of the Royal Commission on the Historical Monuments of England.

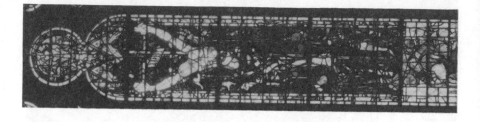

4. (At left.) Placing Christ on the Cross. Woodcut, Dutch version of the *Speculum humanae salvationis* (*Spiegel der menscheliker behoudenisse*, chap. XXIII). Courtesy of the Huntington Library.

5. (At right.) Crucifixion. Painted glass, York Minster, south nave aisle. By permission of the Royal Commission on the Historical Monuments of England.

6. Doom. Painted glass, west window, Fairford, Gloucestershire. The top
portion is "restored." By permission of the Royal Commission on the
Historical Monuments of England.

7. Brigittine Nativity. Painted glass, Great Malvern Priory Church, transept window. By permission of the Royal Commission on the Historical Monuments of England.

8. The world upside down. Woodcut on title page of John Taylor, *Mad Fashions, Od Fashions, All Out of Fashions* (1642). Courtesy of the Huntington Library.

9. (Above.) *Bonta*. Engraving from Cesare Ripa, *Iconologia* (Venice, 1669).

10. Interior of All Saints, Margaret Street. Photograph, c.1890. By permission of the Royal Commission on the Historical Monuments of England.

11. Virgin and Child. Nineteenth-century replacement, altered in line with contemporary taste. The original boss illustrated the Christ Child at his mother's breast. Roof boss, York Minster nave. By permission of the Royal Commission on the Historical Monuments of England.

8

Tradition and Imitation

Richard Hooker, answering Puritan objections to the making of the sign of the cross in baptism, provided an extensive defense of this practice within the context of this sacrament.[1] The widespread revival in the Church of England on numerous other occasions of the use of the sign of the cross, a traditional gesture dating from the early Church, was, however, an outgrowth of the Ritualism that emerged in earliest phase of the Oxford Movement, some members of which recommended following continental Roman Catholic conventions.[2] Though he was not himself a Ritualist, John Henry Newman's poem "The Cross of Christ" celebrating this gesture is indicative of the Romanticism that helped to inspire the early phase of Ritualism in England:

> Whene'er across this sinful flesh of mine
> I draw the Holy Sign,
> All good thoughts stir within me, and collect
> Their slumbering strength divine;
> Till there springs that hope of GOD'S elect
> My faith shall ne'er be wrecked.
>
> And who shall say, but hateful spirits around,
> For their brief hour unbound,
> Shudder to see, and wail their overthrow?
> While on far heathen ground
> Some lonely Saint hails the fresh odour, though
> Its source he cannot know.[3]

The effect of the sign of the cross resonates in the other world where the unholy spirits of the air are restrained, even in lands as yet unconverted to Christianity. Such a miracle, possible for the mind of the Romantic, may hardly have convinced a hardheaded man of the Enlightenment such as David Hume,[4] but at least in the realm of the imagination apparently proved inspiring to those who would revive a traditional practice along with an understanding of it that had been long out of fashion.

Newman's use of the sign of the cross involves the imitation of a traditional form, and in a sense establishes for us a model of nineteenth-century insistence on imitation, in this case of a lost practice (though one still to be found among Roman Catholics), of a traditional form. Naturally there was much resistance to this model, which is to be sure most closely associated with one ecclesiastical party. A generation later a writer in the short-lived Low Church periodical called the *Anti-Ritualist* proclaimed:

> The time for silence is past. It is useless to attempt to conceal any longer that a struggle is imminent. Deadly error must be met. Mediaevalism must be banished, and a simple, spiritual, and hearty worship restored. The real question is, Whether Christianity or mimic Popery shall prevail? whether Christ or anti-Christ shall reign?[5]

Repeating the hostile view of the Roman Catholic Church that had been found in such Reformation writers as John Foxe, this commentator saw the imitation of Catholic practice as the antithesis of true religion. "Ritualism we abhor," another article in the same periodical declared, ". . . because it is a religion of sight, not of faith."[6] And again, in commenting on a harvest celebration: "The processions . . . are not only . . . 'superfluous,' but they are a daring revival of an obsolete dark-age custom in palpable opposition to royal and episcopal injunctions."[7]

John Ruskin too resented the ritual—and the theology—that was being imitated along with medieval architecture in English churches. The *Anti-Ritualist* would comment: "Ritualism is the butterfly in gorgeous attire luring on its fascinated devotees to the vanguard."[8] These words seem almost to echo Ruskin's denunciation of Catholic ritual in an appendix to the first volume of *The Stones of Venice* (1851):

But of all these fatuities, the basest is the being lured into the Romanist Church by the glitter of it, like larks into a trap by broken glass; to be blown into a change of religion by the whine of an organ-pipe; stitched into a new creed by gold threads on a priest's petticoats; jangled into a change of conscience by the chimes of a belfry. I know nothing in the shape of error so dark as this, no embicility so absolute, no treachery so contemptible.[9]

With reference to liturgical practice, it indeed became usual to use the word 'medieval' as an emotionally loaded term according to one's preferences; by the last year of the nineteenth century, J. Wickham Legg, in an essay on "Mediaeval Ceremonial," could comment that "The word 'mediaeval' is often used to express mere like or dislike. By it some mean what is in their eyes perfect or almost divine; with others it is synonymous with what is weak-minded and contemptible."[10]

Newman's poem was written in 1832 and eventually included along with the more famous "Lead, Kindly Light" in the collection *Lyra Apostolica* in 1836. In the same year as the publication of the *Lyra Apostolica*, A. N. W. Pugin, an architect and Roman Catholic convert, published the first edition of his *Contrasts* in which he illustrated idealized Gothic buildings set off against ugly modern structures. The book was calculated to shock. "The so-called Reformation," he claimed, "is now regarded by many men of learning and of unprejudiced minds as a dreadful scourge, permitted by divine Providence in punishment for its decayed faith; and those by whom it was carried on are now considered in the true light of Church plunderers and crafty political intriguers, instead of holy martyrs and modern apostles."[11] Especially he takes aim at those buildings which have imitated Greek and Roman forms—"all revived classic buildings, whether erected in Catholic or Protestant countries, are evidences of a lamentable departure from true Catholic principles and feelings"[12]—and instead argues for the substitution of medieval forms as designs to follow in the architecture of the present time.

The sharp shift in taste to the Gothic style by c.1840 was not, of course, due entirely to Pugin, who as a Roman Catholic would by himself have had only limited influence. Antiquarian research dating from the seventeenth century had laid the groundwork for serious interest in medieval architecture and other aspects of medieval culture.[13] Literary developments also must be taken in to account,[14] especially those associated with the Romantic movement and popular literature such as the novels of Sir Walter Scott. But literature by itself was only an indirect influence; it could, for example, corroborate a taste for ruined abbeys such as the Cistercian house named in the title of Wordsworth's "Lines Composed a Few Miles above Tintern Abbey." But a taste for actual Gothic designs had to come from other sources, which included publication of illustrations as well as specific arguments in favor of medieval forms. The arguments were articulated by John Carter, whose *Specimens of Ancient Sculpture and Painting* had appeared in 1786 and whose letters in the *Gentleman's Magazine* appeared at regular intervals between the closing years of the eighteenth century and his death in 1817. His first communication, entitled "Pursuits of Architectural Innovation," appeared in the 1798 volume of the periodical and was signed, as were all the rest, by "An Architect."[15] Charles L. Eastlake, who appears to have been responsible for popularizing the term 'Gothic Revival,' credits Carter with spreading respect for earlier styles of architecture,[16] though John Britton was recognized as an even more important figure in a change of taste[17] that was so revolutionary that when the houses of Parliament were rebuilt after the conflagration of 1834 the design that was adopted was Gothic.[18] Britton's *Architectural Antiquities of Great Britain*[19] and other publications included engravings which were detailed and accurate illustrations of ancient architecture, often with commentary that remains of significance today to art historians and archaeologists. In Eastlake's opinion, he may have been the most important person among those who played a role in developing an appreciation for medieval art and architecture, for he was extremely successful in securing "for Mediaeval remains the kind of interest which a sense of the picturesque and a respect for historical associations are likely to create."[20] Some buildings were in ruins. In his description of Croyland Abbey in Lincolnshire, Britton lamented:

> The day is not far distant, when the most valuable of the present re-
> mains must fall in ruin, and the ill-judged zeal of the inhabitants in the
> repair of the west front has tended to accelerate its approach. History
> will proclaim what Croyland was, though its glories shall be no more;
> and the *nominis umbra* keep alive the respect which is due to the re-
> mains of antiquity, and to the abode of religion.[21]

The work of Carter, Britton, and others forcefully called attention to the fact that much of the extant medieval architecture in
England was ecclesiastical—Britton's uncompleted *Cathedral Antiquities*, for example, displayed the glories of these splendid buildings
in which people began to take serious national pride—and that it
was in poor condition. Outside of London where the fire of 1666
had made rebuilding necessary, the majority of churches were pre-
Reformation, though with the addition of box pews ("dozing-pens,"
Pugin called them[22]), ostentatious pulpits, and galleries and re-
arranged for a Protestant style of worship; through neglect of the
fabric and of the liturgical traditions which had originally determined the shape and form of the medieval church, there was much
to lament in England's heritage of medieval buildings.[23] Eighteenth-
and early nineteenth-century restorations could also be disastrous.
Concerning the Round Church (Holy Sepulchre) in Cambridge, Britton would lament that "Much of the original design and pristine
character of this building have been altered and injured by late alterations, and by the injudicious operations of the carpenter, white-
washer, and bricklayer, whose performances are commonly, though
really ironically, called '*beautifying*'."[24]

It seemed an event of momentous importance, therefore, in
May 1839, nearly six years after Keble's Assize Sermon marked the
beginning of the Oxford Movement, that the Cambridge Camden
Society was formed. This organization, which was far more significant from an architectural, artistic, and liturgical standpoint than the
Oxford Tractarians, was to encourage the restoration of churches
and the return to traditional worship with its influence felt throughout the English-speaking world.[25] Its periodical, the *Ecclesiologist*,
which began publication in 1841, immediately became influential
through its denunciation of new construction and restoration which

was disliked and through its role of calling attention to the dilapidated condition of English churches. The Society's Rules in 1842 indicated that its "object" was "to promote study of Ecclesiastical Architecture and Antiquities, and the restoration of mutilated Architectural remains."[26] Following a crisis in the mid-1840's, it was reorganized and its name changed to the Ecclesiological Late Cambridge Camden Society, with the "object" of promoting "the study of Christian Art and Antiquities, more especially in whatever relates to the architecture, arrangement, and decoration of churches; the *recognition of correct principles and taste* in the erection of new churches; and the restoration of ancient ecclesiastical remains."[27] The doctrinaire attitude which characterized the Cambridge Ritualists, who sought "correctness" in the imitation of traditional medieval forms within extremely narrow limits, was to be harshly argued in various publications.

The Society's encouragement of church visitation for the purpose of study and evaluation was to become a regular feature of archaeological association meetings in England. But members of the Society were encouraged to look at the structures and their fabric from a particular point of view. The *Report of the Cambridge Camden Society* for 1841 included an insert, called "A Church Scheme," which provided an extensive check-list for use when visiting churches.[28] Since some of the terminology was quite technical, *A Handbook of English Ecclesiology* was also eventually issued which demonstrated its bias about style and taste very clearly. "About the time of the Reformation," the *Handbook* complained, "the partial recurrence to classical forms, induced by the vitiated and unhappy taste for Italian architecture, completely corrupted the pure Pointed style by giving birth to various anomalous compositions, generally termed Debased."[29] Readers were advised, for example, to be alert for aumbries, rood screens, the location of the font (near the entrance), clerestories (which were disliked), vestments (traditional ones were preferred), and so forth.[30]

The medieval church structure was in every way to be regarded as laden with symbolism. For example, the chancel, which had been a neglected portion of the structure in many churches since the Reformation, was to be understood as symbolic of the kingdom of heaven while the nave was to be seen as symbolic of this world striving toward such a heavenly goal.[31] While this view was consistent with the late-medieval understanding of the orientation of the church structure, there was otherwise no guarantee that whatever symbolism was being discovered was being accurately described. E. H. Gombrich wisely argues that the institutional context of symbolism needs to be examined prior to the symbols themselves,[32] and herein the Ecclesiologists failed. Their attempt to create a *science* of ecclesiology was destined to arrive only at a misguided codification that was enforced by a false appeal to the authority of a traditional practice, which is given the status of law—an artificial attempt, no doubt, to achieve stability in an age when the social structure under pressure of the Industrial Revolution was anything but stable.

The tradition that is singled out for imitation is fourteenth-century English, chosen perhaps unconsciously for patriotic reasons ill understood by the Ecclesiologists, who found the earlier Norman and the later Perpendicular styles defective. This is the style that architects were told they must master and follow. John Mason Neale and Benjamin Webb, in their extended introduction to their translation of Book I of Durandus' *Rationale divinorum officiorum*, made the matter plain:

> For the Anglican architect, it will be necessary to know enough of the earlier styles to be able to restore the deeply interesting churches, which they have left us as precious heirlooms; enough of the Debased styles, to take warning from their decline: but for his own style, he should choose the glorious architecture of the fourteenth century; and, just as no man has more than one hand-writing, so in this one language alone will he express his architectural ideas.[33]

This is the route that Neale and Webb insist is the route to "symbolical truthfulness" in church building, which ought to result in a building possessing the quality of "*Sacramentality*."[34] Naturally, the principal symbol described by the plan of the church structure is the cross, which is related to the sign of the cross adopted by early Christians.[35] But there are many other complexities which the architect must command if he is to find approval and any number of rules that he must follow. However, from the standpoint of the twentieth century the most lasting contribution of the Ecclesiologists' aesthetic is that the form of the building must follow its function—in this case, a form determined by the ritual which would be celebrated in the building. As Neale and Webb articulate the principle, "church architecture is the eldest daughter of Ritual."[36] Apparently the term 'Ritual' in this context is intended to be understood as the Prayer Book service with addition of Catholic rubrics; in contrast to the generation of George Herbert, the nineteenth-century Ritualists in their concern for the recovery of liturgical tradition were not as aware as they should have been of the principles inherent in liturgy.[37]

It will now be clear that what was meant by imitation in its architectural sense was not a mechanical replication of medieval buildings. Yet, quite surprisingly, when we encounter the church that received the most approval by the Ecclesiologists we find that it is not in the least like a mere copy of a fourteenth-century English church. The structure is William Butterfield's Church of All Saints, Margaret Street, in London, which was under construction in 1850-52[38] but not finished until 1859 and thereafter looked after and altered by its architect in the succeeding decades. A remarkable building set on a limited plot of land as a deliberate Catholic challenge to "the haughty and Protestantized shopocracy" of the area,[39] All Saints was the work of an architect whose taste was for orderliness as opposed to what he identified as "lawlessness." His taste in liturgy was for a much less ritualistic service than would be instituted at All Saints, and in fact he actively disapproved of such innovations as Benediction that had been imported from the continental Roman practice.[40] But his respect for liturgical forms and for his materials, especially as the plans for the church developed and the influence of Ruskin was felt,[41] meant that the church would be exactly suited to Eucharistic worship.

The basic plan of All Saints was relatively uncomplicated.[42] There was only a small amount of space for an enclosed courtyard through which one crossed to enter the nave, which was, of course, oriented to the east. To the left of the entrance and under the tower is the baptistry with its font. The chancel is the divided chancel that had been introduced in 1841 in the Leeds Parish Church with a view to choral services,[43] and has a low screen with a gate separating this area from the nave. The focus of the building is upon the high altar above which the suspended pyx contains the reserved sacrament. Butterfield's original plan does not note the use to be made of the space to the north of the chancel which now holds the organ. The Lady Altar currently at the east end of the north aisle was not Butterfield's work but was added in the early twentieth century.[44]

The plan, however, can give only a vague impression of the building, its complexity of design, or its avoidance of the strictly imitative in its handling of color or form. According to an entry in his journal on the site of Tintern Abbey on 18 June 1866, Gerard Manley Hopkins was impressed by the way in which the style of the abbey, in ruins but nevertheless "typical English work," reminded him of the work of Butterfield, although it is not necessary that he had All Saints, Margaret Street, specifically in mind.[45] Yet the windows of All Saints are in fact very like fourteenth-century work. Returning to look at All Saints on 12 June 1874 to "see if my old enthusiasm was a mistake," Hopkins seems to have been somewhat disappointed. Nevertheless, he admired the "rich nobility of the tracery" in the chancel, and "the touching and passionate curves of the lilyings in the ironwork under the baptistery arch marked his genius to me as before."[46] The exterior is of black and red brick, a material scorned in early issues of the *Ecclesiologist*, and its use seems, like the design of the steeple, to be based on North German models.[47] But it is the inside of the church, with its extensive use of what the Ecclesiologists had called "constructional polychrome,"[48] that gives it its distinctive character (fig. 10). Early Victorian architects had frequently used paint with the result that their buildings were designed for the addition of color to the structure; Butterfield in All Saints made the color an integral part of the building.[49] The influence of Ruskin will be most obvious in the use of encaustic tiles and marble and in the balancing of colors which would not always be expected normally in Victorian work. Butterfield traveled to the continent to make direct observations of south European use of polychrome techniques, which he then applied in his work on All Saints.[50] But nowhere did he slavishly copy any of his models; his imitation was far more innovative—more innovative with regard to his use of color than was generally appreciated in his own time.

Butterfield was criticized for the harshness of his color and his designs. Even the *Ecclesiologist* complained about the "dread of beauty" that was believed to characterize All Saints Church.[51] But the building, in all its luxuriance and richness and in spite of damage done to some of the tiles in the twentieth century by wrong-headed painting, demonstrates an architectural honesty in its use of materials that looks forward to the dogged integrity of the American Frank Lloyd Wright, whose comments on structural fakery are well known. All Saints, however, is primarily a functional building, a sacred space wherein the liturgy and its music can function as intended. Butterfield's achievement at All Saints was ultimately a triumph over mere imitation in the service of tradition.

The liturgy which found its shape in such churches as All Saints, Margaret Street, was apparently at first a rather stiff ceremonial that in spite of its medieval intent did not come very close to the Sarum ritual which had dominated much of England in the late Middle Ages. The traditional medieval vestments would be returned, along with gestures and many other accouterments of medieval ceremonial. At All Saints, the building was designed so that there could be a Gospel procession, with the reading of the most important lesson of the service in the midst of the people. Incense would be returned, following continental practice.

In such churches, services would ideally be sung, with unaccompanied singing preferred, and even very serious attempts would be made to bring back the practice of Gregorian chant. W. S. Rockstro, writing in the first edition of Grove's *Dictionary of Music and Musicians* which was published in 1880, suggested that chant, or "Plain Song," is "rich enough to supply the Church's every need, so long as her present form of Ritual remains in use, and sufficiently varied to adapt itself to any imaginable contingency."[52] But he also warns against corrupting these melodies, which exist, according to his view, in pure form in medieval manuscripts once the variants are studied and the best sources chosen for use. His article concludes:

> Those, then, who are really in earnest in their desire to preserve both the letter and the spirit of our store of antient Melodies from unauthorised interference, will do well to fortify their own taste and judgment by careful study; remembering, that, however worthy of our reverence the true Music of the Early Christian Church may be, modernised Plain Song is an abomination which neither gods nor men can tolerate.[53]

The belief that the Church was somehow required to imitate only traditional medieval forms, which were thought to be handed down from the earliest years of Christianity, involved a flaw of the most serious kind, since the knowledge of chant prior to 1880 in England was itself imperfect. There apparently was no realization that chant was not a fixed and unchanging tradition throughout history, and that the late medieval manuscripts which contain readable notation cannot always be relied upon to verify the usage of earlier periods with precision. The major research and transcriptions of the abbey at Solesmes were yet to come, and in England the scholarly and practical work of the Plainsong and Mediaeval Music Society was only to begin in 1888.

Neale and Webb had insisted that the form of the church building necessarily was determined by the ritual that was celebrated within it; the architecture therefore was "a petrifaction of our religion."[54] This unfortunate metaphor perhaps reveals the narrowness with which they understood liturgical practice and the architecture in which ceremonial was to be enacted, and it is hence not surprising to find later scholars taking issue with the views of those who would prematurely codify even the most trivial gestures which they supposed were required in the English rite. J. T. Micklethwaite, writing in 1897, could refer ironically in his Alcuin Club tract on *The Ornaments of the Rubric* to the "science of Ecclesiology" which had been "invented" in the middle of the nineteenth century. The result of the founding of this "science" was "the setting up of the standard called *correctness* which has ruled the planning and ornaments of churches for many years." However, *"Correctness* has no definite principle underlying it. . . ."[55] While approving the dramatic changes in worship which have added to its dignity and vitality since the 1840's, Micklethwaite is among those who would limit practice to the imitation of past traditions, and thus he objects to "things strange and modern" in ceremonial. He approves of change only so far as it is within the limits established by tradition and permitted by the rubrics of the *Book of Common Prayer.*[56]

In mid-century, Ritualists in many instances set aside customs that had been in use for the three hundred years since Edward VI's time and replaced them with imitations of far less ancient continental practices.[57] Imitation of this sort led to the codification of rigid rules for gestures during the Eucharist, for example. Legg has commented on the wide variations in ritual that obtained in the Middle Ages and further has noted the adoption of a set of rubrics that were designed to impose "exactness" in the early sixteenth century.[58] These rubrics are were compiled by one John Burckard of Strassbourg, recommended by Pope Alexander VI, and after 1570 attached to the printed editions of the Roman Missal. Burckard had complained about the ways in which priests were "incorrect" in their liturgical practices in saying the Mass—a sign, actually, that medieval practice was flexible rather than affixed to a certain set of rigid practices.[59] The imitation of a medieval ceremonial that existed only as a Romantic chimera rather than as a real tradition was thus the fate of the earlier Ecclesiologists, and yet they did manage to return liturgy to an active practice in the Church of England—no mean achievement in the light of the hostility that Ritualism faced.

After the 1850's, the imitation of medieval styles in church architecture took different forms both in England and in America. In English-speaking lands, the underlying design of the ecclesiastical building became more or less fixed (except for sects that remained insulated from the main trends), and it conformed to the general outlines of the church plan established by the Ecclesiologists. Gothic remained in fact the preferred style of church building up to World War II, and was utilized in those two very prominent American cathedrals, the Cathedral of St. John the Divine in New York

City—the largest Gothic cathedral in the world—and the National
Cathedral in Washington, D.C.—a structure that was only completed
in 1990. The immense funds that were made available for church
building in the United States, often through the philanthropy of extremely rich industrialists, sometimes resulted in very elaborate
churches, as in the case of Christ Church, Cranbrook, Michigan, or
Grosse Pointe Memorial Church in the Detroit suburb of Grosse
Pointe Farms. The latter, a Presbyterian church donated to the congregation by a single family in the late 1920's, nevertheless was
designed with a chancel, albeit a small one, for a vested professional
choir. Churches of this kind in the United States, however, derive
less from the new Gothic Revival churches of England than from
the restoration work that was undertaken on the actual medieval
churches and cathedrals of England. The American architect Ralph
Adams Cram, noted for his neo-medievalism and writing at the turn
of the last century, insisted that "In England the Catholic and Gothic
restorations have succeeded at last in getting back to basic principles; and, as a result, the only vital, modern, consistent church
building to-day is that of England"[60]—a statement unfair to the developments that had also brought many on the continent of Europe
to an awareness of its medieval ecclesiastical heritage. For Cram, as
for the Ecclesiologists, church buildings should be "solid and endur-
ing temples" that, though they may not be equal to medieval work,
nevertheless "would at least take place with it in point of honor";
further, such churches should provide "a place apart where may be
solemnized the sublime mysteries of the Catholic faith; a temple
reared about the altar, and subordinate to it."[61]

The English restorers have been said, however, to have been
vandals as well as "Goths" in taste. In addition to imposing their
views of what a medieval building should be like, they tended to
"restore" aspects of the structure that they felt needed to be made to
look new and fresh. Conformity with the preferred style was often
enforced. Roofs would be raised, walls scraped—a process that removed the plaster and along with it countless medieval wall paintings—and sculptures recarved.[62] The early members of the Society
for the Protection of Ancient Buildings were appalled, and in a

statement dating from their founding in 1877 commented about the "Restoration" of medieval structures:

> No doubt within the last fifty years a new interest, almost like another sense, has arisen in these monuments of art; and they have become the subject of one of the most interesting of studies, and of an enthusiasm, religous, historical, artistic, which is one of the undoubted gains of our time; yet we think that, if the present treatment of them be continued, our descendants will find them useless for study and chilling to enthusiasm. We think that these last fifty years of knowledge and attention have done more for their destruction than all the foregoing centuries of revolution, violence and contempt. . . .
>
> But those who make the changes wrought in our day under the name of Restoration, while professing to bring back a building to the best time of its history, have no guide but each his own individual whim to point out to them what is admirable and what contemptible; while the very nature of their task compels them to destroy something and to supply the gap by imagining what the early builders should or might have done. Moreover, in the course of this double process of destruction and addition, the whole surface of the building is necessarily tampered with; so that the appearance of antiquity is taken away from such old parts of the fabrics as are left, and there is no laying to rest in the spectator the suspicion of what may have been lost; and in short, a feeble and lifeless forgery is the final result of all the wasted labour.[63]

Such vandalism was not, of course, confined to England. Lund Cathedral in Sweden lost its fifteenth-century west front to a restoration which removed all signs of Gothic in the interest of "preserving" a pure Romanesque building and which added newly rebuilt western towers in Romanesque style as well as other details in 1860–80.[64] In England, however, the Gothic reigned, and Romanesque or "Norman" was regarded patronizingly even in the case of a structure as glorious as Peterborough Cathedral.

The church restorer who worked most widely throughout England—and, some would say, who did the most damage—was George Gilbert Scott. Scott, who though converted to the Gothic style as described by Pugin was not a through-and-through medievalist, was allowed to restore such cathedrals as St. Albans and Ely, at the latter rebuilding the wooden lantern atop the octagon of 1322–42 according to a plan that would be controversial and yet, though not warranted perhaps by the extant documentation, may not have been so wrongheaded after all.[65] In all he worked on thirty-nine cathedrals and more than four hundred churches as well as numerous other buildings after his conversion to Gothic.[66] As one who wished always to please the Ecclesiologists (more often than not unsuccessfully, though for reasons that had little to do with architecture), he tended to prefer the fourteenth-century English style, and would do such things as to remove late Gothic windows and to replace them with windows in the approved style so that they would match other parts of a building. Incredibly, he considered himself a "Conservative" in church restoration as opposed to the "Eclectic" procedures favored by many Ecclesiologists, but his approach was little different from the solutions to restoration problems that were proposed by the "Eclectic" school.[67] Eventually, the twentieth century would bring the "Conservative" school to the fore as embodying the dominant attitude toward restoration, although violations of its tenets occur on a regular basis as restorers attempt to imitate medieval art and architecture rather than to preserve the artifacts as representative of past traditions with their own integrity.[68] Scott failed to see that his work treated very cavalierly the structures that he was called to work upon—a failure to respect the integrity of the buildings under restoration.

"Restoration," to be sure, sometimes meant absolute or nearly absolute destruction of a medieval original, which would be replaced by a copy, sometimes a fairly close imitation. In the case of the upper portion of the Great West Window at Fairford, where the glass illustrating the Doom was restored in c.1861–61, the restorers reported that "so much of the glass as could possibly be retained"[69] had been preserved, but this statement is misleading since *none* of the glass from this section of the window was in fact replaced in it. To be sure, the window had been damaged severely in a storm in 1703, but, as Hilary Wayment points out, the iconographic scheme was still in place with details such as Christ seated on his rainbow very much visible at the time the glass was taken down for restoration.[70] There were also a number of drawings and sketches of the glass available from the period before the "restoration." Such procedures, often resulting in the acquisition of old glass by unscrupulous glass "restorers," were not uncommon.

In York Minster, numerous examples of copies by "restorers" exist, including some rather good imitations, the most recent being dated 1903.[71] The Mauley Window on the south side of the nave was packed off to London to the firm of Burlison and Grylls in that year, and when it was returned much of the original glass had been replaced with new glass.[72] O'Connor and Haselock write: "While regretting the principles behind this kind of restoration, the skill with which the work was carried out must be admired."[73] But sometimes copies were felt to be necessary when the originals had been lost or destroyed, as in the case of the oak roof bosses in the roof of the nave of York Minster which were destroyed by fire in 1840. The original bosses had been carefully drawn to scale by John Browne,[74] and hence a decision could be made to replicate them in the course of necessary restoration work. All the original designs were imitated except one—the Nativity scene in which the Child was originally sucking at the breast of the Virgin Mary. In the Victorian copy, prudery won out: the new design (fig. 11) has the Child sucking a baby bottle![75] There were limits to imitation of traditional iconography, obviously.

Clever imitations have, not surprisingly, frequently confused or deceived numerous art historians and archaeologists during the past century. For example, the well-known thirteenth-century sculptures showing the Virtues and Vices in the Chapter House Vestibule at Salisbury Cathedral were restored in 1856 with the result that there has been disagreement about the extent of the mutilation which they had previously suffered and about their restoration, though answers to such questions may in this case be found in earlier documentation.[76] At Beverley Minster, careful study of the musicians carved on the label stops shows the extent of restoration, mainly by John Percy Baker, and indicates the extent to which they are reliable (or unreliable) as records of the early instruments played in fourteenth-century England.[77] For example, a man playing a hurdy-gurdy is entirely a "restoration" imitated from another sculpture in the building, while a man playing a plucked fiddle and singing has a head which is a replacement—a "restoration" which is obviously misleading with regard to performance practice.[78]

Considering the amount of interest in imitating medieval forms in ecclesiastical architecture, art, and liturgy, it comes as some surprise that there was so little interest in the religious drama of the Middle Ages. Some of the religious plays, especially the liturgical music-dramas, were designed for presentation in churches, and indeed were at times indistinguishable from ceremony or ritual. A collection of these Latin plays was published by Coussemaker in 1860,[79] but in England there seems to have been only a little scholarly interest—and no interest in performance. The closest to drama that perhaps was actually achieved involved the singing of the St. John Passion on Good Friday, which is remarked upon by Neale and Webb: "We enter a darkened church, illuminated only by the lighted 'Sepulchre': we hear the history of the Passion chaunted by three voices in three recitatives," whereupon the service continues with the "Reproaches."[80]

However, since the drama of the Visit to the Sepulcher and related quasi-dramatic rituals were associated with the Easter sepulcher which was frequently a part of the fabric of a medieval church and hence might require the attention of the restorers, knowledge about them was required. The Easter sepulcher, often a permanent fixture on the north side of the chancel near the altar,[81] thus would be a challenge to architects and scholars alike. Attempting to supersede the superficial commentary that had previously appeared, Alfred Heales surveyed both the traditional rites and their architectural setting in his article "Easter Sepulchres; their Object, Nature, and History" in 1869.[82] Included in his survey is a summary of the content of the *Visitatio Sepulchri*, and as part of his commentary he also quotes Lambarde's description of the puppet Resurrection show at Witney in Oxfordshire.[83] Though Heales believed that there was a distinction to be made between the liturgical plays and vernacular plays on similar subjects, he nevertheless provided a short discussion of the latter. He concluded that "Quaint as this Mystery was, irreverent as, from its complete discordance with modern associations, many may deem it," we should nevertheless attempt to understand its context and its usefulness to another age in spite of its lack of usefulness at the present time.[84] Some years later Henry John Feasey provided more extensive surveys in his *Ancient Holy Week Ceremonial* and an article in *The Ecclesiastical Review*.[85] Meticulous study of the texts of the ceremonies and the *Visitatio Sepulchri*, however, had to wait until 1933 when the principal examples were collected, with commentary, in Karl Young's monumental *Drama of the Medieval Church*[86]—a work of scholarship, not meant to inspire imitation in liturgy or dramatic presentation.

As the comments cited above from Heales' work on the Easter sepulcher suggest, the vernacular plays aroused even less enthusiasm than the liturgical drama. It is hard to imagine either the Oxford Tractarians or the Cambridge Ecclesiologists very interested in texts they would have seen as lacking in the dignity befitting the subject matter, and—the point will be discussed more fully in the final chapter of this book—many of these plays could not in any case have been staged because of the prohibition against representing God in a theatrical presentation. Further, because of their associations with the Middle Class citizens of medieval cities and with popular audiences, they would have found the plays suspect for their supposed lack of sophistication.

The first book that focuses on the vernacular religious drama of England was published in 1823: William Hone's journalistic and unsophisticated *Ancient Mysteries Described*.[87] Hone's attitude toward the Catholicism of the plays was uniformly hostile in spite of his interest in popular arts such as the mystery plays. The members of the London Trinity Guild, for example, were said by Hone to have "contributed their share to the vulgar gratification of the deluded people" through their patronage of popular shows and plays, while "Of pure devotion toward the Supreme Being, they appear to have been wholly ignorant."[88] However, when two years later a carefully researched and written book on early drama appeared— Thomas Sharp's *A Dissertation on the Pageants or Dramatic Mys-*

teries Anciently Performed at Coventry (1825), which published a considerable portion of what we know about the religious drama associated with one major medieval city—there was no sense of widespread approval of his topic or his methodology in spite of a favorable review in the December issue of the *Gentleman's Magazine*. Like the earlier Protestant writers on the plays, Sharp's critics looked upon the religious drama of the late Middle Ages as rife with superstition and hence upon the technology of its performance as irrelevant. A review in *The Monthly Magazine*[89] thundered against any interest in the minutiae of the traditional theatrical performance practice of the Middle Ages:

> Whatever certain antiquarians may delight to believe, the useful end of investigation does not consist in the laborious trifling with which attention is frittered away upon minute certainties and petty doubts. The scholar of enlarged mind and philosophical reflection will view such enquiries as those before us with reference only to the light which they can shed upon the progress of intellect, manners, and literature: he will take care to examine only the great operations of the machinery of society, not to count every nail and peg in its rude and original structure. We cannot choose but smile . . . at the solemnity with which he dwells on the uses of iron pins and clamps, "tenter-hooks, rings, wire, thread, and small cord." Neither can we sympathise in his grievous lamentation over the loss of some "draper's book of accounts," which could only have accumulated his sufficient catalogue of important articles. . . . (pp. 2–3)

Concerning the text of the Shearmen and Taylors' play which Sharp had included, the anonymous reviewer also had nothing good to say: "There is no intrinsic merit in this wretched and doggerel piece to render its publication at all necessary" since enough has already been made available in the published specimens from the Chester plays (p. 12). One can imagine what the outcry would have been had anyone dared at that time to suggest the revival of this drama as living theater.

Unfortunately, the texts of many of the medieval plays of England had the ill luck to be prepared for the press by scholars who detested or at the very least disliked their theology.[90] When the first edition of the Towneley plays, issued in 1836 by the Surtees Society, was published, the explanation for its appearance was that the cycle had been made available because "next to the Continuation of Wills and Inventories it received the greatest number of votes."[91]

Such lack of enthusiasm was hardly calculated to inspire excitement about medieval drama. The most glaring example of editorial prejudice involves the text of the Digby plays published under Frederick J. Furnivall's name first under the imprint of the New Shakspere Society in 1882 and then by the Early English Text Society in its "Extra Series." Furnivall (who in fact did not even prepare the text, since he thanks "Mr George Parker, our careful copier and collator at Oxford," for his assistance in this regard) wrote an incredibly patronizing introduction in which he admits that the plays have some interest "independent of their literary merit" as predecessors of Shakespeare, though the examples in the Digby manuscript are said to be "poorer than the Towneley [plays]" and "point to the decay of the old religious Drama in England." Thus "the student sees . . . only the greater need for Shakspere to arise, replace the old Religionism with the new Humanity, and take as his themes the loves, fears, hates, ambitions of men, the World and its Ruler, instead of Judæa and its King."[92] These plays were, he was convinced, "but parts of the Romish Church service, developt and taken out into the streets,"[93] and for this Church service he clearly has no liking. In a note of explanation appended to the book, he prints a translation of a relevant segment of Guérenger's *The Liturgical Year* "as most of our members probably know nothing (like I do) about Papal services."[94] He thus assumes that few members of the Shakspere Society (or, presumably, of the Early English Text Society) will have acquaintance with the very liturgical forms that had been the center of interest for the liturgical reformers of the century.

Furnivall, whose purpose in editing dramatic texts had more to do with exploration of the language in preparation for the compilation of the *Oxford English Dictionary* than anything else,[95] is representative of those habits of scholarship that would culminate in E. K. Chambers' *Mediaeval Stage*, a work which is sympathetic to the medieval drama only insofar as it stood in the line of evolutionary development to the great Elizabethans.[96] Even the earliest modern professional production of an English medieval play (*Everyman*) was directed by a man who was essentially hostile to medieval traditions and medieval religion.[97]

Quite curiously, therefore, the century which more than any previous age attempted to return to medieval traditions also in its scholarly community resisted that return. Tory churchmen and Whig scholars between them brought their prodigious energy to bear on the medieval cultural traditions; one group wanted to imitate the past, which was selectively studied in order to filter out all that did not fit the dignity of religious practices it wished to see, while the other was devoted to scholarly progress which would establish the nature of the English language and wipe the mote of superstition from every eye.

9

T. S. Eliot's *Murder in the Cathedral*: Reviving the Saint Play Tradition

When T. S. Eliot was invited to write a play for the Canterbury Festival in 1935, he chose a topic that had been treated in theatrical presentations at previous Canterbury festivals, where Tennyson's *Becket* had been staged in 1932–33 and Laurence Binyon's *The Young King* in 1934.[1] Eliot's treatment was, however, to be significantly different from the previously produced plays on the Becket story. *Murder in the Cathedral*, which would be directed by E. Martin Browne, was designed to touch on contemporary affairs of great interest in the mid-1930's and to pay tribute to the greatest Canterbury saint, Thomas Becket, whose martyrdom was to be approached in a way that varied greatly from the usual handling of the historical drama in the twentieth century. In fact, this drama may be seen as a modern example of a genre that we regard as particularly medieval: the saint play. Thus it is possible to consider *Murder in the Cathedral* as indicative of Eliot's choice of "medievalism" over "modernism" and to recognize this as the result of his conversion to Anglo-Catholicism in 1927.[2] Eliot's transformation of a medieval genre, however, involved a relatively complex decision on the playwright's part and also attempted to draw upon some facts of theatrical history which he probably understood imperfectly. He saw his modern saint play in terms of a connection with ritual and liturgy—a connection which, he believed, would have been present in the medieval genre —and through his interest in ritual forms his drama was greatly enriched.

Eliot may well have known that plays on the subject of St. Thomas Becket existed in the Middle Ages. Interested as the writer was in this medieval saint,[3] it is not impossible that he could have learned from E. K. Chambers' *Mediaeval Stage*, published in 1903 and well known to students of the drama, or from other sources, such as Tancred Borenius' *St. Thomas Becket in Art* or Arthur P. Stanley's *Historical Memorials of Canterbury*, that plays on the subject of Becket were apparently staged at King's Lynn in Norfolk in 1385, where persons were paid for "playing the interlude of St. Thomas the Martyr," and at Canterbury itself, where a "pagent of St. Thomas" was recorded in the sixteenth century on one of his feast days, thought by Chambers to be 29 December, until the suppression of his cult.[4] Concerning the Canterbury presentation, Alan Nelson has suggested that it was not a true drama but merely a *tableau vivant* and not presented for the feast day celebrating Thomas' martyrdom on 29 December but for the eve of his translation, 2 July—a much more attractive time of year for an outdoor spectacle.[5] Chambers prints, however, some interesting accounts for 1504–05 and later years, including payments for new gloves for St. Thomas and the painting of his "hede"; "a new leder bag for the blode"; armor for the knights and, on one occasion, the necessity of hiring a sword are recorded. The accounts also indicate that a mechanical angel, moved by some kind of device, played a role in the show.[6]

Eliot would have had no way of knowing of further examples of saint plays of St. Thomas Becket, one recorded at Mildenhall, Suffolk, in 1505,[7] and another at London and recorded in the Skinners' Renter Wardens' Accounts for 1518–19.[8] The London play, unlike Eliot's, apparently presented the entire story of the Archbishop from his parents' legendary courtship to his murder at Canterbury in 1170. These examples of saint plays on the subject of Becket were apparently entirely unknown prior to World War II.

There is no question, however, about Eliot's enthusiasm for medieval literature in general and medieval drama in particular.[9] He had studied the medieval theater at Harvard under George Pierce Baker, whose interest in the "pre-Shakespearian" drama included the vernacular plays, most conveniently available to students then in the textbook edited by Alfred Pollard, *English Miracle Plays, Moralities, and Interludes* (1890).[10] This collection included not only examples of biblical plays from the great medieval cycles but also an abridged *Everyman*, which Eliot claimed as a direct influence on the style adopted in *Murder in the Cathedral*,[11] as well as selections from the Digby *Mary Magdalene*, one of the two extant saint plays in Middle English. Professor Baker had also insisted that his students should know about the early sources of the medieval drama, and advised them to read the liturgical "tropes" which were the presumed fountainhead of medieval drama.[12]

The Latin liturgical drama, designed to be sung as part of—or as additions to—the liturgy on certain feast days such as Easter or the Feast of St. Nicholas at monastic (usually Benedictine) houses and at cathedrals in the Middle Ages, may be significant for our understanding of *Murder in the Cathedral* because these dramas are ritual forms, and Eliot frequently, even before his conversion, spoke of the close connection which exists—or ought to exist—between ritual and drama. In 1933, Karl Young's monumental *Drama of the Medieval Church* was published by the Clarendon Press. The publication of this book was an event so significant that it is impossible that Eliot, involved as he was in the business of publishing through his association with Faber and Faber, could have failed to know about it. This does not mean, of course, that we can assume Eliot's intimate knowledge of Young's book—indeed, it is likely that he had only a passing knowledge of its contents. Nevertheless, certain aspects of Young's argument seem to agree with Eliot's achievement in *Murder in the Cathedral*, especially his insistence on the close relation of these Latin plays to the liturgy of the Mass and Office. One can only surmise that Eliot would have found the comments on the St. Nicholas plays and their Latin texts most useful as background to his own plan for *Murder in the Cathedral*. As in the liturgical plays, Eliot in his modern saint play insisted on a close association with the liturgy, utilizing in the Canterbury production the antiphons appropriate to the feast day of the martyr and ending the action with the *Te Deum*, regarded as a traditional conclusion for a liturgical drama and here transferred from Matins to Vespers to preserve this association. Perceptively, Joseph Wood Krutch, reviewing the Federal Theater Project production of *Murder in the Cathedral* in the *Nation* in 1936, comments that the play is reminiscent of

"the liturgical drama of the church not the popular if exalted entertainment of the sixteenth-century inn yard."[13] Similarly, Lionel J.
Pike has noted that the drama unquestionably "is nearer to medieval
liturgical drama than to modern theatre."[14]

Yet David E. Jones can insist that *Murder in the Cathedral* is
more closely modelled on Greek tragedy than upon medieval drama,
with the exception of "the use of allegorical figures in the temptations scene" and the influence of the versification of *Everyman*.[15] To
be sure, the Chorus is adapted from the Greek drama, and additionally the narrative of the play is reduced to its essence, the final
period of the saint's life following his return to England and continuing until his death at the hands of his murderers—reminding us
more of the condensation of the Greek theater than of the extended
story normally told in the medieval saint play which was based on
the saint's legend. Jones' objection, however, must be placed in
context, for Eliot saw both medieval drama (especially the liturgical
drama) and Greek drama as having evolved out of religious rituals.
This understanding of the Greek drama owes much to the Cambridge critics whose view of the theater related it directly to its
source in the rituals of the cult of Dionysius in ancient Greece.
Medieval drama likewise was seen as an evolutionary development,
a view that was implicitly set forth by Chambers and explicitly by
John M. Manly, whose "Literary Forms and the New Theory of the
Origin of the Species" was published in *Modern Philology* in 1907.
Young's work likewise was dependent upon the idea of the evolutionary development of drama out of ritual and utilized the notion
that such development must be from simple to complex forms as the
organizing principle of his *Drama of the Medieval Church*.[16] As
unlikely as Eliot was to have been sympathetic to the idea of the
progress of drama from sacred to secular, from simple ritual to
complex and humanizing drama, he nevertheless was clearly influenced very deeply by his understanding of the relationship between
the forms of worship and the forms of theatrical display. In invok-
ing ritual elements, Eliot therefore felt that in *Murder in the Cathedral* he was returning to elements derived from tradition upon which
modern drama had unwisely turned its back.

It would thus seem to be crucial to have in mind exactly how Eliot perceived the structure and function of the ritual that, in turn, would so significantly influence *Murder in the Cathedral*. First, it must be understood that he accepted the Sacramentalism and Ritualism of the Anglo-Catholic theologians of the Church of England which had re-affirmed the role of the Eucharist in establishing the framework around which life ought to be lived. Richard Hooker, in a passage quoted by Paul Elmer More and F. L. Cross in *Anglicanism* (1935), insisted that the sacraments' "chiefest force and virtue consisteth . . . in that they are heavenly ceremonies, which God hath sanctified and ordained to be administered in his Church" and through which grace might be imparted.[17] Also, the rites for the Anglo-Catholic included acts which in some sense not only provide a memory (*anamnesis*) of the past historical events of the Incarnation and Crucifixion but also somehow bring the events into the present and make the present-day worshippers participants in these events that are made contemporary with them. This view is set forth in the sermon which functions as an interlude in *Murder in the Cathedral*: "whenever Mass is said, we re-enact the Passion and Death of Our Lord."[18] As such, the Mass culminates in the canon in sacrifice, and thus may be called a 'Sacrifice.'[19] In the rites, God comes into the presence of men, who become actors in the divine drama of suffering, death, and resurrection. So, too, in *Murder in the Cathedral*; the members of the audience are actively brought into the play through the Chorus of women of Canterbury, with whom they are invited to identify themselves, while the action culminates in a death which ultimately is redemptive within the context of the cult. This action, like the ritual of the Eucharist, is fixed, with specified words and actions repeated each time the play is presented for an audience.

Also, this understanding of Catholic ritual was quite clearly reinforced for Eliot through the intellectual stimulus of early twentieth-century anthropology as applied to the origins of Greek drama. For Jane Harrison, 'ritual' was to be defined in terms of the definition of its Greek equivalent, '*dromenon*,' 'a thing done.'[20] As such, the rite was an act of participation in which the viewers were not merely passive onlookers; in contrast, in drama we have the spectator—for example, one who merely looks on as the action is presented before him or her. "It is in this new attitude of the spectator that we touch on the difference between ritual and art," Harrison wrote; "the *dromenon*, the thing actually done by yourself has become a *drama*, a thing also done, but abstracted from your doing."[21] Further, she defines the starting point of ritual in the lack of division between actor and spectator: "It is in the common act, the common or collective emotion, that ritual starts."[22] Thus Eliot in his Chorus uses the women of Canterbury to draw the audience into the "common act," the community of feeling which will respond to the making of the martyr. Rejecting the distinction established between rite and drama by such writers as Harrison, Eliot attempts to mediate between these two categories in his work.

Already in 1923, in the first volume of the *Criterion*, Eliot had insisted that "the stage—not only in its remote origins, but always— is a ritual, and the failure of the contemporary stage to satisfy the craving for ritual is one of the reasons why it is not a living art." The failure of the realism of the "ordinary stage" thus needs to be exchanged for a different mode, "a literal untruth, a thorough-going convention, a ritual."[23] At this point in his development, Eliot's definition of 'ritual' seems vague, requiring the kind of examination that he would give this matter during the next decade or so. Eventually he was to take the traditional Catholic liturgy as a standard by which he would view the concept of ritual, which at least after his conversion in 1927 would hardly be visualized merely in terms of "convention" or "literal untruth." Even by 1926 he saw drama as a form that stands in relation to the liturgy,[24] while in 1928 one of the characters in his "Dialogue on Dramatic Poetry" insisted that "Drama springs from religious liturgy. . . . [T]he only dramatic satisfaction that I find now is in a High Mass well performed."[25] Further clarification, however, is provided by Eliot in an article published after the success of *Murder in the Cathedral*:

> I would go so far as to say that a religious play, to be good, must not
> be purely religious. If it is, it is simply doing something that the liturgy

does better; and the religious play is not a substitute for liturgical ob-
servance and ceremonial, but something different. It is a combination of
religious with ordinary dramatic interest.[26]

In other words, a play such as *Murder in the Cathedral* may reflect
the secular interests of the viewers and comment directly on the
world as normally perceived by ordinary people, while at the same
time it looks back at a religiously significant event and presents it
imaginatively in a way that breaks the normal mould of verisimilitude. But as in ritual, the audience must become a congregation and
participate in the act shown on stage.[27]

The role of participation in drama is perhaps to be bracketed
with the kind of thinking that Owen Barfield, an author whose work
Eliot published in the *Criterion*, later defined as the antithesis of
modern scientific and rationalist thought in *Saving the Appearances*.[28] The typical inhabitant of the modern world, characterized
by an indifference to tradition and by scientific and rationalistic
modes of thought that are ultimately destructive, will normally analyze rather than participate, in contrast to medieval people, whose
thinking was more likely to be functional—that is, symptomatic of
integration into the order of things. Eliot's early poetry was dedicated to the examination of the alienation and fragmentation that
characterize existence on the level of the analytic and rational as di-
vorced from feeling and tradition. Realism in the theater was, therefore, seen by him as a mechanical contrivance which out of necessity he set out to transcend in his own drama.

As a play on the life of a saint, *Murder in the Cathedral* establishes meaning on several levels at once, though at the same time it
appears to eschew excessive reliance on *gnosis*, which would stress
the didactic at the expense of the emotional and spiritual planes that
are probed in the work. In this respect, it may seem to aim to some
degree at a devotional response such as that achieved by medieval
saint plays. Deeply steeped in the Sacramentalism which it shares
with traditional medieval Christianity—a Sacramentalism that had
been revived by the Oxford Movement and the Anglo-Catholic revival of the nineteenth century—*Murder in the Cathedral* thus dra-

matizes a classically restricted segment of the hero's life: "I wanted to concentrate on death and martyrdom," Eliot has written.[29] Though the actor Robert Speaight, who originally played the role of Becket, apparently never warmed to the personality of the Archbishop, the action with its tragic and yet untragic death nevertheless was exactly right for the audiences before which it was presented in the 1930's.[30] Becket's temptations and his stoic Christian resolution in the face of death won him the respect of those who came to see the drama first in the Chapter House of Canterbury Cathedral and then in the various theaters in which it played.[31] Thus Eliot could convincingly present a story of a churchman who won the crown of a martyr and who hence could be invoked by members of his cult even unto the present day, his cult having been revived in the Church of England through the efforts of the Anglo-Catholic movement that originated with Newman, Keble, and Pusey at Oxford and also included the Ecclesiologists, at Cambridge and elsewhere, who focused on architecture (including shrines and relics) and the ritual appropriate to sacred buildings. Canterbury Cathedral, which served as sponsor of the first performances of the play, was itself a shrine dedicated to Becket, who also stood in opposition to the officialdom of the state in his day in a way that Anglo-Catholicism had come to appreciate. As we might expect in a drama written by Eliot, its devotionalism is thus far more complicated than that of any actual saint play from the Middle Ages.

In writing *Murder in the Cathedral*, Eliot had apparently consciously attempted to set aside the kind of treatment that George Bernard Shaw had given to St. Joan and tried instead to establish some continuity with medieval tradition, which he wished to treat with integrity. To be sure, Eliot admitted tht he had been influenced by Shaw in his presentation of the arguments of the knights following the murder,[32] but on the whole Eliot's play represents a study of a historical martyrdom in a play which is far more serious than any other English drama on such a topic since the end of the Middle Ages. Thus the hero is a sacrificial victim whose very sacrifice is beneficial to later generations. The dynamics of the martyrdom are identified with considerable clarity by W. H. Auden in an article in the *Listener* of 4 January 1968: "The martyr is a sacrificial victim, but in his case it is he who chooses to be sacrificed. . . . Those for whose sake he sacrifices himself do not choose him as an atoning sacrifice."[33] Hence the martyr is modelling his experience of martyrdom on the Passion and Crucifixion of Christ, who also chose a sacrificial death which his executioners did not appreciate or understand. Eliot's treatment of the martyr's death, we should note, is thus deepened by relating the fate of the Archbishop—the inheritor of the apostolic authority handed over from previous generations through the power of the keys originally delegated to St. Peter—to the central myths of the Christian religion. The relationship between Christ and the martyr, whether he be St. Stephen the proto-martyr or St. Elphege of Canterbury, or Thomas Becket, is not figural in the technical theological sense, but rather the martyr imitates or repeats the events of the suffering and death of the Savior Christ.[34] So, too, in the medieval play of *Mary Magdalene* in the Digby manuscript, the saint at the end not only becomes the model contemplative in her denial of her bodily needs—self-induced suffering, if you will—but also is taken up into heaven first to be fed and then, following the death of her body, to the salvation of her soul. In the Digby play, these effects would have utilized machinery identical with that used for the Ascension of Christ. Thus Becket, for example, will be identified ironically by the Second Tempter as like an "old stag, circled with hounds."[35] The reference here is to a verse of the twenty-second psalm, "For many dogs are come about me" (v. 16), specified in the *Book of Common Prayer* as a reading to be read or chanted on Good Friday and understood as a prophecy of the form of the Crucifixion of Christ. Since Becket lives in Christian time, he cannot be a figure or type of Christ, but he can echo in his life the agony experienced by the Son of God who was made to suffer and die as a man, according to medieval theologians. The drunken knights, who enter the cathedral to kill Becket, are appropriately identified as "Like maddened beasts."[36] Such details as these also have some important implications for our interpretation of the tempters. By extension, these tempters who come to Becket, internalized and mental as they are,[37] nevertheless do in some sense reflect the temptations that Jesus according to the Gospels had to endure in the desert.[38] The suffering must be preceded by temptations that, to be efficacious, need to be resisted by the martyr prior to his fated end—a fated end that requires acceptance of a higher design.

The pattern of Becket's return and his martyrdom as well as the subsequent rise of his cult are for Eliot also analogous to a cosmic pattern that may be observed in nature. As *The Waste Land* illustrates, he was interested in the ritual theories of death and renewal as developed especially in the work of Jesse Weston, whose *From Ritual to Romance* was published in 1920. Eliot would have regarded such theories as indicative of the underpinnings of medieval courtly romance and of traditional folk rituals such as the mummers' plays; additionally, he would likely have included the St. George and the dragon pageants presented in civic pageantry in the late Middle Ages on St. George's Day, 23 April, among the items illustrating such themes. Seasonal imagery and the imagery of death and renewal are especially strong in *Murder in the Cathedral*. In the case of one example, the reference to the ploughman's repetition of the turning of the soil in preparation for planting in March,[39] a further level of signification is established, since such a tableau is frequently shown in medieval representations illustrating this month of the year—representations which are part of the traditional series of the Months.[40] In spite of Eliot's now outdated anthropology here, there is nevertheless an element of considerable significance that is added through his references to the cycle of the seasons and to the great pattern of death and renewal, which would see Easter itself as a great festival that parallels patterns established by pre-Christian pagans who in darkness thus pre-figured the death and resurrection of the Christian Savior. It is a pattern which includes desecration, pictured in terms of sexual violence and pollution. The sacred place has been made dirty, unclean, as if the very altar has been befouled.[41] In the end, even the air needs to be cleaned in a "world that is wholly foul."[42] That cleansing will be associated with the spring, a season which is as closely identified with hope as the coming of winter is with despair.

The most striking imagery of the play text of *Murder in the Cathedral*, however, is that of the Wheel of Fortune, a ubiquitous medieval symbol which was universally regarded as illustrative of life in the world where ambition and secular *rising* might precipitate a quite different effect from the one desired. Traditionally the figure of Fortuna, blind or blindfolded to represent her indifference to the fate of individual men, was placed at the center of the wheel, sometimes turning a crank which then turns the wheel; thus she was presented, though without the crank, as a crowned figure in the frontispiece to the famous Benediktbeuern manuscript which contains the mixture of sacred and profane verse and drama known as the *Carmina Burana*.[43] The modern playwright, who admired medieval Latin verse,[44] undoubtedly knew the lyrics of the *Carmina Burana* (some of which would be set to music by Carl Orff two years after Eliot's *Murder in the Cathedral*), though possibly he may not have known the illumination in the Benediktbeuern manuscript. In any case, his drama insists on seeing the wheel almost in Eastern terms as a variant of the Western traditional image—not surprising for one who had studied Indic Philology at Harvard and who for a time had been deeply attracted to Buddhism.[45] Because it is constantly turning, the wheel itself is thus symbolic of the flux of time—the process of temporal transformation—and hence impossible to control by anyone within time: "Only/ The fool, fixed in his folly, may think/ He can turn the wheel on which he turns."[46] At the center of the wheel, however, is a still point that is not turning, and from the perspective of this point the turning of the wheel is a pattern apart from the appearance of movement.[47] Understood in this way, the Wheel of Fortune image in the play is absorbed—perhaps through the mediation of an Eastern understanding of the image of the wheel—into another image, which, however, appeared in Western medieval tradition. This wheel seems reasonably identical to the Wheel of Life illustrated in the Robert De Lisle Psalter (British Library Arundel MS. 83, fol. 126ᵛ), which shows God at the center of the wheel. The still point is Eternity, which is beyond time but which provides a point of reference for all time. There is little likelihood that Eliot would have known the De Lisle Psalter's illuminations, and in any case his choice of this image would more likely have been derived most immediately from Dante (for example, *Paradiso* III.79–81) and other literary sources.[48] Certainly the image of the wheel is introduced to provide an explanation for the act of martyrdom, which must be beyond this world's flux and the turning of the wheel if the act is to be efficacious. The lesson is identical to the teaching of the *Commedia*, for example, that the "peace which the world cannot give," of which the *Book of Common Prayer* speaks, is the peace which can be found only at the center of the wheel. "His will is our peace," as Dante learned in the *Paradiso* (III.85)—a passage echoed in Eliot's *Ash Wednesday*: "our peace in His will."[49]

For his sources for the dramatization of the martyrdom of Thomas Becket, Eliot chose to go to historical documents not so different from the ones that might have been available to a medieval playwright preparing a saint play. Eliot himself denied any extensive research in historical documents.[50] Study of the sources has shown that he was familiar with some of the early accounts of the martyrdom of Becket and not simply with the version that is told in the *Golden Legend*.[51] Hence he is indebted to Herbert of Bosham, who was to have had a speaking role in an early draft of the play,[52] as well as to William Fitzstephen and the monk Edward Grim.[53] From such sources as these he learned that Becket had returned to England in early December, arriving on Tuesday, 1 December 1170. He was welcomed along the way from Sandwich, where he had landed, to Canterbury in a manner reminiscent of the Palm Sunday liturgy and the account of Christ's entry into Jerusalem. He further learned the topic of Becket's Christmas sermon, along with a summary of the saint's concluding remarks in that sermon. So, too, he discovered much about the confrontation with the knights of Henry II which led to Becket's death, as well as about the Archbishop's final words before his end. Since Eliot was concerned to present an authentic representation of the martyrdom, the material in the sources is not distorted but handled with the integrity that would be expected of the author of a saint play in medieval tradition. "I did not want to write a chronicle of twelfth-century politics, nor did I want to tamper unscrupulously with the meagre records as Tennyson did (in unscrupulously introducing Fair Rosamund, and in suggesting that Becket had been crossed in love in early youth)," Eliot explained in his essay "Poetry and Drama."[54]

Access for Eliot to the historical sources would have been easy if he was himself familiar with Borenius' *St. Thomas Becket in Art* (1932), which was reviewed in the October 1933 issue of the *Criterion* by Francis Wormald.[55] Borenius' book thoroughly examines the extant iconography of Becket from the first representation, a mosaic showing the Archbishop at Monreale Cathedral, Sicily, from perhaps no more than a decade after the martyrdom. Borenius' first chapter further treats the "life and personality" of Becket and provides, in the notes, references to the biography of Edwin A. Abbott (1898), Latin hymnody in the *Analecta Hymnica*, medieval saints' lives, and the writings of Herbert of Bosham and John of Salisbury, both contained in *Materials for the Study of Thomas Becket* in the Rolls Series, as well as information about the suppression of Thomas' cult by Henry VIII. A quotation on page 8 from the *South English Legendary* likens the progress of the saint from Sandwich to Canterbury to the honor given by the people to Christ as "he rod into Jerusalem"; further, the quotation notes, Becket's death is appropriately compared to the death on the cross of "ore louerd."[56]

Wormald's review in the *Criterion* may well be of the greatest significance for Eliot's understanding of the Becket martyrdom. The distinguished art critic and scholar noted not only Borenius' documentation of the swift dissemination of the cult of Thomas but also pointed out the three feast days of this saint, which in addition to the feast of his Translation included the *Regressio S. Thomae* found in books for Christ Church Cathedral at Canterbury (2 December) and the feast day of the martyrdom (29 December). These dates in December frame the action of *Murder in the Cathedral*, which dramatizes the return of the Archbishop, his Christmas sermon, and the events of the day of his death. According to the *South English Legendary*, the day of his return to England, 1 December 1170, was the third day of Advent.[57] This penitential season of the Church year—a season when in the English Church the *Kyrie* is substituted for the

Gloria in excelsis in the Eucharistic liturgy and the *Alleluia* is omitted—was, of course, very much in Eliot's mind throughout the writing of Part 1 of the play, which quite appropriately shows the hero of the drama turning away from one temptation after another until, in an ambiguous encounter with a final tempter, he must confront the question of doing the right thing for the wrong reason. Ironically, Advent is the beginning of the Church year, and the warning contained in the Epistle (*Romans* 13.8) for the first Sunday of the season in the Prayer Book is apt: "The night is far spent, the day is at hand." In the penultimate sentence from the Epistle, the order of all except the last of the temptations in *Murder in the Cathedral* would appear to be established: "Let us walk honestly, as in the day; not in rioting and drunkenness, not in chambering and wantonness, not in strife and envying." The Gospel lesson for this day, from *Matthew* 21, describes the triumphal Entry into Jerusalem, an event that, as we have seen, was important for both the traditional understanding of Becket's return to Canterbury and Eliot's handling of it in his modern saint play. Advent is also a period of waiting— waiting in expectation for the celebration of Christ's Incarnation, for Christmas, which also functions as the time of the central segment of *Murder in the Cathedral.*[58]

"The iconography of the martyrdom is fairly simple," Wormald wrote in his review in the *Criterion.* Nevertheless, he notes that depictions of the martyrdom in the arts normally contain three errors. The first, added as early as the twelfth century, was the placement of an altar in the scene, though the murder did not in fact take place at Mass but during an evening service. The second and third errors, both logical extensions of the first, show the Archbishop dressed in a chasuble and then as celebrant celebrating the Eucharist.[59] Eliot, though he allows an altar on stage and, as we have seen, uses the structure of the Mass as a device for shaping the play, locates the martyrdom in the cathedral at the time of vespers ("My Lord, to vespers!" the priests urge, and then they will literally carry him to the cathedral for the service). In the Canterbury festival production, however, the priests began singing the Introit for the saint, *Gaudeamus [omnes in Domino, diem festum celebrantes sub honore*

Thomae Martyris],"[60] though no martyrdom has yet occurred.[61] E. Martin Browne thought this liturgical touch was "a brilliant stroke," apparently not recognizing that it was very much like another event told in the early versions of the Becket story. This is the narrative account of Becket's requiem Mass; in the *Golden Legend*, the clergy of Canterbury Cathedral were about to chant *Requiem eternam*: "whan the quer began to synge Requiem/ An angelle on hye aboue began thoffyce of a martir: *Laetabitur iustus.*"[62] Further, the introduction of the *Te Deum* "sung in Latin by a choir in the distance," against which the Chorus recites an English paraphrase of the text of this item, seems to make much less specific the liturgical setting for the martyrdom, especially since, as noted above, the *Te Deum* is an intrusion from Matins. Finally, the play ends with the litany of the saints, which was sung in procession by the Chorus in the Canterbury Cathedral production, when at the end of the procession there followed the body of Becket, who was carried out through the audience.[63] The conclusion with the litany is a final Anglo-Catholic touch, and we are reminded that even today Mass at an Anglo-Catholic church such as All Saints, Margaret Street, may conclude with a similarly devotional prayer.

In *Ash Wednesday* Eliot had made much of the internal struggle of the modern Christian between disbelief and despair, on the one hand, and religious belief, on the other.[64] If we keep in mind that St. Thomas Becket possessed the same given name ('Thomas') as the author, we may come to the conclusion that he exemplifies some of the playwright's own agonizings before, during, and after his conversion. Yet such a conclusion is very risky, for Eliot was not writing a personal confession but an impersonal play about a historical figure with whom, paradoxically, he closely identified and sympathized deeply.[65] Like a medieval writer creating a saint play, he was anxious to present an objective drama—but also a drama which would accurately portray the modern dilemma of both religious and non-religious men and women. Thus, having constraints which differ from those of the medieval writer, he would need to suppress certain devotional elements, though through the Chorus, the tempters, the sermon, and various other devices he could nevertheless directly make a religious appeal to those sitting at the play, whose participation in the action he clearly regarded as necessary for the success of the production. Unlike Shaw's *Saint Joan*, which is at once entertainment and a didactic experience, *Murder in the Cathedral* illustrates its affinities with the medieval drama of the saints, the miracle plays which were staged primarily as spectacles designed to stimulate the cults of the saints and to provide an impetus toward devotion directed to them. "Blessed Thomas, pray for us," the Chorus pleads at the end of the drama. Thus, too, at the conclusion of the late medieval Cornish play of *St. Meriasek*, after the death and burial of the saint, the Earl of Vannes speaks to the audience: "Whoever trust in him/ And loyally pray to him/ Jesu has granted to them/ Their desire readily."[66]

St. Thomas Becket's death in *Murder in the Cathedral* comes after a short speech which reads like the opening passage of a medieval will: "Now to Almighty God, to the Blessed Virgin Mary ever Virgin, to the blessed John the Baptist, the holy apostles Peter and Paul, to the blessed martyr Denys, and to all the Saints, I commend my cause and that of the Church."[67] His final statement, however, is only slightly an expansion of his words as recorded in Eliot's source.[68] The result is particularly happy since it is precisely appropriate for a saint play, for a play which delineates the actions of one who follows in the way of Christ. The Digby *Mary Magdalene* is even more explicit at the heroine's death, for she is made to use language which yet more precisely contains an echo of Jesus' dying words: "*In manus tuas, Domine!/ . . . Commendo spiritum meum! Redemisti me./ Domine Deus veritatis*" (ll. 2115, 2117–18), a passage which is translated as follows: "Into your hands, Lord[,] . . . I commend my spirit. You have redeemed me, Lord God of truth."[69]

Murder in the Cathedral is a play which, as Eliot explains in "Poetry and Drama,"[70] is designed "to bring poetry into the world in which the audience lives and to which it returns when it leaves the theatre." But the drama is much more than a formal exercise in poetic language; it is designed to bring the saint play of the past into the present and to make it relevant to the full range of human experience in our time.

10

Modern and Medieval

While no great wisdom is required to discover that the human race cannot escape its past, recent admiration for "innovation," novelty, and post-modern ideology as well as contempt for tradition have characterized much thinking in the West. In the visual arts, for example, the practical result has often been the denigration of older techniques and also often of culturally preferred ways of preserving paintings and other works in museums where the public may view them. The attitudes of artists, including practicing artists in art departments of contemporary colleges and universities, are relevant here. In an interview with Jim Dine, a formerly avant-garde artist whose drawings of classical subjects were on exhibit at the Nelson-Atkins Museum of Art in Kansas City, Missouri, in 1990, the statement was made that "it is unusual for a contemporary artist to refer to the past without a sneer."[1] The Nelson-Atkins Museum's brochure for the exhibit comments that while "Modernism has proposed to reject all references to the past, and so-called Post Modernism will only permit them for ironic effect," Dine expresses "his impatience with the constant, implicit pressures on artists to be 'new' or 'cutting edge'."[2] Such pressure starts with young art students. In one case that has been brought to my attention, a beginning art student found already that her least competent drawings were the ones that received praise from her instructors, while the best among the others received only criticism.

The above comments are not meant to be unreasonably critical of the numerous artists working in modernist and post-modernist styles who have been remarkably successful. I have over my desk in my office an artist's sketch (1970) by Francis Littna which shows a dancer, with legs stretched to right and left and a body that fragments into abstractions; three faces are added above instead of a single head—indicative of the movement of the dancer. The composition, balanced and alive to motion, is a satisfactory and sophisticated work of art. The symbolism of such a sketch, with its colors and shapes indicating the distortions inherent in a cultural milieu that has been subjected to the historical dislocations of the traumatic twentieth century, marks it as resisting the positivism of much scientific thought and the shallow realism of popular culture.

In the theater, there is likewise a trend toward innovation and newness rather than tradition—in strong contrast to the popular realism of television. Whether we like it or not, however, the theater too is part of our inheritance delivered over to us by tradition—tradition which extends back to the Middle Ages and, to a lesser degree, even earlier. The logical starting point for any discussion of the medieval dramatic tradition is the Carolingian period and the century following since several practices relevant to drama—e.g., troping as a liturgical practice—seem then to have developed. Also, in spite of the wreckage of classical traditions including traditions surrounding theatrical performance, knowledge of antiquity—often, it is true, filtered through the continued popularity of the writings of Isidore of Seville (d. 636)—was an influence in the retention of practices related to the theater at this time.[3] Yet, keeping in mind observations made in Chapter 2 of this book, it is extremely important to make adequate distinctions concerning drama during this extended period in history leading up to our own day. While until relatively recently drama and theater critics have been too ready to see the development of theater as evolutionary—as a case of the survival of the fittest, resulting in automatic secularization and improvement within the context of historical time—such a biological model cannot any longer be applied to what happened in theater history during the past millenium.[4]

Thus the practice described in the *Regularis Concordia* in the tenth century—a practice which introduces mimetic ceremony into the service of the Church on Easter morning when four Benedictine brothers imitate the angel at the tomb and the three holy women on the original day of the Resurrection[5]—bears little resemblance to the vernacular drama of the late Middle Ages, and in fact very different genres are involved in the theatrical practices which we label "medieval."[6] Nor does one kind of practice lead directly or indirectly to the other, for the medieval music-dramas for Easter and similar feasts were very widespread indeed until the Reformation and Counter-Reformation, and the vernacular dramas surely were made possible more by the developing conditions and social contexts favorable for such production in the growing cities of the Middle Ages than by any crucial dependence on allegedly "earlier" forms. Yet the theatrical practices and dramaturgy of the medieval period, especially in the case of the vernacular plays, did in fact establish patterns which persist in the theater unto the present. The heritage is, however, complex.

The raised platform on which medieval vernacular plays were set, whether on wagons—as at York, Coventry, or Lille—or, probably far more commonly, on scaffolds,[7] became absorbed into the platform stage of Shakespeare's time. The Globe, like the medieval stage, did not use either perspective scenery or a set which in other ways might be construed as realistic. As a symbolic construct, the stage for which Shakespeare wrote was representative of reality as he and the other playwrights saw it. Thus the stage was *positional*, the place where the actors could imitate actions in this middle earth, located as it was between the "mighty opposites" of heaven and hell. For Shakespeare and his contemporaries, the theater was a location where actors might dramatize the great conflict that had set the forces of good against the potential for evil and deception throughout history. So too had been the case in the medieval theater, which would allow a character like Lucifer even before the beginning of human history to usurp God's own throne—an act which would demand the downfall of the would-be ruler of heaven who is transformed into his opposite and as part of the transformation is dropped from the high seat to the low pit of hell. So too would Shakespeare's Richard III raise himself up to regal power in the kingdom, and thus also would Marlowe's Tamburlaine and Doctor Faustus reach for power and glory beyond the limits set for earthly creatures.

On such a platform stage, whether or not enclosed in the proscenium or fitted with perspective scenery, modern actors continue to present the rise and fall of Shakespeare's tragic heroes, sometimes with less than satisfactory results when directors and actors fail to take into account the visual effects which seem to be demanded if we are sensitive to what we may regard as the original intent of the author and those who collaborated with him in producing the drama. In the current fashion, the platform stage has in fact been reintroduced in a form more or less consistent with medieval and early modern forms, but plays presented on such a stage paradoxically may differ substantially from what would have been *seen* in earlier times. I have previously used as an example David Hare's 1987 production of *King Lear*, staged at the National Theatre, London.[8] In this production, though a platform stage was used, the director's indifference to verticality—i.e., to hierarchy—simply destroys the basic structure since the lines of authority and of power thus become totally muddled. The play collapses as a moral statement, while the denial of its basis in early modern political thought serves as a reminder that the context of its symbolism has been totally set aside with the result of making the play a senseless power struggle rather lacking in dramatic interest. In Mary Douglas' terminology, "positional symbolic patterns" are abandoned,[9] and hence even the aged King Lear seemed unconvincing (I have reported that he appeared like a committee chairman rather than someone having a divine mandate to rule his kingdom[10]). Too, characters were not sufficiently differentiated by costume, and on the whole all coherence seemed lost.

Decadence in performance practices aside, the early modern stage of Shakespeare's time usefully mediates between the older theatrical forms of the past and the newer forms which were to be developed. It is thus unfortunate that in this portion of the twentieth century there is a tendency among many theater people, who sometimes can be remarkably retrophobic, to reject what they feel might be an imitation of an imitation. It would thus now be regarded as illegitimate to pretend first to be an actor of Shakespeare's or Chaucer's time performing in a play of the sixteenth or fourteenth century. Visually, and in the use of music, therefore, the modern production might deliberately distance itself from earlier traditions, yet the text would be the same as that which had been presented on the early modern or medieval stage. Hard hats and fork lifts in the presentation of medieval religious drama may, however, only create a modern parody of the original theatrical event,[11] which is not only torn out of its context but also subjected to desacralization. How far may we allow the visual effect and function of a play to drift from the original intent of its framers without seeing the resulting production disintegrate into nonsense? In my opinion, the visual effect implied by the text may be as much a part of the performance as the words spoken by the characters who take part in the action.

Attention to very precise visual effects on the contemporary stage by such dramatists as Samuel Beckett has been noted,[12] and recently theater critics like Martin Esslin have finally recognized that "*All* dramatic performance is basically iconic."[13] A similar claim for medieval dramaturgy has been put forth by Pamela Sheingorn, who insists upon the "fundamentally visual nature" of the medieval stage.[14] Our modern inheritance here is very clear, and we are reminded that the very word 'theater'—a term adapted from the classical term *theatron* in the Middle Ages—means a place where things are *seen*. The events dramatized on the stage therefore qualify (if we may return to Jane Harrison's terminology to which attention was called in the previous chapter) as *things seen*—in contrast to the *things done* in ritual.[15] The theater is a *locus* where the imagination is displayed, for in no sense will the happening that is staged be regarded by its audience as *real* to the extent of effects achieved by ritual acts. In the ritual of the Church, the participants can be made to stand before the miracle of transubstantiation which takes them back in time to the central events of history; memory is invoked, but we are in the presence of something that dissolves time and participates directly in the transcendent reality of the Incarnation. Drama never quite does that, though at least the medieval religious drama, assisting the audience to remember events of sacred history, intentionally helps people to *imagine* what those events might have been like. Insofar as possible, the words of the patriarchs and apostles are repeated from the narrative accounts, and the visual display is deliberately conventional rather than iconographically innovative in order to preserve the feeling of authenticity.

The lack of iconographic innovation, however, does not mean that the medieval stage was necessarily dull—or even that it lacked innovation in technical matters. Furnivall's view that the people must have become bored with the mystery and saint plays, whereupon they turned to the production of moralities and hence began a process of secularization,[16] is most curious since it suggests that pressure to produce less boring plays was the engine driving the move toward secularization—i.e., he cannot but believe that medieval people were, underneath the surface, as impatient with religion as he himself was. The evidence would suggest otherwise. A conventional religious subject matter, excitement, and even technological ingenuity could go together, as, for example, in the Paris *Resurrection* in the spectacular scene showing Pentecost which involved tongues of fire created by burning alcohol that "should fall on Our Lady, on the women, on the apostles and disciples."[17] Even more spectacular seem to have been the effects used in raising characters into heaven, as in plays that dramatize the Assumption of the Virgin or the Ascension of Christ. Elaborate machinery was used to raise the Blessed Virgin and to lift her up to be crowned Queen of Heaven, and we know that the resulting spectacle was something that we would still potentially find impressive today. We can be certain about this since the effect is still utilized in a music-drama of the Assumption and Coronation presented annually at Elche in Spain on 14–15 August.[18] In the Basilica de Santa Maria in Elche, there is on the first day a spectacular descent of the angel from heaven (located in the dome) to announce to the Virgin that she is about to die, while during the second part of the play on the next day a statue of the Virgin—a devotional image from a shrine in the apse—is raised in the *araceli*. At each side of the Virgin are angel musicians, played by two men and two boys, accompanying her into the dome of the cathedral. Before the *araceli* with the statue, which wears an elaborate costume, disappears, it will stop twice, once at the late appearance of the Apostle Thomas who sees her in her ascent, and again for the Coronation by the Trinity. In spite of the early modern and modern alterations and additions to this play, we can be reasonably certain that the dramatic impact of the statue being raised has not been substantially diminished since medieval times.

In the Paris *Resurrection*, the Ascension used similar machinery:

> And he should be pulled gradually, and his legs should show below the machine (*engin*), and above his head and joined hands, and over the machine should be a cloth (*toille*) painted all over with the souls of the holy patriarchs (who shall enter Paradise secretly by ladders under Paradise). And the cords pulling the device (*instrument*) on which Jesus should be hidden by cloth looking like a cloud (*en maniere de nue*). . . . And the Virgin Mary and her noble company, kneeling with joined hands, should watch our Lord ascending thus until they have lost sight of him.[19]

Here the machinery, which but presumably for the lack of counterweights in earlier times may be regarded as technically similar to that used for the apotheosis of Gisabella when she is raised "Up up up past the Russell Hotel,/ Up up up up to the Heavyside Layer" in the musical *Cats*,[20] must have been ingenious enough, but the iconography of the Ascension in this French play was absolutely conventional, with Christ's feet and robe appearing beneath the cloud in which he ascends into bliss while below the apostles and his mother stand watching.[21] The scene duplicates in lively motion precisely what was otherwise made visible in the static painting and sculpture of the visual artists.

Defenders of the stage thus not surprisingly spoke of the superiority of the theatrical scene over the scene depicted in the visual arts. The Wycliffite *Tretise of Miraclis Pleyinge*, though of course hostile, reports the current defense of the religious stage: the visual arts are a substitute for books of learning for illiterate people, but compared to the lively art of the religious theater they are like "deed" books. In comparison with the effectiveness of a scene which is merely painted by an artist, the scene as played by actors is better held in men's minds.[22] The *Tretise* hence emphasizes the effectiveness of the drama, in which each member of the audience will potentially participate imaginatively as his or her mental powers are engaged. Such an experience in the theater will be familiar enough to almost everyone today, and in it the person seems almost absorbed into the events and characters that are displayed in the action of the play.

The author of the Wycliffite *Tretise* seems to object most strongly to the *play* aspect of the theater, and we are reminded again of the close relationship that existed between a drama and a game.[23] In games also we tend to lose ourselves and to become engaged in the event to the exclusion of thoughts about other things. Like games, the theater therefore may be subject to the damning charge of being "entertainment"—unserious, even frivolous, insincere, and, worse yet, handling lightly the most urgent topics upon which we might focus our minds. Quite importantly the Old English word 'spilera' designated not only players in plays but also jesters,[24] while 'plega' was defined as both "play" and "sport" and thus functioned as a direct translation of the Latin *ludus*.[25] The tendency to see the theater as a form of entertainment rather than as a serious art form is still with us, and also we still use the same word that was established in medieval tradition for an actor—i.e., 'player.'[26] We also retain the word 'play' to designate the drama, its text and performance, and we speak of 'playing' as the thing that the actor does when he or she remembers both lines and actions required to flesh out the performance and to make it seem "real." As an act of *anamnesis* (remembering), playing brings the imagination quite literally into the picture. Belief is made visible for all to see.

Because the imagination is brought into play in the medieval religious drama, the result is not always comfortable, and we need to remember that such drama would be prohibited on the English stage for several centuries on account of Protestant hostility; this is a topic that will require further analysis in the second half of this chapter. Subversive elements are introduced even into the early music-drama. In Hildegard of Bingen's *Ordo Virtutum*, the Devil is introduced as a real threat that perhaps caused both fear and laughter in the twelfth-century audience, while the same drama also allows the Soul to be seduced, though of course she returns to achieve regeneration in the course of the play.[27] Similarly, in the eleventh-century *Sponsus* from St. Martial, the Foolish Virgins seem more lively and present fewer problems for the director than the Wise Virgins,[28] but they illustrate misguided behavior that nevertheless may capture the sympathy of the audience and insure that their consignment in the end to smoking hell will have a considerable impact on viewers.

It is worth mentioning again the Towneley *Mactacio Abel*, a play which is probably very late (the manuscript may have been copied as late as the early part of Queen Elizabeth I's reign), for in this pageant the character of Cain points up the most hostile feelings toward the proper order of things.[29] Cain's vocabulary is replete with scatological references, which are presumably translated into obscene gestures. When his unsatisfactory sacrifice burns, it is with a smudge that "stank like the dwill in hell" (1. 283)—a detail that will remind us of the scene in the famous fourteenth-century *Holkham Bible Picture Book*[30] which shows the smoke from Cain's sacrifice blending with smoke from the mouth of hell. This play, attributed to the so-called Wakefield Master, is not the stuff of a bland Sunday School lesson, but rather makes visible for us the full range of human experience as it was pictured in the later Middle Ages. In the end Cain's existence is an explication of the absurd as much as Samuel Beckett's *Waiting for Godot* or Alain Resnais' film *Last Year at Marienbad*,[31] for in a world which for him lacks order, hope, or forgiveness he will command his boy to leave the playing area with the team and plough and then will surrender himself to despair. The scene is one that in itself is hardly edifying, and yet it echoes forbidden ways of thinking which we all as human beings have shared (or repressed). Interestingly, James Gordon, the first editor of the Towneley plays for the Surtees Society, found himself disapproving of this aspect of the cycle. Archival research by Barbara Palmer has recently uncovered a report by Raine that the edition was for Gordon "an undertaking which gave him very great pain on his death-bed. He was a highly religious man, and it grieved him to think that he had been instruemental [sic] in bringing to light such apparent profanity as the book contains."[32] But such insolent profanity as Cain's also looks ahead directly to the final scene of the cycle when he and his kin are indeed herded into the mouth of hell to suffer in pitch and tar and unbearable heat forever and ever. In contrast to a play like *King Lear* with its ambiguous fifth act, the Towneley cycle, like the other extant cycles of the type presented in civic festivals in England at Corpus Christi or Whitsuntide nearly every year until they were suspended in the late sixteenth century, concludes with an assertion of order and the ultimate suppression of all that is subversive.

While it is true that twentieth-century drama, except in such popular forms as television series on commercial networks, often fails to reinforce any principles of order or hierarchy in the end of the play, its presentation of rebelliousness and of subversive elements will in fact need to be seen as the result of dissolving transcendental principles that had been inherited from the early theater. If such a drama seems desacralized and at times critical of all that might be held holy, its energy nevertheless is directed against something of considerable historical force. The modern world is one in which language and picture are both often squeezed into a reductive positivism, and, following the philosophy of motion championed by Thomas Hobbes in the seventeenth century, action is merely rooted in previous effects. So already in nineteenth-century naturalism, as in Ibsen's *Ghosts* in which the young Osvald Alving's tragedy is the result of occurrences in the past that are not reversible, events tend to be serially ordered. While in the hands of dramatists like the later Strindberg such a world view is shattered, the world nevertheless has frequently been one in which God seems absent or unnecessary, reduced from All Powerful to a figure, as in a modern parable by Pär Lagerkvist, of an obstinate old workman who is encountered sawing wood by the light of a lantern.[33] But when this world is evoked in the most thoughtful dramatists and film-makers of our century, something tends frequently to break through. The world upside down of modern literature and theater is in fact undercut, and the audience is encouraged, whether intentionally or not, to wonder if the positioning of the action of the drama within perverse cultural values in fact validates something other than what appears on the surface.

As an example I know of no better drama to cite than Ingmar

Bergman's film trilogy which, beginning with *Through a Glass Darkly*, explores the twentieth-century predicament and confronts madness, irrationality, and alienation. The terrifying mystical vision of *Through a Glass Darkly* is the inverse of the ecstatic experiences of the saints; God appears, but to a disturbed mind and in the most horrible form imaginable—in the form of a creature that resembled a spider threatening rape.[34] Life separated from the comfort of traditional belief may be intolerable. The point is continued in the second segment of the trilogy, *Winter Light*, a study of doubt and despair which concludes with a most powerful scene—a scene that I have remarked upon in Chapter 1 above. Tomas Eriksson, the priest who has lost his faith, has traveled to a church in a village with a name that implies coldness. In the dusk he waits for a congregation that does not arrive.[35] The only other persons in the church at Fröstnas are the sexton Algot, the organist Blom, who would be most happy not to be required to play the service, and the priest's mistress, Märta Lundberg. Yet the priest, even in the midst of his doubt, personal agony, and physical illness, begins the Swedish Mass with the traditional words.[36] If Bergman intended this ending to be merely an ironic touch in his film, he misjudged his material in a very real way. The words, which invoke the Holy, place the events of the action of the drama in a perspective that strongly denies the positivist view of language and of images. The intrusion of ceremony, however fragmentary, returns the film to the questions raised by some of the vernacular cycle plays or even by such a music-drama as the twelfth-century *Peregrinus* plays for Monday of Easter week which depict the meal at Emmaus—a meal which begins by celebrating the absent God but in the end affirms transcendence.

Medieval drama, even the plays on religious subjects which perhaps formed the bulk of theatrical productions during this period,[37] were naturally of different kinds and consisted of different genres. The plays were given remarkable support from their producers, which might, as at York, be the city corporation itself. Some of the motives for play production were not strictly religious; at Coventry, for example, the vernacular cycle plays on the Nativity, Passion, Resurrection, and Last Judgment coincided with the great Coventry Corpus Christi fair to which people flocked from all over England.[38] There was also a social element in the festivals that were the occasions for the plays. But the popularity of drama—mystery plays, saint plays, interludes, folk drama, liturgical ceremonies and plays—in medieval Europe, its forms, its traditions of staging, and even its treatment of transcendental issues of the greatest significance laid the groundwork for subsequent drama and theater down to the present day.

The revival of the early religious drama—especially drama written in early English—in our time has been another matter and itself involves a rather curious history which will be best told by returning to some aspects of prejudice against representing God on stage from Patristic and medieval times. In contrast to other countries such as Spain and Germany which have had a continuous tradition of religious drama, England and English-speaking countries tended to be wary of producing medieval plays in modern times, often for reasons delineated in Chapter 8 above. In England particularly, it was the playing of God on stage that proved to be the great stumbling block to religious plays. Stage censorship had been very strict, especially watching for signs of blasphemy, which was held by many to be inherent in any attempt to represent God by a human actor. Thus Nugent Monck had not been allowed to stage a Passion play even though he had planned to represent the crucifixion itself behind a curtain.[39]

E. Martin Browne, serving as director of the newly formed Religious Drama Society in the early 1930's, felt at that time unable to allow God or Jesus to appear in a theatrical performance in spite of the fact that the power of the Lord Chamberlain as theatrical censor did not extend to the church.[40] Consistent with the thinking among supporters of the Religious Drama Society, every attempt was made to see "that great reserve should be exercised in representing the Deity."[41] Indeed, whenever God might have appeared in any form other than as the newborn infant Jesus, he simply was not literally present. For example, The Play of Maid Mary was performed, leading up only to the Annunciation, adapted from the N-

town cycle, and when in a modern play a stage reference to the
Crucifixion was required, "the nearest one could get to Jesus was
the tip of his cross passing outside the window."[42] Nevertheless,
Browne found resistance to his efforts in the Religious Drama Society. For example, an article in *The English Churchman* attacked his
staging of a play on St. Francis at Brighton:

> But, for ourselves, we cannot agree that they have any legitimate place
> within the walls of our churches. We have spoken of them as a "devel-
> opment". . . . The demand "ornate" services has prevailed for many
> years to change the simplicity and purity of common Prayer and Praise
> and the ministry of the Word and Sacraments into spectacular and
> sensuous ceremonial, a fit stepping stone to the further advance which
> has now been staged in Brighton Parish Church. Passion plays, miracle
> plays and the like make their appeal to the emotions, but we believe
> that they have no warrant of Scripture and that the introduction as "acts
> of worship" in our churches is a retrograde step and one which will
> prove to be detrimental. . . .[43]

Normally, however, plays that did not attempt to introduce God or
Christ did not suffer from actual interference. For example, the *Second Shepherds' Play* and other Nativity dramas seem to have been
performed on a number of occasions, sometimes in sanitized versions, and were also popular in America.[44]

Not until 1951 was the taboo broken. The first full-scale modern revival of an English cycle of medieval religious plays, at York
and under the direction of E. Martin Browne, began with the story
of the Creation and the fall of Adam and Eve—wearing body stock-
ings—in the Garden of Eden. In this case it was not allowing simu-
lated nudity in the presentation of the first parents of the race that
marked a change in the official attitude toward plays (actual nudity,
though in a film rather than a stage play, was to be allowed by the
Lord Chamberlain only in 1953[45]), but rather the allowing of actors
to play God and to show his works on stage. At York, such
daring—actors playing God openly on stage, albeit in this case in
the almost hallowed ruins of St. Mary's Abbey—had not happened
in England for more than 350 years. At the same time, little could

anyone in 1951 have predicted the treatment such "medieval" plays would receive in the 1980's when, though using a reasonably attractive text adapted by Tony Harrison,[46] a beardless and bald God would nevertheless enter on the National Theatre's Cottesloe stage dressed in a plain gown, with a miner's hat, and hoisted up on a fork lift—a stage character recognizable by his words and not at all by his appearance. One might confidently predict that those who had barely approved of E. Martin Browne's production in 1951 would have been utterly scandalized had they seen anything even remotely like the National Theatre's *The Mysteries*, a production loudly asserting man's post-lapsarian nature with all the tricks of modern stagecraft—and doing it without any sense of guilt.

Resistance to the idea of playing God on stage, then, had already reached a crucial stage in the early 1950's when the old prejudices were beginning to evaporate, perhaps under the influence of Hollywood extravaganzas which had dared to place imaginary events of biblical times on film—performances that audiences attended with almost the reverence shown to Oberammergau, which had long been exempt from the normal prejudice against playing God among English-speaking people who flocked to productions.[47] But condemnations of actors playing God did not originate merely with the Reformation, and may be traced in the late Roman empire when the tension between the secular culture of ancient Rome and the new Christian religion was documented in numerous writings.

In pre-Carolingian times in the Christian West, the very idea of actors playing God would have seemed quite scandalous—an imitation of the practices of the allegedly demonic stage of antiquity when the pagan gods, regarded by early Christianity as demons, were thus presented before the eyes of audiences. The Church Fathers and the Church Councils had condemned not only the theater but also acting itself. For Tertullian, play-acting meant pretending to be a person which one in fact was not—a falsification of identity.[48] To act a role would be to take on the characteristics of that role, as when one might act a vicious person or devil, but to assume the role of a better person than oneself or of God would be an insufferable fraud. For the Council of Arles in 314 A.D., actors were to "be separated from the body of the faithful for as long as they are in the acting profession."[49] In the eighth century, the Council of Nicea denounced actors as unrighteous, and an episcopal edict specified corporal punishment for actors who dared to dress themselves as priests, monks, or nuns.[50] As late as the twelfth century, John of Salisbury in his *Policraticus* still reminded his readers that "by the authority of the Christian Fathers the sacrament of holy communion is forbidden actors and mimics as long as they persist in their evil career,"[51] and even St. Thomas Aquinas' more relaxed attitude toward them does not suggest full approval: "the occupation of play-actors, the object of which is to cheer the heart of man, is not unlawful in itself; nor are they in a state of sin *provided that their playing be moderated, namely that they use no unlawful words or deeds to amuse, and that they do not introduce play into undue matters and seasons.*"[52]

Where was the line to be drawn between lawful and unlawful? Did the playing of God fall within the category of the lawful or of the unlawful? Perhaps significantly, in the earliest liturgical drama and quasi-dramatic ceremony for Holy Week and Easter (briefly discussed in Chapter 3, above), Christ is not represented. In the *Visitatio Sepulchri*, the angel or angels and holy women at the Easter sepulchcr on Easter morning appear in a music-drama—documented as early as the tenth century but continuing through thc entire Middle Ages until its suppression by Reformation and Counter-Reformation alike in the sixteenth century—that presents the Resurrection story, only in a few later versions introducing the Risen Christ.[53] The core of this devotional drama is the visit to the *empty* sepulcher and the announcement that the Lord is risen, a fact that is also verified by the sight of the grave clothes. Only in the most complex later versions of the *Visitatio Sepulchri*, such as the example in the Fleury Playbook of the twelfth century, do we find Christ included in the play, and here his presence is made known in the added scene of Mary Magdalene meeting the one whom she takes to be the Gardener.[54] Would such a scene, though ritualized in form and presentation, have been accepted even two or three hundred years earlier? I suspect not.

Some clues in this regard are to be found in the *Depositio* or Burial ceremony for Good Friday. This devotional rite, representing the Deposition from the Cross and the Burial, principally utilized a consecrated Host, often along with a Crucifix, that would be "buried" in a specially constructed tomb-like structure on or near the altar.[55] Like the dramatized Visit to the Sepulcher, the ceremony was designed to make visible in some way an event, in this case the Burial, for the congregation in order that they might become in some sense contemporary with the original happenings in sacred time. But direct *mimesis* was avoided, and the consecrated Host, implicitly participating in the actual Body of Christ, served to make the present scene an immediate reflection of the events following the Crucifixion.[56] Enveloped within the liturgy, the *Depositio* or Burial did not attempt to place a clergyman-actor in the role of Christ; impersonation, or role-playing, was strictly avoided.

There would seem to have been a real danger of being perceived as promulgating blasphemy as well as idolatry in the playing of the divine role, whether of Christ or of the Father. St. Thomas Aquinas' definition of blasphemy may indeed touch on any playing of God that is at least not incredibly tactful, for he sees this sin as attributing to the deity that which does not appropriately belong to him or, conversely, denying to him that which is properly his with the effect of "disparag[ing] the Divine goodness."[57] For St. Thomas, this sin of blasphemy is grievous and potentially worse than murder.[58] Medieval punishment for blasphemy was severe, even including death, the punishment assigned in the Old Testament (*Lev.* 24.15-16), for which we may cite the sixth-century Justinian Code or the Frankish law ratified by the Diet of Aachen in 818 A.D.[59] The medieval reaction was thus not likely to have been entirely dissimilar to the current Islamic intolerance of blasphemy—as revealed in the furor over Salman Rushdie's *Satanic Verses*—or to the fundamentalist objections to the depiction of Jesus in a film such as *The Last Temptation of Christ*. That this can lead very quickly to a prejudice against any theatrical depiction of Christ or the Father may, in my opinion, be signaled in a not perfectly coherent (or, for that matter, grammatical) letter to editor of the local paper in my city: "Those protesting against the 'Last Temptation of Christ' are trying to separate Jesus' human nature from his divinity or God incarnate. That cannot be separated. When anyone mocks and blasphemes Jesus, they do the same to God. When somebody acts or takes the place of Jesus, it is a sacrilege."[60] The words of this amateur theologian have a long historical resonance.

In the twelfth-century Anglo-Norman *Adam*, God as Creator appears as an actor in the play, which extends from the creation of Adam to the story of Nebuchadnezzar, at which point the manuscript breaks off. Here God, depicted as the Second Person of the Trinity who was traditionally given credit for the Creation, is identified as *Figura*, and he wears a dalmatic. The garment is a significant one, since it is the vestment still worn by the deacon, whose role in the Mass is to read the Gospel—a role which, according to the tradition established by Amalarius of Metz, places the deacon in the place of the apostles who would proclaim Christ himself.[61] In the play, the actor is likewise not playing Christ directly, but is only playing a role which at one remove represents the *figure* of Christ; in other words, he appears in place of the Second Person in order to present the scene of the Creation and subsequent events of primordial time, and this is done in imitation of the way in which Christ himself appeared as the *figura* of the Father during the historical acts of creation.[62] Playing God, like the act of visualizing him in the visual arts, becomes possible because of the Incarnation which revealed the Trinity to men in human form, having been born of a human mother, albeit an unusually perfect one.

In the late medieval drama in England, to be sure, more freedom was allowed in the depiction of God on the stage. In the plays which are extant, he is most in evidence in the great play cycles such as those associated with the cities of York and Chester. Presumably the presentation of the deity in such cycles, which were expected to reflect on the honor of the city in a rather direct way and which were extremely lavish productions involving not only heavy expenditure but also personal commitment from the citizens, was carefully designed so as not to offend more sensitive viewers. One such potentially sensitive viewer at York in 1426 was the friar

William Melton, who commended the play as "good in itself and most laudable,"[63] though he complained about the way in which it conflicted with the Corpus Christi procession scheduled for the same day and the same crowded streets. The city corporation was encouraged to move the plays, presented on pageant wagons, to another day, to which they appeared to agree; but in fact the city failed to do this, and later in the century it was the ecclesiastical procession that was moved to another day.[64]

The dialogue attributed to God or Christ in these plays is always dignified and, whenever possible, adapted, either directly or indirectly, from the biblical text and the traditions surrounding it. The intent was clearly to achieve an effect analogous to that achieved in the visual arts—i.e., figures that could be regarded as devotionally useful and as somehow pointing beyond themselves to the reality depicted by the work of art. From the point of view of the Franciscans, there was, as we know, a necessity of helping people to achieve an imaginative identification with the suffering Savior, and by what better way could such an effect be brought into being than through playing the Passion? Actors playing God therefore must have been chosen with great care for impressive rather than weak voices and for strong stage presence. At York in 1476, for example, there was a record of the city Corporation (the sponsor of the plays) wishing to find competent actors—those "sufficiant in personne and Connyng"[65]—and presumably to sift out the incompetent ones. And what more important roles were included in the play cycle than those representing the Creator and Savior of the world? At Coventry in 1573 when its Corpus Christi cycle was still being performed, the Drapers for their pageant of Doomsday paid "to god" 3s. 4d., exactly the amount paid to *two* demons in the same play and far more than the two shillings for the trumpeter, normally the most expensive of musicians.[66]

While the amount paid to "god" at Coventry in 1573, only a few years before the play cycle was suppressed, may have involved reimbursement for out-of-pocket expenses as well as a fee for playing, we can be reasonably certain, I believe, that from the standpoint of costume the roles of God and Christ were intentionally impressive. An inventory of costumes and properties for the Doomsday play of the York Mercers dated 1433 lists "Array for god that ys to say a Sirke Wounded a diademe With a veseme [mask] gilted."[67] The Savior, who descended from the heavens on a contraption which included a "Rainbow of tymber" for him to sit upon, not only had a gold mask—a feature that may be noted to this day in the depiction of God in the stained glass of the Te Deum windows in the transept of York Minster—but also a body garment that would at once clothe the actor's nudity and display the wounds which were a center of Northern piety in the late Middle Ages. In continental documents we learn of the concern for appropriate and differentiating costume that not only was indicative of the character represented but also assisted the audience in knowing one social position from another.[68] God and Christ required such differentiation—and hence for them and for no other characters the gold mask would be appropriate.

Conversely, an animal mask such as was common enough in folk entertainments, if we can believe the evidence of later survivals, would never do. A number of years ago one of my former students, attempting to be innovative, directed an Old Testament play from one of the medieval cycles in which God appeared in just such an animal mask. Recalling Aquinas' definition of blasphemy, can we expect that such a characterization of God would have been accepted in the West in the fifteenth or sixteenth century? God is herein given characteristics that the Judeo-Christian tradition declares he does not in fact have, and this sort of thing could never achieve approval, at least in a play that was designed to do honor to a city or town as well as to the deity. But thus the question of the leeway appropriate for a director arises, and the question is very much with us when we consider the amount of imaginative improvisation that characterized the National Theatre's production of *The Mysteries*. A bald and beardless God the Father on a forklift would have been no more acceptable than the aging Blessed Virgin Mary in a funny hat who also appeared in that Rabelaisian production. Perhaps even more outrageously, in this production the Flight into Egypt was depicted by having Joseph tow Mary, who was holding a bundle of cloth representing the Child Jesus, off stage on a toy donkey. Such staging in my view is patronizing[69] and, like Shakespeare's play-within-a-play in *A Midsummer Night's Dream*, amounts to parody; unfortunately, in *The Mysteries* the failure to come to terms with the theatrical effects demanded by the text and the ignoring of the original context of the symbolism resulted in something less than successful theater.

Naturally, audience reaction can be unpredictable, and there is the case at York of one pageant, *Fergus*, dramatizing the funeral of the Virgin, in which boisterous spectators embarrassed the actors; noise and disorder were the result instead of the intended devotional tableau, and thus the guild responsible for this play requested in 1431-32 to be relieved of responsibility for it.[70] At every moment, therefore, the play cycle at a city such as York or Chester may not have produced the effect desired by those who were most anxious for a production which would do honor to the city, but it is important to see the early productions of these plays as necessarily skirting any potential charge of blasphemy at the same time that they were directed at performance which would credibly enhance the reputation of the city.

The author of the Wycliffite *Tretise of Miraclis Pleyinge* not only noted widespread support for the religious stage and provided a listing of its alleged merits but also, like the writer cited above in the twentieth century periodical *The English Churchman*, rejected absolutely all arguments in its defense. He pointed to the rules which had long forbidden priests to participate in plays, and indeed identified the act of playing in a religious play as the "verre taking of Goddis name in idil."[71] Plays reverse God, and make the One who stands for absolute Truth into a figure of hypocrisy and deceit. Instead of performing a religious function, those who act in plays are to be seen as similar to Christ's tormentors. Further, actors who play God may even be regarded as Luciferian, since their act of imitating the deity is reminiscent of the pride of Lucifer at the beginning of the Creation. In short, playing reduces what should be earnest to utter game—a blasphemous act, since actions are attributed to God in play that are not in fact accurate portrayals of earnest historical fact.

While there is no evidence that the *Tretise* itself had any influence on the aesthetics of religious drama in the following century and more—and quite clearly all the followers of Wyclif did not have such a negative view of the religious stage—Protestantism nevertheless eventually did take an anti-dramatic stance with regard to the religious plays that had been favored in Roman Catholic times. Not only did these plays have a Catholic bias which revision of the text could fix only to a certain extent, but also they presented God on the stage directly both in the form of the Father and of the Son. Resistance to such depiction of God helped to signal the end of the mysteries in England.

In 1568, Matthew Hutton, then Dean of York Minster, requested to see the Register or master copy of the York Creed Play, which was sometimes substituted for the usual Creation to Doom cycle. This play, for which the text is now lost, was organized according to the clauses of the Apostles' Creed and almost certainly included all the apostles (St. Peter is mentioned in an earlier document) in the course of its action, and, like the mystery cycle, was seen in a very negative light by the Reformers and Church authorities. Dean Hutton's response was that "as I finde manie thinges that I muche like because of thantiquitie, so see I manie thinges, that I can not allowe, because they be Disagreinge from the *senceritie* of the gospell. . . ." In conclusion, his letter claimed that "thoghe it was plausible 40 yeares agoe, and wold now also of the ignorant sort be well liked: yet now in this happie time of the gospell, I knowe the learned will mislike it and how the state will beare with it I knowe not."[72] His objections to this type of drama, which he felt would need massive revision so that "the wholle drift of the play shuld be altered"[73] to make it viable, were both humanist and Protestant. Such plays, like the statues, wall paintings, relief sculptures, vestments, candles, holy water, and relics that had been made strictly illegal under Queen Elizabeth,[74] allegedly contained too much of the stuff of "superstition" to be allowed to survive in their medieval form.

David Rogers, in his *Breviary* in which he had copied the late banns of the Chester Whitsun cycle and other information about these plays, concluded that they only reflected "the Ignorance of oure forefathers"; further, he prayed that "neither wee. nor oure posterities after us. maye neuar see the like Abomination of Desolation, with suche a Clowde of Ignorance to defile with so highe a hand. the moste sacred scriptures of god."[75] By the time Rogers wrote these words, the medieval religious stage was almost entirely suppressed—a religious Corpus Christi play seems to have continued into the seventeenth century only at such a remote place as Kendal in Cumberland in the far north of England[76]—and after 1612 God was not to be represented as a character in an English play until modern times.

The Puritan element—many of whom, like William Prynne whose *Histrio-Mastix* of 1633 is perhaps the most elaborate attack on the stage ever written, despised what they saw as the inherent hypocrisy of the stage—could rejoice at the suppression of the religious stage even if the secular stage would rear its head once more under the Restoration after 1660. One document dated 1644 which included a notice of the Kendal play by John Shaw, records Shaw's meeting with "an old man (about 60) sensible enough in other things," who seemed appallingly ignorant of Calvinist theology or even of events which prior to the Reformation had been familiar to medieval men and women through wall paintings, sculpture, and other ecclesiastical art that functioned as laymen's books—which is what Gregory the Great had claimed for such art.[77] Questioned by the ideological Shaw about God, the cross, and salvation, the old man only remembered in his youth seeing the Kendal Corpus Christi play "where there was a man on a tree, and blood ran downe, etc."[78] Shaw's attitude, far from expressing gratitude for the role of the play in teaching a theological lesson however imperfectly, was that the old man and others like him needed to be catechized in the right way of understanding reality and one's own spriritual predicament.

Even puppets representing God were seen as illegitimate, as we might expect. A statue of the Crucified Second Person of the Trinity with wires that animated the eyes and chin at Boxley had been called an "idolle," in one writer's opinion "a very monstrows sight." William Lambarde believed that the Boxley Rood, as it was called, had been a player in a game of "imposture, fraud, juggling, and Legierdemain" which the monks had used to entrap "the sillie lambes of Gods flocke" for economic gain.[79] Reference has been made above to Lambarde's reporting of an annual Easter puppet show at Witney, Oxfordshire, which he identified as having the dual purpose of bringing customers to the town and of entertaining "the comon Sort" in order to attract them to Catholic ritual. He insisted that such a show reflected only the "Shadowe" rather than the "Bodye" or substance, and that the result was a blasphemous jesting with religion—"Religion rather jested at then digested."[80] Lambarde was no more impressed by the white dove that was used to impersonate the Holy Spirit or third person of the Trinity on Pentecost at St. Paul's Cathedral in London. The dove was allowed "to fly out of a Hole . . . in the mydst of the Roofe of the great Ile," an action which was accompanied "by a long Censer, which descendinge out of the same Place almost to the verie Grounde, was swinged up and downe at suche a Lengthe, that it reached with thone Swepe almost to the West Gate of the Churche, and with the other to the Quyre Staires of the same, breathinge out over the whole Churche and Companie a most pleasant Perfume of suche swete Thinges as burned thearin."[81] Curiously, the inheritors of such Protestant hostile reporting about ceremonies and plays seem to have been those nineteenth-century scholars who, like Furnivall, showed no interest in actually reviving the early plays on the stage.

The major role played by legislation in inhibiting any early revival in the theater of the medieval religious drama involved both the Blasphemy Act and the rules of stage censorship established in 1843 by the Theatres Act.[82] Daringly, Adonai appeared in William Poel's *Everyman* in 1901, and was played by the director himself wearing a curious costume and beard, not at all like a medieval costume for God and perhaps foreshadowing the thoroughly untraditional costume worn by God in *The Mysteries* at the National Theatre in the 1980's.[83] But in 1951 God returned in religious drama in E. Martin Browne's revival of the York Corpus Christi cycle at York. Not surprisingly, there was a certain amount of nervousness in the air at the opening of Browne's York cycle, though the legal opinion had been that a play written prior to the Theatres Act was exempt from censorship. Even the Archbishop of York confessed his "doubts about the production of the play."[84] But Browne's work was successful in that it broke through a facet of anti-theatrical prejudice—a prejudice against playing God that had existed in England for more than 350 years.

There was a distinct difference between E. Martin Browne's approach to the plays, which in his handling were intended to be devotional in their reception, and the way that God and Christ have been depicted in the National Theatre's *Mysteries*, where the effects were marred by a constant striving for innovation in visual effect (e.g., Peter was to cut off Malchus' ear with a putty knife at the Betrayal, and the crown of thorns was made of barbed wire) and by thoroughly inappropriate music, including some songs by Bob Dylan—for example, his "When my Ship Comes in" with its reference not to the "hills of Armenie" but to "the sands [that] will roll out a carpet of gold" during the Noah segment.[85] The National Theatre production was admittedly mounted by agnostics for an audience of agnostics, though obviously not all those who saw it would fit into this category.[86] Nevertheless, the party atmosphere that prevailed through the six hours of the show indicated that in the case of this production we have come full circle from those who in earlier times would banish the theater on account of their fear of offending God.

The mood of the twentieth century has on the whole been iconoclastic, destructive not only of images which previous ages have held to be holy but also of texts and ideas formerly revered or admired. This has led, for example, to the fragmenting of the visual arts (resulting in abstract art which quite literally deconstructs natural forms) and also to a disregard for architectural and artistic treasures, especially in ecclesiastical buildings. Coming against the background of such attitudes, the pronouncements of the Second Vatican Council were used as an excuse for widespread vandalism in churches and cathedrals.[87] Secular buildings have also suffered, of course, and it is with regard to the latter that the historical preservation movement in the United States has been most active. In England, fortunately, the Council for the Care of Churches has been a significant force in attempting to prevent wrongheaded restorations and other damage, but even the twentieth-century pollution in the air has been revealed to be a great enemy of stone and glass, the materials of which the finest medieval buildings were constructed. (The greatest damage may have been in Eastern Europe—e.g., Cracow —where pollution controls have been non-existent and soft coal has been burned, but the situation in the West is also critical.) Furthermore, iconoclastic attitudes must be seen as having a very definite effect on the other arts in the contemporary setting.

Paradoxically, there is another side to the picture, a hint of which we may receive from the high value of art-as-investment, especially in the view of corporations; incredible prices are being paid for art that is held to be increasing in monetary value. The purpose of such purchases seems far removed from any urge to preserve, and the aesthetic is not preservationist but economic. Sometimes the high price is the result of the celebrity status of the artist, but there may also be a residue here of the presumed worth assigned to certain examples of the arts in prior centuries. The high valuation of certain examples of the visual arts may have its roots in those crafts which served religion in the Middle Ages—crafts which produced cult images of the saints and other representations that were allowed to have a larger meaning than would be the case if the art work were merely decorative. In spite of the objections of some modernists and post-modernists who believe that at least certain objects have been overvalued either by museums or private collectors, the contemporary work of art may be a secular cult object as the result of a historical development in the past which has handed down to us certain attitudes toward the arts.

In drama, there has likewise been been a double movement, both aspects of which perhaps owe something to the mood that also has informed iconoclasm in this century. On the one hand, though there has been borrowing from the past (as in the case of the platform stage, which has been found widely useful), there has been a denial of the context of early plays, even Shakespeare's, as these derive from a social order which gives meaning to their structure and symbolism. Early religious drama, when presented like the National Theatre's *The Mysteries*, are about as faithful to the traditions from which the original texts are derived as William Mountfort's *The Life and Death of Doctor Faustus, made into a Farce*, the late seventeenth-century parodying of Marlowe's famous play.[88] On the other hand, the dissolving of the fear of blasphemy has led to the freedom to perform traditional religious plays in England and other English-speaking countries where there had been a conspiracy of attitudes and laws, the latter derived from a staunchly Protestant heritage, that previously had limited such freedom.

In T. S. Eliot's *Four Quartets*, the poet had introduced the first of four poems with a brief and teasing meditation on *time* which begins:

> Time present and time past
> Are both perhaps present in time future,
> And the time future contained in time past.
>   (*Burnt Norton*, ll. 1–3)

The passage teases because of the word "perhaps," which must be ironic since "time future" indeed cannot exist without both past and present any more than the present can exist without the past. Is the word "perhaps" an acknowledgment that there are some who would see the past, present, and future artificially disconnected? But such disconnectedness involves the threat of alienation, social dissolution such as we are seeing in American cities in the end of this century, and the terror which comes when we are asked to live as strangers in a world of uncomprehended innovation—that is, like people visiting a foreign land where the language of the local people cannot be understood.[89] Attention may be called to the motto that stands at the beginning of E. M. Forster's *Howards End*: "Only connect . . ." Tradition connects us with our past, and what better way to make such connections than through theatrical and artistic—and religious —experience, which may serve to heal the wound of post-modernity and to make its skepticism seem irrelevant.

Notes

Chapter 1
Tradition and the Individual Scholar

1. Hans Robert Jauss, *Aesthetic Experience and Literary Hermeneutics*, trans. Michael Shaw (Minneapolis: Univ. of Minnesota Press, 1982), p. 260.

2. Frank Kermode, *Forms of Attention* (Chicago: Univ. of Chicago Press, 1985), p. 89.

3. See especially the biography by E. H. Gombrich, *Aby Warburg* (London: Warburg Institute, 1970), *passim*.

4. Rona Wilensky, Letter to the Editor, *New York Times*, 30 June 1985.

5. Ibid.

6. Glynne Wickham, *Early English Stages, 1300–1660* (London: Routledge and Kegan Paul, 1963), II, Pt. 1, 2–8 and *passim*.

7. See Paul Thompson, *William Butterfield* (Cambridge: M.I.T. Press, 1971), *passim*; James Stevens Curl, "All Saints', Margaret Street," *Architects' Journal*, 25, No. 191 (June 1990), 36ff.

8. See the summary and bibliography in *The Oxford Dictionary of the Christian Church*, ed. F. L. Cross, 2nd ed. (London: Oxford Univ. Press, 1974), pp. 1388–89.

9. Gervase Mathew, *Byzantine Aesthetics* (New York: Viking, 1964), p. 50.

10. See especially Lynn White, Jr., *Medieval Technology and Social Change* (New York: Oxford Univ. Press, 1962), and "Medieval Borrowings from Further Asia," *Medieval and Renaissance Studies*, 5, ed. O. B. Hardison, Jr. (Chapel Hill: Univ. of North Carolina Press, 1971), pp. 3–26.

177

11. Christopher Page, "The Earliest English Keyboard," *Early Music*, 7 (1979), 308–14.

12. Early Drama, Art, and Music, Monograph Ser., 4 (1983).

13. "Renaissance Dramatic Forms, Cosmic Perspective, and Alienation," *Cahiers Elisabéthains*, No. 27 (April 1985), pp. 1–16.

14. See the classic study by Brents Stirling, *Unity in Shakespearian Tragedy* (New York: Columbia Univ. Press, 1956), pp. 40–54.

15. Harrison Salisbury, Letter to the Editor, *New York Times*, 30 June 1985.

16. London, 1493, fol. 394.

17. See the statement by Robert Scholes, "Deconstruction and Communication," *Critical Inquiry*, 14 (1988), 284–85; deconstruction, according to Scholes, has a strong appeal to those who were influenced by the anarchism of the 1960's since it "allows a displacement of political activism into a textual world where anarchy can *become* the establishment without threatening the actual seats of political and economic power. Political radicalism may be thus drained off or sublimated into a textual radicalism that can happily theorize its own disconnection from unpleasant realities." This passage is quoted by Frank Kermode, *An Appetite for Poetry* (Cambridge: Harvard Univ. Press, 1989), p. 25, in a chapter which deserves to be read by every scholar (pp. 1–46).

18. The term is Robert J. Lifton's.

19. *Reflections on the Revolution in France*, as quoted by Jaroslav Pelikan, *The Rediscovery of Tradition* (New Haven: Yale Univ. Press, 1984), p. 20.

20. Ingmar Bergman, *A Film Trilogy*, trans. Paul Britten Austin (London: Calder and Boyars, 1967), p. 104; for the original Swedish text, see *En filmtrilogi* (Stockholm: P. A. Norstedt och Soners Forlag, 1963).

Chapter 2
The Sociology of Visual Forms, Tradition, and the Late Medieval English Theater

1. C. Clifford Flanigan, "Rezeptionsästhetik and Critic," read at the Twentieth International Congress on Medieval Studies (1985); see Hans Robert Jauss, *Toward an Aesthetic of Reception*, trans. Timothy Bahti (Minneapolis: Univ. of Minnesota Press, 1982).

2. Jauss, *Toward an Aesthetic of Reception*, p, 15. See also the criticism, from the standpoint of the social historian rather than the theater historian, of Peter Clark in his review of Lawrence Clopper's edition of the dramatic records of Chester (*Renaissance and Reformation*, n.s. 5 [1981], 239).

3. Compare the important comments on method of Rudolf Bultmann, *The History of the Synoptic Tradition* (New York: Harper and Row, 1963), pp. 1–7, esp. 5.

4. Clifford Davidson, "Space and Time in Medieval Drama: Meditations on Orientation in the Early Theater," in *Word, Picture, and Spectacle*, ed. Clifford Davidson, Early Drama, Art, and Music, Monograph Ser., 5 (Kalamazoo: Medieval Institute Publications, 1984), pp. 39–93.

5. Charles Phythian-Adams, *Desolation of a City: Coventry and the Urban Crisis of the Late Middle Ages* (Cambridge: Cambridge Univ. Press, 1979), and the same author's "Ceremony and the Citizen: The Communal Year at Coventry 1450–1550," in *Crisis and Order in English Towns, 1500–1700*, ed. Peter Clark and Paul Slack (Toronto: Univ. of Toronto Press, 1972), pp. 57–85.

6. Keith Thomas, *Religion and the Decline of Magic* (New York: Charles Scribner's Sons, 1971), esp. p. 27.

7. *York*, ed. Alexandra F. Johnston and Margaret Rogerson, Records of Early English Drama (Toronto: Univ. of Toronto Press, 1981), I, 55.

8. *Coventry*, ed. R. W. Ingram, Records of Early English Drama (Toronto: Univ. of Toronto Press, 1981), pp. 60, 167, 259.

9. Thomas, *Religion and the Decline of Magic*, p. 470.

10. *The York Plays*, ed. Richard Beadle (London: Edward Arnold, 1982), p. 52 (ll. 97–117).

11. See the chapter entitled "Medieval Celebrations of Corpus Christi: A Formal Analysis," in Peter W. Travis, *Dramatic Design in the Chester Cycle* (Chicago: Univ. of Chicago Press, 1982), pp. 1–29, though here the connection between the doctrinal content of the Festival and the plays is exaggerated in my opinion, especially with regard to the Chester Whitsun plays. Even at Coventry, the connection between the plays and the Corpus Christi Festival is complicated by the fact that this was the date of an important annual fair, to which people came from long distances to buy and sell.

12. Susan Brigden, "Religion and Social Obligation in Early Sixteenth-Century London," *Past and Present*, No. 103 (May 1984), pp. 73–81.

13. Mervyn James, "Ritual, Drama and Social Body in the Late Medieval Town," *Past and Present*, No. 98 (Feb. 1983), p. 11. This entire article is a most valuable contribution to our understanding of the function of the cycle drama within the civic context, although it makes assumptions about the nature of this drama and about its association with the Feast of Corpus Christi that are not warranted in the light of recent scholarship.

14. *The Wakefield Pageants in the Towneley Cycle*, ed. A. C. Cawley (Manchester: Manchester Univ. Press, 1958), pp. 1–13.

15. Clifford Davidson and David E. O'Connor, *York Art: A Subject List of Extant and Lost Art Including Items Relevant to Early Drama*, Early Drama, Art, and Music, Reference Ser., 1 (Kalamazoo: Medieval Institute Publications, 1978), p. 182; see also my *From Creation to Doom* (New York: AMS Press, 1984), pp. 45–46.

16. *York*, ed. Johnston and Rogerson, I, 186; see also James, "Ritual, Drama and Social Body," p. 11.

17. Phythian-Adams, *Desolation of a City*, p. 116.

18. Cf. Gordon Kipling, "Richard II's 'Sumptuous Pageants' and the Idea of the Civic Triumph," in *Pageantry in the Shakespearean Theater*, ed. David Bergeron (Athens: Univ. of Georgia Press, 1985), pp. 88ff, for commentary which links the city of London with the idea of Jerusalem.

19. James, "Ritual, Drama and Social Body," pp. 11–12. This writer cites a legal opinion of the time of Edward IV that declares: "The political body is made up of men like us. If the man's head is decapitated, he himself is dead. In the same way, if the mayor who is the head of the 'corps politike' die, the writ abates. And if the community without the mayor wish to enforce such an act, it cannot be done, because the mayor did not give his assent."

20. Grocers' Inventory; see *Norwich 1540–1642*, ed. David Galloway, Records of Early English Drama (Toronto: Univ. of Toronto Press, 1984), p. 53.

21. See *York Plays*, III.21–22.

22. See especially Rosemary Woolf, *The English Mystery Plays* (Berkeley and Los Angeles: Univ. of California Press, 1972), pp. 136–45, for commentary on this depiction of Noah's wife.

23. Clifford Davidson and Jennifer Alexander, *The Early Art of Coventry, Warwick, Stratford-upon-Avon, and Lesser Sites in Warwickshire: A Subject List*, Early Drama, Art, and Music, Reference Ser., 4 (Kalamazoo: Medieval Institute Publications, 1985), p. 80; Mary Frances White, *Fifteenth Century Misericords in the Collegiate Church of Holy Trinity, Stratford-upon-Avon* (Stratford-upon-Avon: Philip Bennett, 1974), figs. 25–26.

24. See the chapter entitled "Women on Top," in Natalie Zemon Davis, *Society and Culture in Early Modern France* (Stanford: Stanford Univ. Press, 1975), pp. 124–51.

25. Lawrence Stone reports that children in England in the sixteenth century were commonly expected "to kneel before their parents to ask their blessing every morning, and even as adults on arrival at and departure from the home" (*The Family, Sex and Marriage in England 1500–1800* [New York: Harper and Row, 1977], p. 171). The importance of such gestures by children for the stage is noted by David Bevington, *Action Is Eloquence* (Cambridge: Harvard Univ. Press, 1984), pp. 183–84.

26. See Stone, *The Family, Sex and Marriage*, pp. 169–71.

27. See Hilary Wayment, *The Stained Glass of the Church of St. Mary, Fairford, Gloucestershire* (London: Society of Antiquaries, 1984), pp. 79–80, Pl. XXXVIII.

28. See especially M. D. Anderson, *Drama and Imagery in English Medieval Churches* (Cambridge: Cambridge Univ. Press, 1963), pp. 95–98.

29. Miriam Skey, "Herod's Demon Crown," *Journal of the Warburg and Courtauld Institutes*, 40 (1977), 274–76. A broad survey of the iconography involved is presented in the same author's "The Iconography of Herod in Medieval Art," *EDAM Newsletter*, 3, No. 1 (1980), 4–10, while for a study of Herod in the English cycles see also David Staines, "To Out-Herod Herod: The Development of a Dramatic Character," *Comparative Drama*, 1976), 29–53; rpt. in *Drama in the Middle Ages*, ed. Clifford Davidson, C. J. Gianakaris, and John H. Stroupe (New York: AMS Press, 1982), pp. 207–31.

30. *The Paston Letters*, ed. James Gairdner (1904; rpt. New York: AMS Press, 1965), V, 321; see also Alan H. Nelson, *The Medieval English Stage* (Chicago: Univ. of Chicago Press, 1974), p. 131.

31. See, for example, Francis Cheetham, *English Medieval Alabasters* (Oxford: Phaidon-Christie's, 1984), pp. 180–88 (Nos. 107–15).

32. *The Chester Mystery Plays*, ed. R. M. Lumiansky and David Mills, EETS, s.s. 3 (1974), p. 181n, where Jesus' words are quoted from British Library MS. Add. 10305 and Harley MS. 2013. See also R. M. Lumiansky and David Mills, *The Chester Mystery Cycle: Essays and Documents* (Chapel Hill: Univ. of North Carolina Press, 1983), p. 197.

33. Sally-Beth MacLean, *Chester Art: A Subject List of Extant and Lost Art Including Items Relevant to Early Drama*, Early Drama, Art, and Music, Reference Ser., 3 (Kalamazoo: Medieval Institute Publications, 1982), p. 32, fig. 13. Normally genuflection involved kneeling on the *right* knee, however.

34. Cheetham, *English Medieval Alabasters*, p. 113 (No. 113); cf. W. L. Hildburgh, "English Alabaster Carvings as Records of the Medieval Religious Drama," *Archaeologia*, 93 (1949), 58, Pl. XIb.

35. *Chester*, ed. Clopper, p. 243.

36. Lumiansky and Mills, *The Chester Mystery Cycle: Essays and Documents*, pp. 197, 259; *Chester*, ed. Clopper, p. 32.

37. See especially Sixten Ringbom, "Devotional Images and Imaginative Devotions," *Gazette des Beaux-Arts*, 111 (1969), 159–70.

38. MacLean, *Chester Art*, p. 32, citing Raymond Richards, *Old Cheshire Churches*, revised ed. (Didsbury, Manchester: E. J. Morten, 1973), p. 122.

39. See *Iconoclasm vs. Drama and Art*, ed. Clifford Davidson and Ann Eljenholm Nichols, Early Drama, Art, and Music, Monograph Ser., 11 (Kalamazoo: Medieval Institute Publications, 1989).

40. *Chester*, ed. Clopper, pp. 35–36.

41. Ibid., pp. 34, 39.

42. James, "Ritual, Drama and Social Body," p. 17. For a petition of 1523–24 in which the Cappers of Chester, objecting to the Mercers and other guilds who encroached on their privileges, threatened to request to be released from "the bryngynge forthe of the sayd playe/ Whe[r]of they wolde be right sorye," see *Chester*, ed. Clopper, pp. 25–26.

43. For the script, with stage directions, see Tony Harrison, *The Mysteries* (London: Faber and Faber, 1985).

44. Ibid., p. 209.

Chapter 3
Northern Spirituality
and the Late Medieval Drama and Art of York

1. In particular, see O. B. Hardison, Jr., *Christian Rite and Christian Drama in the Middle Ages* (Baltimore: Johns Hopkins Press, 1965), pp. 1–34; Thomas Munro, *Evolution in the Arts and Other Theories of Culture* (Cleveland: Cleveland Museum of Art, 1963).

2. A narrow perspective artificially cuts off aspects which are necessary to know if we are to understand a play or work of visual art properly; no expert in chess can understand a chess game well under way if he (or she) knows only the moves that have been made by a single piece on the chess-board. (This analogy is derived from Ferdinand de Saussure's comparison of language and a chess game as summarized in Susan Wittig, "The Historical Development of Structuralism," *Soundings*, 58 [1975], 146–47.)

3. For a recent appreciation of image theology, see Margaret Miles, *Image as Insight: Visual Understanding in Western Christianity and Secular Culture* (Boston: Beacon Press, 1985).

4. George Benson, *Later Medieval York* (York, 1919), p. 128; *The Fabric Rolls of York Minster*, ed. James Raine, Surtees Soc., 35 (Durham, 1859), p. 218.

5. *Fabric Rolls*, p. 218.

6. John A. Knowles, *The York School of Glass Painting* (London: SPCK, 1936), p. 42; David E. O'Connor and Jeremy Haselock, "The Stained and Painted Glass," in *A History of York Minster*, ed. G. E. Aylmer and Reginald Cant (Oxford: Clarendon Press, 1977), pp. 350, 352–53.

7. See Knowles, *York School*, pp. 215–21; E. A. Gee, "The Painted Glass of All Saints' Church, York," *Archaeologia*, 102 (1969), 190.

8. See Davidson, *From Creation to Doom*, pp. 118–23.

9. *The Hours of Catherine of Cleves*, Guennol Collection, Fol. 60^v; ed. John Plummer (New York: Braziller, n.d.), Pl. 22.

10. Francisco de Hollandia, *Diologos de Hollandia*, as quoted by Johan Huizinga, *The Waning of the Middle Ages* (1949; rpt. Garden City, N.Y., 1954), p. 265; see also Erwin Panofsky, *Early Netherlandish Painting* (Cambridge: Harvard Univ. Press, 1953), p. 2.

11. On my own "pilgrimage" to the Basilica of the Holy Blood in Bruges some years ago, I saw no tears; nevertheless, it was clear that those in attendance at the Mass when the Holy Blood was displayed were deeply affected by the presence of the relic.

12. *A Middle English Treatise on the Playing of Miracles*, ed. Clifford Davidson (Washington, D.C.: Univ. Press of America, 1981), p. 39.

13. See, for example, Sandro Sticca, "Drama and Spirituality in the Middle Ages," *Medievalia et Humanistica*, n.s. 4 (1973), 69–87.

14. Karl Young, *The Drama of the Medieval Church* (Oxford: Clarendon Press, 1933), I, 239–306.

15. Ibid., I, 249–52.

16. See especially the collection of edited texts by Walther Lipphardt, *Latein-ische Osterfeiern und Osterspiele* (Berlin: Walter de Gruyter, 1975–81), 6 vols.; for collections including texts and facsimiles for national areas, see Pamela Sheingorn, *The Easter Sepulchre in England*, Early Drama, Art, and Music, Reference Ser., 5 (1987), and, including also transcriptions of the music, *Holy Week and Easter Ceremonies and Dramas from Medieval Sweden*, ed. Audrey Ekdahl Davidson, Early Drama, Art, and Music, Monograph Ser., 13 (Kalamazoo: Medieval Institute Publications, 1990), and Máire Egan-Buffet and Alan J. Fletcher, "The Dublin *Visitatio Sepulchri* Play," *Proceedings of the Royal Irish Academy*, Sec. C, 90, No. 7 (1990), 159–241.

17. Conveniently included in *The Play of Herod*, ed. Noah Greenberg and William L. Smoldon (New York: Oxford Univ. Press, 1965). On the Herod of this drama, see Miriam Anne Skey, "The Iconography of Herod in the Fleury *Playbook* and in the Visual Arts," in *The Fleury* Playbook: *Essays and Studies*, ed. Thomas Campbell and Clifford Davidson, Early Drama, Art, and Music, Monograph Ser., 7 (Kalamazoo: Medieval Institute Publications, 1985), pp. 120–43.

18. *Wakefield Pageants*, ed. Cawley, pp. 64–77. For a penetrating discussion of this pageant, see J. W. Robinson, *Studies in Fifteenth-Century Stagecraft*, Early Drama, Art, and Music, Monograph Ser., 14 (Kalamazoo: Medieval Institute Publications, 1991), pp. 145–75.

19. *Two Coventry Corpus Christi Plays*, ed. Hardin Craig, EETS, e.s. 87 (London, 1957), p. 26. On the madness of Herod, see the discussion by Penelope Doob, *Nebuchadnezzar's Children* (New Haven: Yale Univ. Press, 1974), pp. 115–30.

20. *The Late Medieval Religious Plays of Bodleian MSS Digby 133 and e museo 160*, ed. Donald C. Baker, John L. Murphy, and Louis B. Hall, Jr., EETS, 283 (London, 1982), pp. 101–03.

21. Cuthbert Butler, *Western Mysticism* (1922; rpt. New York: Harper and Row, 1966), p. 119.

22. E. W. Tristram, *English Medieval Wall Painting: The Thirteenth Century* (London: Oxford Univ. Press, 1950), I, 47. See also Patrick J. Collins, "Narrative Bible Cycles in Medieval Art and Drama," *Comparative Drama*, 9 (1975), 125–46.

23. Margaret Aston, *England's Iconoclasts*, I (Oxford: Clarendon Press, 1988), 287.

24. *Meditations on the Life of Christ*, trans. Isa Ragusa (Princeton: Princeton Univ. Press, 1861), p. 333. See also David L. Jeffrey, *The Early English Lyric and Franciscan Spirituality* (Lincoln: Univ. of Nebraska Press, 1975), *passim*.

25. *Meditations on the Life of Christ*, p. 333.

26. Ibid., p. 334.

27. Davidson and O'Connor, *York Art*, pp. 75–76, and the discussion in Davidson, *From Creation to Doom*, pp. 125–27.

28. *York Plays*, ed. Beadle, pp. 315–23.

29. F. P. Pickering, *Literature and Art* (Coral Gables: Univ. of Miami Press, 1970), pp. 238–41, but see also the very detailed discussion by James Marrow, *Passion Iconography in Northern European Art of the Late Middle Ages and Early Renaissance* (Kortrijk: Van Ghemmert, 1979).

30. See Gordon McN. Rushforth, *Mediaeval Christian Imagery* (Oxford: Clarendon Press, 1936), p. 72; Max Friedländler, *Die altniederländische Malerei* (Leiden: Sijthoff, 1934), VI, Pl. LXIX; and, for commentary on fig. 4 in my plates, Adrian Wilson and Joyce Lancaster Wilson, *A Medieval Mirror: Speculum humanae salvationis 1324–1500* (Berkeley and Los Angeles: Univ. of California Press, 1984), p. 124.

31. *The "Painter's Manual" of Dionysius of Fourna*, trans. Paul Hetherington (London: Sagittarius Press, 1974), p. 38.

32. Pickering, *Literature and Art*, pp. 285–301.

33. Johannes Tinctorus, *Proportionale musicae*, in *Source Readings in Music History*, ed. Oliver Strunk (New York: Norton, 1950), p. 194.

34. Thomas French and David E. O'Connor, *York Minster: A Catalogue of Medieval Stained Glass*, Fascicule 1: *The West Windows of the Nave*, Corpus Vitrearum Medii Aevi, Great Britain, 3 (Oxford: Oxford Univ. Press, 1987), p. 4.

35. E. W. Tristram, *English Wall Paintings of the Fourteenth Century* (London: Routledge and Kegan Paul, 1955), pp. 21–22.

36. Gunennol Collection, fol. 66^v; ed. Plummer, Pl. 26.

37. *The Lay Folks Mass Book*, ed. Thomas Frederick Simmons, EETS, o.s. 71 (London, 1879), p. 109.

38. Ibid., p. 42.

39. J. D. Chambers, *Population, Economy, and Society in Pre-Industrial England* (Oxford: Oxford Univ. Press, 1972), p. 19 and *passim*; but cf. Robert Gottfried, *Epidemic Disease in Fifteenth Century England* (New Brunswick, N.J.: Rutgers Univ. Press, 1978), who argues that the major demographic factor in population decline was indeed disease.

40. See H. F. Westlake, *The Parish Guilds of Mediaeval England* (London: SPCK, 1919), pp. 26ff.

41. Maud Sellers, ed., *York Memorandum Book A/Y*, Pt. II (Durham, 1915), p. lxiii.

42. Ibid., p. lix; translation from p. 19.

43. *Chantry Surveys*, Pt. I, Surtees Soc., 91 (Durham, 1894), p. 61; see also the discussion in Davidson, *From Creation to Doom*, pp. 94–95.

44. *Testamenta Eboracensia*, Pt. II, Surtees Soc., 30 (Durham, 1855), p. 21. The Blackburn chantry in St. Anne's Chapel on Foss Bridge continued to be maintained by the Corporation in the sixteenth century even after others had been dissolved; see A. G. Dickens, "A Municipal Dissolution of Chantries at York, 1536," *Yorkshire Archaeological Journal*, 36 (1947), 164–72.

45. Eileen Power, *The Wool Trade in English Medieval History* (London: Oxford Univ. Press, 1941), pp. 104–05. On the Blackburn window, see Eric A. Gee, "The Painted Glass of All Saints' Church, North Street, York," *Archaeologia*, 102 (1969), 153–57.

46. Gee, "The Painted Glass of All Saints' Church," p. 156; translation of Latin text.

47. Douay-Rheims, verse 17; see Gee, "The Painted Glass of All Saints' Church," p. 156.

48. *Letters Patent, Edward III*, Jan. 1349, as quoted by G. H. Cook, *Mediaeval Chantries and Chantry Chapels* (London: Phoenix House, 1963), p. 73.

49. *York*, ed. Johnston and Rogerson, I, 3.

50. Ibid., I, 11–12.

51. Ibid., I, 25–26.

52. Ibid., I, 24–25.

53. Ibid.

54. Edwin Benson, *Life in a Mediaeval City* (London: SPCK, 1920), p. 10; see also D. M. Palliser, *Tudor York* (Oxford: Oxford Univ. Press, 1979), pp. 26–27.

55. See *York*, ed. Johnston and Rogerson, I, 12, 29.

56. Ibid., II, 728; for the Latin text, see I, 43.

57. Ibid., I, 109.

58. Ibid., I, 278, quoting the City Chamberlain's Books for the year 1541.

59. Benson, *Later Medieval York*, p. 41.

60. *York*, ed. Johnston and Rogerson, I, 56.

61. For an illustration of this wall painting, see David Bevington *et al.*, *Homo, Memento Finis: The Iconography of Just Judgment in Medieval Drama and Art*, Early Drama, Art, and Music, Monograph Ser., 6 (Kalamazoo: Medieval Institute Publications, 1985), fig. 14.

62. Davidson and O'Connor, *York Art*, p. 114.

63. Davidson and O'Connor, *York Art*, pp. 115–16, and Eric Milner-White and F. Harrison, in *The Friends of York Minster: Sixteenth Annual Report* (1944), pp. 14–18.

64. *York*, ed. Johnston and Rogerson, I, 55–56.

65. See also Wayment, *The Stained Glass of the Church of St. Mary*, p. 56, Pls. XXII–XXIII.

66. Tristram, *Fourteenth Century*, p. 19.

67. Louis Bouyer, *Rite and Man*, trans. M. Joseph Costelloe (Notre Dame, Indiana: Univ of Notre Dame Press, 1963), p. 170.

68. See *Lay Folks Mass Book*, ed. Simmons, pp. 38–41.

69. See Émile Mâle, *Religious Art in France: The Thirteenth Century*, trans. Marthiel H. Matthews, ed. Harry Bober (Princeton: Princeton Univ. Press, 1985), pp. 362, 367–70.

70. C. J. P. Cave, "The Bosses on the Vault of Winchester Cathedral," *Archaeologia*, 76 (1927), Pl. XXVIII, fig. 3.

71. "A Relic of the Pilgrimage of Grace," *Yorkshire Archaeological Journal*, 21 (1910–11), 108–09.

72. *York*, ed. Johnston and Rogerson, I, 55.

73. Davidson and O'Connor, *York Art*, pp. 77–78.

74. J. W. Robinson, "The Late Medieval Cult of Jesus," *PMLA*, 80 (1965), 508–14.

75. *York Civic Records*, ed. Angelo Raine (York, 1946), V, 173.

76. Davidson and O'Connor, *York Art*, p. 116.

77. O. Elfrida Saunders, *A History of English Art in the Middle Ages* (Oxford: Clarendon Press, 1932), p. 131.

78. Ibid., fig. 65; E. W. Tristram, "'Piers Plowman' in English Wall Painting," *Burlington Magazine*, 31 (1917), 140. However, Tristram's association of the Christ of the Trades at Breage, Cornwall, with Piers Plowman, though repeated in Tancred Borenius and E. W. Tristram, *English Mediaeval Painting* (Paris: Pegasus Press, 1927), is refuted by Ruth Ryan in the *Art Bulletin*, 11 (1929), 302–03.

79. Saunders, *A History*, p. 131.

80. See Palliser, *Tudor York*, pp. 231–37.

81. Alexandra F. Johnston, "The Plays of the Religious Guilds of York: The Creed Play and the Pater Noster Play," *Speculum*, 50 (1975), 55–90.

82. Quoted by Robert Davies, *Extracts from the Municipal Records of the City of York* (London, 1843), p. 270.

83. Young, *Drama of the Medieval Church*, II, 14–15.

84. *Ludus Coventriae*, ed. K. S. Block, EETS, e.s. 120 (London, 1922); on this episode and a related episode during the funeral procession of the Virgin, see also Ann Eljenholm Nichols, "The Hierosphthitic Topos or the Fate of Fergus: Notes on the N-Town *Assumption*," *Comparative Drama*, 25 (1991), 29–41.

85. Quoted in translation by Henrik Cornell, *The Iconography of the Nativity of Christ*, Uppsala Universitets Årsskrift (Uppsala, 1924), pp. 12–13. For comment on this scene in drama, see Davidson, *From Creation to Doom*, pp. 16–18, and Robinson, *Studies in Fifteenth-Century Stagecraft*, pp. 60–80.

86. Oscar G. Farmer, *Fairford Church and Its Stained Glass Windows*, 8th ed. (1968), p. 9; see also Wayment, *The Stained Glass of the Church of St. Mary*, p. 26.

87. See especially, in relation to the English vernacular drama, Anderson, *Drama and Imagery in English Medieval Churches*, and Hildburgh, "English Alabaster Carvings as Records of the Medieval Religious Drama," pp. 51–101.

88. Beadle, ed., *York Plays*, p. 426; see also Robinson, *Studies in Fifteenth-Century Stagecraft*, pp. 61–62.

89. Davidson and O'Connor, *York Art*, pp. 46–49.

90. James Torre, *The Antiquities of York Minster* and *Antiquities Ecclesiastical of the City of York*, unpublished MSS., York Minster Library.

91. Ann Eljenholm Nichols, "Books-for-Laymen: The Demise of a Commonplace," *Church History*, 56 (1987), 457–73.

Chapter 4
"What hempen home-spuns have we swagg'ring here?"

1. *Minutes and Accounts of the Corporation of Stratford-upon-Avon*, ed. Richard Savage, Dugdale Soc., 1 (1921), I, 128.

2. See Hugh MacLachlin, "St. George," *Spenser Encyclopedia*, ed. A. C. Hamilton *et al.* (Toronto: Univ. of Toronto Press, 1990), pp. 329–30.

3. *Literary Criticism: Plato to Dryden*, ed. Allan H. Gilbert (1940; rpt. Detroit: Wayne State Univ. Press, 1962), pp. 449–53.

4. *York*, ed. Johnston and Rogerson, I, 353.

5. See also Chap. 5, below.

6. Quotations from *A Midsummer Night's Dream* are from *The Riverside Shakespeare*, ed. G. Blakemore Evans *et al.* (Boston: Houghton Mifflin, 1974). For older commentary on the play-within-a-play in this drama, see especially *A Midsummer Nights' Dream*, 6th ed., ed. H. H. Furness, New Variorum Edition (Philadelphia: Lippincott, 1895). For more recent scholarship, see especially J. W. Robinson, "Palpable Hot Ice: Dramatic Burlesque in *A Midsummer Night's Dream*," *Studies in Philology*, 61 (1964), 192–204, and also Robert F. Willson, Jr., "The Plays Within *A Midsummer Night's Dream*," *Shakespeare-Jahrbuch* (Weimar), 110 (1974), 104–05.

7. Robert Weimann, *Shakespeare and the Popular Tradition in the Theater*, ed. Robert Schwartz (Baltimore: Johns Hopkins Univ. Press, 1978), pp. 81–85. See also Robinson, "Palpable Hot Ice," pp. 194–95.

8. S. Schoenbaum, *William Shakespeare: A Documentary Life* (New York: Oxford Univ. Press, 1975), pp. 29–36.

9. For a conjectural list of pageants included in the Coventry cycle, see Craig, ed., *Two Coventry Corpus Christi Plays*, p. xv. The dramatic records of Coventry have been edited for Records of Early English Drama by R. W. Ingram: *Coventry* (Toronto: Univ. of Toronto Press, 1981). For further commentary on the Coventry plays, see Reginald W. Ingram, "'Pleyng geire accustomed belongyng &

necessarie': Guild Records and Pageant Production at Coventry," in *Proceedings of the First Colloquium*, ed. JoAnna Dutka (Toronto: Records of Early English Drama, 1979), pp. 60–92, and "'To find the players and all that longeth therto': Notes on the Production of Medieval Drama in Coventry," *The Elizabethan Theatre*, ed. G. R. Hibbard (London: Macmillan, 1975), pp. 17–44. The civic context is described by Charles Phythian-Adams, "Ceremony and the Citizen: The Communal Year at Coventry, 1450–1550," in *Crisis and Order in English Medieval Towns, 1500–1700*, ed. Peter Clark and Paul Slack (Toronto: Univ. of Toronto Press, 1972), pp. 57–85. On the very close relations which existed between Coventry and Stratford-upon-Avon, see Mary Dormer Harris, ed., *The Coventry Leet Book*, Pt. 4, EETS, o.s. 146 (London, 1913), pp. xlix–l.

10. *Two Coventry Corpus Christi Plays*, ed. Craig, p. 27.

11. J. O. Halliwell-Phillipps, *Outlines of the Life of Shakespeare*, 6th ed. (London: Longman's, Green, 1886), I, 42–47, 309–10.

12. Quoted by Halliwell-Phillipps, I, 310; see also Ingram, ed., *Coventry*, p. xviii.

13. Quoted by Furness in New Variorum Edition, p. 33.

14. Thomas Sharp, *A Dissertation on the Pageants or Dramatic Mysteries* (Coventry, 1825), p. 8.

15. See Ingram, ed., *Coventry*, p. 3.

16. Edited by Craig in *Two Coventry Corpus Christi Plays*.

17. See Ingram, ed., *Coventry*, *passim*, and Clifford Davidson, "The Lost Coventry Drapers' Play of Doomsday and Its Iconographic Context," *Leeds Studies in English*, 17 (1986), 144–58.

18. However, in 1575, for example, the Coventry plays were called off on account of the plague.

19. While their attitude toward theological tradition and to the traditional ecclesiastical hierarchy was uniformly hostile, all Lollards were not as antagonistic to religious drama as the author of *A Tretise of Miraclis Pleyinge*. On Lollards in Coventry, see *The Victoria County History of the County of Warwick*, ed. William

Page, II (London: Constable, 1908), 20–22. See also John Fines, "Heresy Trials in the Diocese of Coventry and Lichfield, 1511–12," *Journal of Ecclesiastical History*, 14 (1963), 160–75.

During the reign of Queen Mary, Coventry was the scene of much religious tension, and ultimately the city took the Protestant side in the controversy; see the *Victoria County History of the County of Warwick*, II, 33–34, and Frederick Smith, *Coventry: Six Hundred Years of Municipal Life*, revised ed. (Coventry, 1946), pp. 79–80.

20. *Coventry*, ed. Ingram, pp. 148–49. On the decline of the Coventry economy in this period, see Phythian-Adams, *Desolation of a City, passim*.

21. See Harold C. Gardiner, *Mysteries' End: An Investigation of the Last Days of the Religious Stage* (1946; rpt. Hamden, Conn.: Archon, 1967), pp. 83–85.

22. John Foxe, *Acts and Monuments*, introd. George Townsend (rpt. New York: AMS Press, 1965), VIII, 163–70; see also *Coventry*, ed. Ingram, pp. 569–70.

23. Quoted by Ingram, ed., *Coventry*, p. 207; see also Foxe, *Acts and Monuments*, VIII, 170.

24. *Coventry*, ed. Ingram, p. 37.

25. Ibid., p. 66; for the visit of Henry VII in 1487 to see plays on St. Peter's Day, see ibid., pp. 67–68.

26. Ibid., p. 234.

27. See Bottom's statement in *A Midsummer Night's Dream* IV.ii.39: "our play is preferr'd."

28. Furness, New Variorum Edition, p. 23

29. Sharp, *Dissertation*, p. 12.

30. On the importance of this feast for *A Midsummer Night's Dream*, see Anca Vlosopolos, "The Ritual of Midsummer: A Pattern for *A Midsummer Night's Dream*," *Renaissance Quarterly*, 31 (1978), 21–29.

31. *Coventry*, ed. Ingram, p. 469.

194

32. Ibid., p. 332. On the *Destruction of Jerusalem*, see also Stephen K. Wright, *The Vengeance of Our Lord: Dramatizations of the Destruction of Jerusalem* (Toronto: Pontifical Institute of Mediaeval Studies, 1989), pp. 194–204.

33. *Coventry*, ed. Ingram, p. 332.

34. See ibid., pp. 303–09, 332–35.

35. See Vlosopolos, "The Ritual of Midsummer," pp. 21–29.

36. Carpenters and joiners in Coventry were related guilds which contributed to the pageants staged respectively by the Pinners, Needlers, and Tilers and by the Cappers.

37. *Coventry*, ed. Ingram, pp. 235–36.

38. Ibid., pp. 186, 188.

39. For additional information about the arrangements for a play and other preparations, see *The Staging of Religious Drama in Europe in the Later Middle Ages*, ed. Peter Meredith and John E. Tailby, Early Drama, Art, and Music, Monograph Ser., 4 (Kalamazoo: Medieval Institute Publications, 1983), pp. 35–61.

40. *Coventry*, ed. Ingram, p. 27.

41. For the addition of a prologue to the Coventry Cappers' play in 1566, see ibid., p. 241.

42. Ibid., pp. 122, 168. However, for an ambiguous reference (to Frauncys Co15ckes who played Salome in 1584), see ibid., p. 208, and William Tydeman, *The Theatre in the Middle Ages* (Cambridge: Cambridge Univ. Press, 1978), p. 200.

43. *Coventry*, ed. Ingram, pp. 86, 93.

44. For remarks which illustrate continuity of practice in the preparation of a play for the stage, see Bernard Beckerman, *Shakespeare at the Globe, 1599–1609* (New York: Macmillan, 1962), pp. 130–31.

45. See *Coventry*, ed. Ingram, pp. 44, 252, 281, 285, 551.

46. See, for example, the 1433 inventory of the York Mercers, transcribed in *York*, ed. Johnston and Rogerson, I, 55–56.

47. *Coventry*, ed. Ingram, pp. 334–35.

48. Richard Axton, *European Drama of the Early Middle Ages* (London: Hutchinson, 1974), p. 162.

49. Meg Twycross and Sarah Carpenter, "Masks in Medieval English Theatre," *Medieval English Theatre*, 3 (1981), 7–44, 69–113; 4 (1982), 28–47.

50. Ibid., 3 (1981), 17; see also *Coventry*, ed. Ingram, p. 240.

51. *Coventry*, ed. Ingram, p. 334; cf. David Bevington, *From* Mankind *to* Marlowe (Cambridge: Harvard Univ. Press, 1962), p. 92.

52. *Coventry*, ed. Ingram, p. 292.

53. Ibid., p. 258.

54. See E. C. Cawte, *Ritual Animal Disguise* (Cambridge: D. S. Brewer, 1978).

55. Axton, *European Drama*, p. 85.

56. Twycross and Carpenter, "Masks," *Medieval English Theatre*, 3 (1981), figs. 4, 5. See also Lilian M. C. Randall, *Images in the Margins of Gothic Manuscripts* (Berkeley and Los Angeles: Univ. of California Press, 1966), p. 165; cf. ibid., fig. 455, for further illustrations showing stag, hare, and bear from MS. Bodley 264, fol. 21^v.

57. Cf., however, Joseph Rosenblum, "Why an Ass?: Cesare Ripa's *Iconologia* as a Source for Bottom's Translation," *Shakespeare Quarterly*, 32 (1981), 357–59.

58. Two or three rehearsals were apparently usual when a play was in repertoire with annual production. However, for the new play of the *Destruction of Jerusalem* in 1584, the Cappers required five rehearsals; see *Coventry*, ed. Ingram, p. 303.

59. Ibid., p. 292.

60. The trumpeter, as the first folio reveals, was William Tawyer, a musician in the pay of John Heminge; see Furness, New Variorum Edition, pp. 214–15.

61. *Coventry*, ed. Ingram, p. 256.

62. Ibid., pp. 307–09.

63. Ibid., p. 77.

Chapter 5
The Phenomenology of Suffering,
Medieval Drama, and *King Lear*

1. John Wasson, "The Morality Play: Ancestor of Elizabethan Drama?" in *Drama in the Middle Ages*, ed. Clifford Davidson, C. J. Gianakaris, and John H. Stroupe (New York: AMS Press, 1982), pp. 316–22.

2. See, for example, Clifford Davidson, "Renaissance Dramatic Forms, Cosmic Perspective, and Alienation," pp. 1–16, but also, for a study which focuses on the "social dimension," Weimann, *Shakespeare and the Popular Tradition in the Theater*. I have previously commented on the shortcomings (and strengths) of the school known as "New Historicism" in a review article focusing on Steven Mullany's *The Place of the Stage* (Chicago: Univ. of Chicago Press, 1989); see "The 'New Historicism' and Early Modern Drama," *Comparative Drama*, 22 (1988–89), 359–69.

3. See the discussion of personified abstractions in Natalie Crohn Schmitt, "The Idea of a Person in Medieval Morality Plays," in *Drama in the Middle Ages*, ed. Davidson *et al.*, pp. 307–09; and also Clifford Davidson, *Visualizing the Moral Life* (New York: AMS Press, 1989), pp. 6–8 and *passim*. For a different and important view of the morality play, see Joanne Spencer Kantrowitz, *Dramatic Allegory* (Lincoln: Univ. of Nebraska Press, 1975), pp. 131–45.

4. *The Très Riches Heures of Jean, Duke of Berry*, introd. Jean Longnon and Raymond Cazelles (New York: Braziller, 1969), Pl. 20.

5. See Erwin Straus, "The Upright Posture," in *Studies in Phenomenology*, ed. Maurice Natanson (The Hague: Martin Nijhoff, 1966), pp. 164–92. Though we may argue with his definition of 'allegory,' Straus notes, otherwise perceptively, that "There are good reasons to assume that the term 'upright' in its moral connotation is more than a mere allegory" (p. 164).

6. Davidson and O'Connor, *York Art*, p. 19.

7. See Rushforth, *Mediaeval Christian Imagery*, p. 161.

8. See especially Edgar Schell, "The Limits of Typology and the Wakefield Master's *Processus Noe*," *Comparative Drama*, 25 (1991), 147-67.

9. See, for example, Nicholas Love's translation of the *Meditations on the Life of Christ* (*The Mirrour of the Blessed Lyf of Jesu Christ* [London, 1486], sig. N3ᵛ) and Davidson, *From Creation to Doom*, pp. 124–32.

10. Carolly Erickson, *The Medieval Vision: Essays in History and Perception* (New York: Oxford Univ. Press, 1976); Thomas, *Religion and the Decline of Magic*, pp. 59–61.

11. C. R. Morley, "A Group of Gothic Ivories in the Walters Art Gallery," *Art Bulletin*, 18 (1936), 199–212.

12. For a convenient explanation of Jung's theory of the *anima*, see M.-L. Franz, "The Process of Individuation," in *Man and His Symbols*, ed. C. G. Jung (New York: Doubleday, 1964), pp. 177–88.

13. *Chester Plays*, ed. Lumiansky and Mills, p. 50.

14. *Non-Cycle Plays and Fragments*, ed. Norman Davis, EETS, s.s. 1 (London, 1970), p. 21.

15. Peter Dronke, *The Medieval Lyric* (New York: Harper and Row, 1969), pp. 26, 86–92; Kemp Malone, "Two English Frauenlieder," *Comparative Literature*, 14 (1962), 106–17; Leo Spitzer, "The Mozarabic Lyric and Theodor Frings' Theories," *Comparative Literature*, 4 (1952), 1–22.

16. Julian of Norwich, *Revelations of Divine Love*, chap. 2.

17. For an important study of the Reformation in England, see J. J. Scarisbrick, *The Reformation and the English People* (Oxford: Blackwell, 1984).

18. Roy Walker, *The Time Is Free: A Study of* Macbeth (London, 1949), p. 53.

19. For additional discussion of the world-upside-down *topos*, see William R. Elton, *King Lear and the Gods* (San Marino, California: Huntington Library, 1966),

pp. 310–16; Clifford Davidson, "The Iconography of Wisdom and Folly in *King Lear*," in *Shakespeare and the Emblem*, ed. Tibor Fabiny (Szeged, Hungary: Department of English, Attila József Univ., 1984), pp. 189–214.

20. Chambers, *Population, Economy, and Society*, pp. 19, 29.

21. Ernst Robert Curtius, *European Literature and the Latin Middle Ages*, trans. Willard R. Trask (1953; rpt. New York: Harper and Row, 1963), pp. 94–98; see also Samuel Chew, *The Pilgrimage of Life* (New Haven: Yale Univ. Press, 1962), pp. 44–45.

22. Curtius, *European Literature and the Latin Middle Ages*, p. 95.

23. John Taylor, *A Plea for Prerogative: or, give Caesar his due, Being the Wheele of Fortune turn'd round: or, The World turned topsie-turvie* (London, 1642), and *Mad Fashions, Od Fashions, All out of Fashions* (London, 1642); see also Chew, *Pilgrimage of Life*, pp. 44–45.

24. Quoted in *King Lear*, ed. H. H. Furness, New Variorum Edition (Philadelphia: Lippincott, 1880), p. 419.

25. Ibid., p. 418.

26. *Narrative and Dramatic Sources of Shakespeare*, ed. Geoffrey Bullough (London: Routledge and Kegan Paul, 1973), VII, 349 (ll. 512–13).

27. *Physiologus*, trans. Michael J. Curley (Austin: Univ. of Texas Press, 1979), pp. 9–10.

28. *Lexikon der christlichen Kunst*, ed. Engelbert Kirschbaum *et al.* (Freiburg: Herder, 1968–76), III, 390–92.

29. Cesare Ripa, *Iconologia*, English trans. (1709), p. 14. *Bonta* is not illustrated in the engravings in the 1603 edition; my illustration (fig. 9) is from the edition printed at Venice in 1669 (p. 95).

30. In recent years, to be sure, social historians have considerably qualified earlier charges that, with the closing of the monasteries, the Protestants were also deliberately harsher in their treatment of the poor. There were immense social pressures brought to bear through social change, and it is undeniable that in many

locales there was lowered access to the means of livelihood at the same time that the structures previously established to cope with poverty were diminished.

31. See J. V. Cunningham, *Woe or Wonder: The Emotional Effect of Shakespearian Tragedy* (1951; rpt. Denver: Alan Swallow, 1960), pp. 36–102.

32. Bertram Joseph, in his *Elizabethan Acting*, 2nd ed. (London: Oxford Univ. Press, 1964), assumes the authenticity of the emotion, as in his statement "With both orator and actor, action was the result of allowing truly felt emotion to communicate itself through trained voice, facial expression, and movement" (p. 22). Like participating in a game, however, the actor's assumption of passion is part of a *play* world rather than the real world. Hamlet, of course, shows awareness of knowing the actor was *playing*, and it is absurd to believe that the audience did not know the actor playing Hamlet was in fact also *playing*. See also the distinctions identified by Hans-Jürgen Diller, "Theatrical Pragmatics: The Actor-Audience Relationship from the Mystery Cycles to the Early Tudor Comedies," *Comparative Drama*, 23 (1989), 156–65.

33. Cunningham, *Woe or Wonder*, pp. 36–102. For Sidney's use of "admiration and commiseration," see *Literary Criticism: Plato to Dryden*, ed. Gilbert, p. 432; Sidney's immediate sources were continental critics such as Scaliger rather than Donatus or Aristotle (see ibid., pp. 459–69).

34. See Jane Harrison, *Ancient Art and Ritual*, rev. ed. (London: Williams and Norgate, 1918), p. 26 and *passim*.

Chapter 6
Jonson's *Bartholomew Fair*, Stage Plays, and Anti-Traditionalism

1. See Douglas Bush, *English Literature in the Earlier Seventeenth Century 1600–1660*, 2nd ed., Oxford History of English Literature, 5 (Oxford: Clarendon Press, 1962), p. 107, who calls Jonson "the first great English theorist and practitioner of neoclassicism, the first really direct, learned, deliberate, and single-hearted heir of antiquity."

2. Ben Jonson, *Poems*, ed. George Burke Johnston (Cambridge: Harvard Univ. Press, 1962), pp. 76–79.

3. See D. J. Gordon, "Poet and Architect: The Intellectual Setting of the Quarrel between Ben Jonson and Inigo Jones," in *The Renaissance Imagination*, ed. Stephen Orgel (Berkeley and Los Angeles: Univ. of California Press, 1975), pp. 77–101.

4. Quotations from *Hymenaei* and *Bartholomew Fair* are from the edition edited by C. H. Herford and Percy and Evelyn Simpson (Oxford: Clarendon Press, 1925-41), Vols. VI and VII; the quotation from *Hymenaei* is from VII, 209.

5. *Literary Criticism: Plato to Dryden*, ed. Gilbert, pp. 431–32.

6. "An Ode. To himselfe," in Jonson, *Poems*, p. 151.

7. Jackson Cope, "*Bartholomew Fair* as Blasphemy," *Renaissance Drama*, 8 (1965), 134-35. Cope sees the rigid standards as associated with an outdated legalism, but such a model does not exactly fit the play. In the case of Busy, the character exhibits an attempt to revive out-of-context biblical standards out of a disrespect for tradition.

8. Jonson's view of the stage, while ambivalent, needs to be understood in terms of his hierarchy of values: the *meaning* is the *soul* of the play, the visible *spectacle* is its *body*. See Gordon, "Poet and Architect," pp. 77-101.

9. "An Ode. To himselfe," ll. 31-35.

10. Cope, p. 144; see Cesare Ripa, *Iconologia* (Venice, 1659), p. 156. Cope (p. 144) also cites Vicenzio Cartari, *Imagini delli dei de gl'antichi* (Venice, 1674), pp. 197-98. For Jonson's use of Ate in a different context, see the *Masque of Queenes*, in Herford and Simpson, VII, 286.

11. T. W. Craik, *The Tudor Interlude* (Leicester: Leicester Univ. Press, 1967), pp. 93-95, Pl. V; Ian Donaldson, *The World Upside-Down: Comedy from Jonson to Fielding* (Oxford: Clarendon Press, 1970), p. 65.

12. *Historical Poems of the XIVth and XVth Centuries*, ed. Rossell Hope Robbins (New York: Columbia Univ. Press, 1959), pp. 121-27.

13. *An Encyclopaedia of London*, ed. William Kent (New York: Dutton, 1937), pp. 581.

14. Charles Wriothesley, *A Chronicle of England*, ed. William Douglas Hamilton, Camden Soc., 11, 20 (London, 1875-77), I, 80.

15. E.g., Wriothesley, II, 127, 129-30, 132, 134, 137; Henry Machyn, *The Diary*, ed. John Gough Nichols, Camden Soc., 42 (London, 1848), pp. 83, 88, 90, 98-99, 104, 130, 157, 161. For accounts of the Protestant martyrs under Queen Mary, see John Foxe's *Acts and Monuments*, Vols. V-VIII.

16. "Bartholomew Legate," *DNB*, XI, 846-47.

17. John Strype, *Annals of the Reformation* (Oxford: Clarendon Press, 1824), I, Pt. 1, 254. The destruction of images by burning is also implied in the folk practice called the Burning of Bartle at West Witton, Yorkshire, formerly on 24 August (now on a Saturday near the feast day). A large effigy, called Bartle (presumably a shortened form of Bartholomew, the patron of the local parish church), is placed on a bonfire at the end of a procession (Christina Hole, *British Folk Customs* [London: Hutchinson, 1976], p. 35).

18. *Liturgies and Occasional Forms of Prayer set forth in the Reign of Queen Elizabeth*, ed. William Keatinge, Parker Soc. (Cambridge: Cambridge Univ. Press, 1847), p. 451.

19. E. A. Webb, *The Records of St. Bartholomew's Priory and of the Church of St. Bartholomew the Great, West Smithfield* (London: Oxford Univ. Press, 1921), II, 104.

20. See Aston, *England's Iconoclasts*, and the survey presented by John Phillips, *The Reformation of Images* (Berkeley and Los Angeles: Univ. of California Press, 1973), as well as *Iconoclasm vs. Art and Drama*, ed. Davidson and Nichols.

21. Helen Wilcox, "Puritans, George Herbert and 'Nose-Twange'," *Notes and Queries*, 224 (1979), 152-53.

22. Quoted by A. C. Moule, ed., *The Cambridge Journal of William Dowsing, 1643* (1926), p. 3.

23. *The Journal of William Dowsing, of Stratford* (Woodbridge: R. Loder, 1786), p. 12.

24. James E. Robinson, "*Bartholomew Fair*: Comedy of Vapours," *Studies in English Literature*, 1, No. 2 (1961), 65-80.

25. John Selden, *The Table Talk*, ed. Samuel Harvey Reynolds (Oxford: Clarendon Press, 1892), pp. 164-65.

26. It is important not to see all Puritans as having identical attitudes toward the stage; only some Puritans, like Prynne, objected to the theater, while others, like Middleton, did not. See especially the controversial work of Margo Heinemann, *Puritanism and Theatre* (Cambridge: Cambridge Univ. Press, 1980), pp. 18-47.

27. E. A. Horsman, ed., *Bartholomew Fair*, The Revels Plays (Cambridge: Harvard Univ. Press, 1962), p. 147.

28. Jonas A. Barish, *Ben Jonson and the Language of Prose Comedy* (Cambridge: Harvard Univ. Press, 1960), p. 232.

29. Jonas Barish, "*Bartholomew Fair* and Its Puppets," *Modern Language Quarterly*, 20 (1959), 13.

30. See Tertullian, *De Spectaculis* x, in *Tertullian*, ed. and trans. Gerald H. Rendall, Loeb Classical Library (Cambridge: Harvard Univ. Press, 1931), pp. 258-61.

31. See Gordon, "Poet and Architect," pp. 77-78, on the beginnings of the quarrel between Jonson and Inigo Jones.

32. *Bartholomew Fair*, ed. Horsman, p. 169.

33. Hyder E. Rollins, "A Contribution to the History of the Commonwealth Drama," *Studies in Philology*, 18 (1921), 281.

34. Henry Morley, *Memoirs of Bartholomew Fair* (London: Chatto and Windus, 1880), p. 183.

35. Thomas D'Urfey, *Wit and Mirth, or Pills to Purge Melancholy* (1719; rpt. New York: Folklore Library, 1959), IV, 169. For another reference to puppet shows at Bartholomew Fair during the Commonwealth period, see the speech by Henry Cromwell in Parliament (1659), as quoted by George Speaight, *The History of the English Puppet Theatre* (London: George G. Harrap, 1955), p. 71.

36. *The Diary of Samuel Pepys*, ed. Robert Latham and William Matthews (London: G. Bell, 1974-76), VIII, 408-09, IX, 293, 296, 299.

37. Frances Teague, *The Curious History of Bartholomew Fair* (Lewisburg: Bucknell Univ. Press, 1985), p. 19.

38. For a typical comment by a Calvinist divine, see the statement by William Perkins, as quoted by Jonas Barish, *The Anti-Theatrical Prejudice* (Berkeley and Los Angeles: Univ. of California Press, 1981), p. 113.

39. William Lambarde, *Dictionarium Angliae Topographicum et Historicum* (London, 1730), pp. 459.

40. Ibid., pp. 459-60.

41. William Prynne, *Histrio-Mastix* (London, 1633), pp. 158-59.

42. Ibid.

43. Barish, *The Anti-Theatrical Prejudice*, p. 151.

44. Ernst Cassirer, *The Platonic Renaissance in England*, trans. James P. Pettegrove (London, 1953), p. 74, as quoted by Barish, *The Anti-Theatrical Prejudice*, p. 173.

45. *De Spectaculis* xxiii (pp. 286-87).

46. Stephen Gosson, *Plays Confuted in fiue actions* (1582), sigs. E3^v-E4^r.

47. Francis Hargrave, *A Complete Collection of State-Trials*, 2nd ed. (London, 1780), I, 400.

48. *Commentary on I John*, as quoted by Carlos M. N. Eire, *War Against the Idols* (Cambridge: Cambridge Univ. Press, 1986), pp. 225-26.

49. John Calvin, *A Very Profitable Treatise . . . declarynge what great profit might come to al christen dome, yf there were a regester made of all Sanctes bodies and other reliques*, trans. Steven Wythers (London, 1561), sig. A5^r.

50. Mary Douglas, *Purity and Danger* (New York: Frederick Praeger, 1966), pp. 41, 113.

51. Meg Twycross, "'Transvestism' in the Mystery Plays," *Medieval English Theatre*, 5 (1983), 123-80.

52. John Selden, *Works* (London, 1726), II, 1690-94, as cited by Carroll Storrs Alden, ed., *Bartholomew Fair*, Yale Studies in English, 25 (New York: Henry Holt, 1904), pp. 217-18. See also Selden, *Table Talk*, pp. 134-35, and the comments of Russell Fraser, *The War Against Poetry* (Princeton: Princeton Univ. Press, 1970), pp. 26-27.

53. Twycross, "'Transvestism' in the Mystery Plays," pp. 137-38.

54. John Rainolds, *Th'Overthrow of Stage-Playes* (London, 1599), pp. 45, 104; cited by Twycross, "'Transvestism' in the Mystery Plays," p. 138.

55. Prynne, *Histrio-Mastix*, p. 208.

56. "An Ode. To himselfe," ll. 36-37.

Chapter 7
George Herbert and Painted Glass Windows

1. George Herbert, *The Works*, ed. F. E. Hutchinson (Oxford: Clarendon Press, 1941), p. 94; all subsequent quotations from Herbert's poetry and prose are from this edition.

2. For Herbert's life, see Amy M. Charles, *A Life of George Herbert* (Ithaca: Cornell Univ. Press, 1977).

3. Margaret Aston, "English Ruins and English History: The Dissolution and the Sense of the Past," in *Lollards and Reformers: Images and Literacy in Late Medieval Religion* (London: Hambledon Press, 1984), pp. 313–37; see also her *England's Iconoclasts*, I, *passim*. For the quotation from Thomas Fuller, *The Church History of Britain*, ed. J. S. Brewer (Oxford, 1845), III, 434, see Aston, "English Ruins and English History," pp. 319–20.

4. Richard Hooker, *Of the Laws of Ecclesiastical Polity* V.vii.1 (introd. Christopher Morris [1907; rpt. London: Dent, 1960], II, 27).

5. *The Great Exemplar* (1649), Pt. II, p. 35, as quoted in *The Golden Grove: Selected Passages from the Sermons and Writings of Jeremy Taylor*, ed. Logan Pearsall Smith (Oxford: Clarendon Press, 1930), p. 139.

6. See Clifford Davidson, "Herbert's 'The Temple': Conflicts, Submission and Freedom," *English Miscellany*, 25 (1975), 163-81. See also G. W. O Addleshaw, *The High Church Tradition* (London: Faber and Faber, 1941), p. 60, for an appreciation of Herbert's understanding of the Christian congregation praying "with one heart and one voice, and in a reverent posture," and expressing the peace of Jerusalem as well as being at peace with itself.

7. Izaak Walton, *The Life of Mr. George Herbert*, in *The Lives*, ed. S. B. Carter (London: Falcon, 1951), p. 235. See also Herbert's poem entitled "Redemption."

8. See Richard Strier, "'To all Angels and Saints': Herbert's Puritan Poem," *Modern Philology*, 77 (1979), 132-45.

9. *Works*, ed. Hutchinson, p. 246. See also Herbert's comments on Baptism and Holy Communion, pp. 257-59. While with regard to the latter he suggests the appropriateness of sitting since it is a feast (the Calvinists insisted that this was the correct posture), he very firmly indicates that kneeling is the proper posture for receiving. The point is an important one.

10. Ibid., p. 246.

11. Ibid.

12. Joseph Hall, *The Works*, VI (Oxford, 1837), 464. See also Hooker, *Of the Laws of Ecclesiastical Polity* V.xxix.3 (introd. Morris, II, 119), for the classic Anglican statement on this matter.

13. *Works*, ed. Hutchinson, p. 246.

14. John Hacket, *Scrinia Reserata*, as quoted by Charles, *A Life of George Herbert*, p. 115.

15. Hooker, *Of the Laws of Ecclesiastical Polity* X.vii.3 (introd. Morris, II, 29).

16. See Walter Blankenburg, "Church Music in Reformed Europe," in Friedrich Blume *et al.*, *Protestant Church Music* (New York: Norton, 1974), pp. 516ff.

17. Peter Smart, *A Sermon preached in the Cathedrall Church of Durham* (1628), p. 22.

18. Ibid., pp. 19-20.

19. Dora H. Robertson, *Sarum Close* (1938; rpt. Bath: Firecrest, 1969), p. 164; Charles, *A Life of George Herbert*, pp. 164-66.

20. Smart, *A Sermon*, pp. 9, 11.

21. *Tudor Royal Proclamations*, ed. Paul L. Hughes and James F. Larkin (New Haven: Yale Univ. Press, 1969), II, 146-48.

22. On Herbert's "Church Monuments," see especially Barbara Leah Harman, *Costly Monuments* (Cambridge: Harvard Univ. Press, 1982), pp. 112-29, 129.

23. The replacement of the altar at the east end of a raised chancel by the Laudian church was especially disliked; see, for example, Smart, *A Sermon*, p. 17.

24. *The Journal of William Dowsing, of Stratford* (Woodbridge, 1786).

25. For an apparent parallel to Herbert's analogy, see T. A. Joscelyne, "George Herbert's 'The Windows': A Parallel in Barbaro's Vitruvius," *Notes and Queries*, 227 (1982), 493-94.

26. It is very significant that Herbert accepts, at least to a limited degree, the Gregorian understanding of pictures as "books for the unlearned"; the Gregorian concept had been all but banished by the English Reformers, as Nichols points out ("Books-for-Laymen: The Demise of a Commonplace," pp. 457-73). For the theology of light, see Otto von Simson, *The Gothic Cathedral*, 2nd ed. (1962; rpt. New York: Harper and Row, n.d.), pp. 120-23.

27. William Shullenberger rightly indicates the way in which light and divine grace are associated in "The Windows" ("Ars praedicandi in George Herbert's Poetry," in *"Bright Shootes of Everlastingnesse": The Seventeenth-Century Religious Lyric*, ed. Claude J. Summers and Ted-Larry Pebworth [Columbia: Univ. of Missouri Press, 1987], pp. 103-04).

28. Richard Strier, *Love Known: Theology and Experience in George Herbert's Poetry* (Chicago: Univ. of Chicago Press, 1983), p. 150.

29. See also Sigrid Renaux, "George Herbert's 'The Windows' Illuminated: A Critical Approach," *George Herbert Journal*, 9 (1985), 31.

30. John M. Fletcher and Christopher A. Upton, "Destruction, Repair and Removal: An Oxford College Chapel during the Reformation," *Oxoniensia*, 48 (1983), 126-27.

31. Robert Benson and Henry Hatcher, *Old and New Sarum* (London, 1843), p. 371; for a more complete report of the trial, see Francis Hargrave, *A Complete Collection of State-Trials*, 2nd ed. (London, 1780), I, 377ff; for a summary of the trial, see Mr. Horman-Fisher, "The Proceedings, in the Star Chamber, against the Recorder of Salisbury in 1632," *British Archaeological Journal*, 15 (1859), 194-98. The context of the urban conflict in Salisbury is analyzed by Paul Slack, "Religous Protest and Urban Authority: The Case of Henry Sherfield, Iconoclast, 1633," in *Schism, Heresy and Religious Protest*, ed. Derek Baker, Studies in Church History, 9 (Cambridge: Cambridge Univ. Press, 1972), pp. 295-302; for this reference I am grateful to Sidney Gottlieb, whose article "Herbert's 'Case of Conscience': Public or Private Poem?" *Studies in English Literature*, 25 (1985), 109-26, briefly notes the relevance of the Sherfield case to the understanding of Herbert (p. 123).

32. *A Complete Collection of State-Trials*, I, 381.

33. Benson and Hatcher, *Old and New Sarum*, pp. 372-73.

34. William Laud, "Speech in the Star Chamber, at the Censure of Henry Sherfield, Esq.," in *Works*, VI (Oxford: John Henry Parker, 1857), 17.

35. *Calendar of State Papers, Domestic, 1631-33*, pp. 538-39; *Calendar of State Papers, Domestic, 1633-34*, p. 19. For a convenient summary of the judgment against Sherfield, see Horman-Fisher, "The Proceedings," pp. 196-98. Sherfield would also have been a member of the anti-music faction in Salisbury—a faction that did not approve of the cathedral music which Herbert loved. That music was silent, of course, following the suppression of the Prayer Book and the confiscation of church property in 1645; see Robertson, *Sarum Close*, p. 195.

36. *The Second Tome of Homilies* (1563), fols. 12^r-83^v. The Book of Homilies would have been included as one of "the books appointed by authority" to be present in the parish church; see Herbert, *Works*, ed. Hutchinson, p. 246.

208

37, *Works*, ed. Hutchinson, p. 309.

38. *A Complete Collection of State Trials*, I, 379. Sherfield complained that "he was placed in the Church in such a Seat, as that the said Window was always in his Eye, during his abode in the Church" (ibid., I, 377). See also Laud, "Speech in the Star Chamber," p. 19.

39. *Anglicanism*, ed. Paul Elmer More and Frank Leslie Cross (London: SPCK, 1935), pp. 737-38.

40. Judy Z. Kronenfeld, "Probing the Relation between Poetry and Ideology: Herbert's 'The Windows'," *John Donne Journal*, 2 (1983), 76.

41. Charles, *A Life of George Herbert*, pp. 127-30, plausibly connects "The Crosse" with the period when Herbert was planning the renovation of the cruciform church at Leighton Bromswold. For a description and praise of the work of the seventeenth-century restoration of this church, see Nikolaus Pevsner, *Bedfordshire and the County of Huntingdon and Peterborough*, Buildings of England (Harmondsworth: Penguin, 1968), pp. 282-83

42. J. M. J. Fletcher, "The Stained Glass in Salisbury Cathedral," *Wiltshire Archaeological and Natural History Magazine*, 45 (1930), 238.

43. Von Simson, *The Gothic Cathedral*, p. 44.

44. *Works*, ed. Hutchinson, p. 286.

Chapter 8
Tradition and Imitation

1. Hooker, *Of the Laws of Ecclesiastical Polity* V.lxv.1–21.

2. See Owen Chadwick, ed., *The Mind of the Oxford Movement* (Stanford: Stanford Univ. Press, 1960), pp. 55–58.

3. *Lyra Apostolica* (Derby: Henry Mozley and Sons; London: J. G. and F. Rivington, 1836), p. 14. "The Cross of Christ" has at its head a quotation from Tertullian. The poems collected in *Lyra Apostolica*, by Newman and others, were reprinted from the *British Magazine*.

Another version of the first stanza of Newman's poem is superior to the one printed in the *Lyra Apostolica*:

When'er across this sinful flesh of mine
   I draw the Holy Sign,
All good thoughts stir within me, and renew
   Their slumbering strength divine;
Till there springs up a courage high and true
   To suffer and to do.

Also of interest in this collection is Newman's "Awe" (p. 13), which begins as follows:

I bow at Jesus' Name, for 'tis the Sign
Of awful mercy toward a guilty line. . . .

The gesture of bowing at the holy name would have been regarded as a sign not of piety but of superstition in many quarters in the England of the 1830's.

4. David Hume, "On Miracles" [*Concerning Human Understanding*, sec. 10], in *Essays Moral, Political, and Literary*, ed. Thomas Hill Green and Thomas Hodge Grose (1882; rpt. Aalen: Scientia Verlag, 1964), II, 88–108. For commentary on Newman's Romanticism and also on the strong anti-Romantic strain in the Anglo-Catholic poetry of the period, see Hoxie Neale Fairchild, *Religious Trends in English Poetry*, IV (New York: Columbia Univ. Press, 1957), 240–57.

5. *Anti-Ritualist*, 1 Sept. 1868, p. 3.

6. *Anti-Ritualist*, 1 Oct. 1868, p. 18.

7. *Anti-Ritualist*, 2 Nov. 1868, p. 49. This seems to have been the last issue of this periodical.

8. *Anti-Ritualist*, 1 Sept. 1868, p. 4.

9. Ruskin, *The Stones of Venice* (New York: John Wiley and Sons, 1860), I, 414; this attack, directed especially at Pugin, is in part quoted from another edition by James F. White, *The Cambridge Movement: The Ecclesiologists and the Gothic Revival* (Cambridge: Cambridge Univ. Press, 1962), p. 175.

10. Wickham Legg, *Ecclesiological Essays*, ed. Vernon Staley (London: Alexander Moring, 1905), p. 27.

11. A. W. N. Pugin, *Contrasts*, introd. H. R. Hitchcock (New York: Humanities Press, 1969), p. iv.

12. Ibid., p. 7.

13. Especially important were works like William Dugdale's *Monasticon Anglicanum* (London, 1655).

14. See Kenneth Clark, *The Gothic Revival: An Essay in the History of Taste*, 3rd ed. (New York: Holt, Rinehart, and Winston, 1962), pp. 78–91.

15. *Gentleman's Magazine*, 68, Pt. 2 (1798), 764–65. For a listing of Carter's contributions to this periodical, see the Index to the volumes for 1797–1818 under the headings *Carter* and *Architectural Innovation.*

16. Charles L. Eastlake, *A History of the Gothic Revival* (London: Longmans, Green, 1872), pp. 103–08.

17. See J. Mordaunt Crook, "John Britton and the Genesis of the Gothic Revival," in *Concerning Architecture*, ed. John Summerson (London: Allen Lane, 1968), pp. 98–119.

18. Clark, *The Gothic Revival*, pp. 108–21.

19. John Britton, *The Architectural Antiquities of Great Britain* (London: Longman, Hurst, Rees, and Orme, 1807–29).

20. Eastlake, *History of the Gothic Revival*, p. 88.

21. Britton, *Architectural Antiquities*, IV, 101.

22. Pugin, *Contrasts*, p. 31.

23. See Nigel Yates, "The Legacy of the Oxford and Cambridge Movements," *Churchscape: Annual Review of the Council for the Care of Churches*, No. 3 (1983–84), pp. 4–20, for a useful survey.

24. Britton, *Architectural Antiquities*, I, 10. This church, however, probably suffered an even worse fate at the hands of the doctrinaire church restorers who "restored" it in the 1840's; for a description of the present condition of the building, see Nikolaus Pevsner, *Cambridgeshire*, 2nd ed. (Harmondsworth: Penguin, 1970), pp. 230–31.

25. See White, *The Cambridge Movement*, p. 37 and *passim*.

26. "Laws of the Cambridge Camden Society," 1842; in White, *The Cambridge Movement*, Appendix A, p. 225.

27. "Laws of the Ecclesiological Late Cambridge Camden Society," 1847–49, in White, *The Cambridge Movement*, Appendix B, p. 228 (italics mine).

28. Ibid., Appendix C, pp. 231–36.

29. *A Handbook of English Ecclesiology* (London: Joseph Masters, 1847), p. 35.

30. Ibid., *passim*.

31. Ibid., p. 71.

32. E. H. Gombrich, *Symbolic Images* (London: Phaidon, 1972), p. 21.

33. *The Symbolism of Churches and Church Ornaments*, trans. John Mason Neale and Benjamin Webb (1843; rpt. London: Gibbings, 1893), p. xxv.

34. Ibid., pp. xxvi–xxvii.

35. See ibid., pp. xl–xli, lv–lvi, lxi, lxvii–lxviii, lxxxiv.

36. Ibid., pp. lix–lx.

37. See Addleshaw, *The High Church Tradition*, p. 37 and *passim*.

38. See "New Churches," *Ecclesiologist*, 9 (1850), 432–33, reporting construction beginning on All Saints' Church.

39. The words are those of Butterfield's patron, Alexander Beresford-Hope; quoted by Paul Thompson, *William Butterfield* (Cambridge, Mass.: M.I.T. Press, 1971), p. 321.

212

40. Ibid., p. 33.

41. Ibid., p. 163.

42. Ibid., p. 322. fig. 272.

43. See G. W. O. Addleshaw, *The Architectural Setting of Anglican Worship* (London: Faber and Faber, 1948), pp. 211–14.

44. Curl, "All Saints', Margaret Street," p. 32.

45. *The Journals and Papers of Gerard Manley Hopkins*, ed. Humphrey House and Graham Storey (London: Oxford Univ. Press, 1959), p. 140; see also the note on p. 357.

47. Ibid., p. 248.

48. See White, *The Cambridge Movement*, p. 196, citing the *Ecclesiologist*, 10 (1850), 432.

49. See Henry Russell Hitchcock, *Early Victorian Architecture* (1954; rpt. New York: Da Capo Press, 1972), p. 574.

50. *The Building News*, 78 (1900), 292, as cited in Curl, "All Saints', Margaret Street," p. 54.

51. *Ecclesiologist*, 20 (1859), 185; cited by Thompson, *William Butterfield*, p. 367.

52. W. S. Rockstro, "Plain Song," *A Dictionary of Music and Musicians*, ed. George Grove (London: Macmillan, 1880), II, 769.

53. Ibid., II, 769.

54. Neale and Webb, *The Symbolism of Churches*, p. lx.

55. J. T. Micklethwaite, *The Ornaments of the Rubric*, Alcuin Club Tracts, 1 (London: Longmans, Green, 1897), p. 13.

56. Ibid., pp. 13–15.

57. Legg, *Ecclesiological Essays*, pp. 29–43.

58. Ibid., pp. 39–40.

59. Ibid., p. 40.

60. Ralph Adams Cram, *Church Building: A Study of the Principles of Architecture in Their Relation to the Church* (Boston: Small, Maynard, 1901), pp. 5–6.

61. Ibid., p. 7. Medieval churches, however, had many altars and an interior arrangement considerably less focused than Cram would have approved; see, for example, G. H. Cook, *The English Mediaeval Parish Church* (London: Phoenix House, 1961), pp. 149–206.

62. See White, *The Cambridge Movement*, pp. 156–77.

63. Quoted by Martin S. Briggs, *Goths and Vandals: A Study of the Destruction, Neglect, and Preservation of Historical Buildings in England* (London: Constable, 1952), pp. 208–09.

64. Otto Rydbeck, *Lunds Domkyrkas Byggnadshistoria* (Lund: Gleerup, 1923), esp. figs. 230–31.

65. Nikolaus Pevsner, Priscilla Metcalf, *et al.*, *The Cathedrals of England* (New York: Viking, 1985), p. 110.

66. *Architectural Review* (1878), p. 185n, as cited in Clark, *The Gothic Revival*, p. 175.

67. White, *The Cambridge Movement*, pp. 166–71, and see also the review of Scott's *A Plea for Faithful Restoration of Our Ancient Churches* in the *Ecclesiologist*, 11 (1850), 12ff. There was additionally a "Destructive" school, led by John Mason Neale who said he would have torn down Peterborough Cathedral if it could have been rebuilt in pure English fourteenth-century style—the style that the Ecclesiologists called "Middle Pointed."

68. Two examples from the city of York may be mentioned. After World War II, Dean Eric Milner-White directed the restoration of the Minster's painted glass, which had been in storage for safe keeping during hostilities. Without maintaining adequate record of what was done in the glass shop, the restorers re-

organized much glass, replaced lost heads with heads from other sources (not always the same size), and otherwise patched the panels to make them look authentic. A second example involves the even more recent restoration of the angel musicians on the roof of All Saints, North Street, York, where some of the carvings have been repainted (they had already been stripped of their polychrome, presumably in the nineteenth century) using the most inappropriate pigments.

69. Wayment, *The Stained Glass of the Church of St. Mary*, p. 56, citing S. Evans, "The Glass in Fairford Church, Gloucestershire," *Ecclesiologist*, 26 (1865), 16–18.

70. Wayment, *The Stained Glass of the Church of St. Mary*, p. 56; see also Hilary Wayment, "Echo answers 'Where': The Victorian Restoration of the West Window at Fairford," *Journal of the British Society of Master Glass Painters*, 17, No. 1 (1980–81), 18–25.

71. Haselock and O'Connor, "The Stained and Painted Glass," pp. 389–92.

72. For the iconography, see Davidson and O'Connor, *York Art*, pp. 60–61, 112, 127, 174, 183.

73. Haselock and O'Connor, "The Stained and Painted Glass," p. 392.

74. John Browne, *The History of the Metropolitan Church of St. Peter, York Minster* (London, 1847), Vol. II. There were also less valuable drawings by John Carter, preserved in British Library MS. Add. 29,929, fols. 106–07.

75. Davidson and O'Connor, *York Art*, p. 47; cf. Browne, *The History of the Metropolitan Church*, Pl. CI (the original design).

76. Rosalie B. Green, "Virtues and Vices in the Chapter House Vestibule in Salisbury," *Journal of the Warburg and Courtauld Institutes*, 31 (1968), 148–58.

77. See Gwen and Jeremy Montagu, "Beverley Minster Reconsidered," *Early Music*, 6 (1978), 401–15.

78. Ibid., pp. 406–07. Another figure, playing an unrecognizable stringed instrument, is very obviously an eighteenth-century carving, though even this example has been mistaken for fourteenth-century.

79. Eduard de Coussemaker, *Drames liturgiques du moyen âge* (Rennes, 1860).

80. Neale and Webb, *The Symbolism of Churches*, p. lxxvii.

81. See Sheingorn, *The Easter Sepulchre in England, passim.*

82. Alfred Heales, "Easter Sepulchres; Their Object, Nature, and History," *Archaeologia*, 42 (1869), 263–308.

83. Ibid., pp. 277–82.

84. Ibid., p. 287.

85. Henry John Feasey, *Ancient Holy Week Ceremonial* (London: Thomas Baker, 1897), and "The Easter Sepulchre," *The Ecclesiastical Review*, 4th ser., 2 (1905), 337–499. The latter article should be sufficient proof that neither the medieval ceremonies nor the liturgical dramas had been revived.

86. See Karl Young, *The Drama of the Medieval Church* (Oxford: Clarendon Press, 1933), Vol. I.

87. William Hone, *Ancient Mysteries Described, Especially the English Miracle Plays, founded on Apocryphal New Testament Story, Extant among the Unpublished Manuscripts in the British Museum; including Notices of Ecclesiastical Shows* (London, 1823).

88. Ibid., pp. 84–85.

89. Clippings of the reviews from the *Gentleman's Magazine* and *The Monthly Review* (pp. 1–12) are preserved in Thomas Sharp's own copy of his *Dissertation* (British Library Add. MS. 43,645). See also "Enlightenment vs. Antiquarianism," *EDAM Newsletter*, 8, No. 1 (1985), 4–5.

90. For a very useful survey of early editions of plays, see Ian Lancashire, "Medieval Drama," in *Editing Medieval Texts English, French, and Latin Written in England*, ed. A. G. Rigg (New York: Garland, 1977), pp. 58–85.

91. *The Towneley Mysteries*, [ed. James Gordon,] Surtees Soc., 3 (London, 1836), p. xviii; the passage is quoted by Lancashire, "Medieval Drama," p. 61.

92. *The Digby Plays*, ed. F. J. Furnivall, EETS, e.s. 70 (London, 1896), pp. vii–viii, xvi.

93. Ibid., p. vii.

94. Ibid., p. 227.

95. See Stanley J. Kahrl, "Editing Texts for Dramatic Performance," in *The Drama of Medieval Europe*, Leeds Medieval Studies, 1 (Leeds: Graduate Center for Medieval Studies, Univ. of Leeds, 1975), pp. 40–45.

96. E. K. Chambers, *The Mediaeval Stage* (London: Oxford Univ. Press, 1903), 2 vols.

97. See Chap. 10, below.

Chapter 9
T. S. Eliot's *Murder in the Cathedral*:
Reviving the Saint Play Tradition

1. E. Martin Browne, *The Making of T. S. Eliot's Plays* (Cambridge: Cambridge Univ. Press, 1969), pp. 34–36; see also E. Martin Browne and Henzie Browne, *Two in One* (Cambridge: Cambridge Univ. Press, 1981), pp. 91–100, and Kenneth W. Pickering, *Drama in the Cathedral: The Canterbury Festival Plays, 1928–1948* (Worthing: Churchman, 1985), pp. 178–95.

2. "Mr. Eliot's New Essays," *Times Literary Supplement*, 6 Dec. 1928, p. 953, as cited by John D. Margolis, *T. S. Eliot's Intellectual Development, 1922–1939* (Chicago: Univ. of Chicago Press, 1972), p. 114. Eliot's previous interest in medievalism has been, however, well documented; see, for example, Leo Shapiro, "The Medievalism of T. S. Eliot," *Poetry*, 56 (1940), 202–13, who notes that approximately half of the notes to *The Waste Land* "relate directly or indirectly to medieval culture" (p. 202).

3. Browne, *The Making of T. S. Eliot's Plays*, p. 36.

4. Chambers, *The Mediaeval Stage*, II, 344–45, 374; Tancred Borenius, *St. Thomas Becket in Art* (1932; rpt. Port Washington, N.Y.: Kennikat Press, 1970), p. 70, who further cites Thomas Wright, "On the Municipal Archives of the City of

Canterbury," *Archaeologia*, 31 (1846), 207–09; Arthur P. Stanley, *Historical Memorials of Canterbury*, 11th ed. (London, 1887), p. 223. Chambers' work was considered the standard study of medieval English drama, and quite appropriately is the primary work on drama recommended in a Bibliographic Note following the chapter on Latin Poetry in Charles Homer Haskins, *The Renaissance of the Twelfth Century* (1927; rpt. New York: Meridian, 1957), p. 192; this bibliography was especially recommended in T. S. Eliot's review of Haskins' book in the *Times Literary Supplement*, 11 Aug. 1927, p. 542. For notice of a review of Borenius' book in the *Criterion*, see below and note 55. Dean Stanley's guide was a widely known and much reprinted introduction to the story of Becket and his cult.

5. Alan H. Nelson, *The Medieval English Stage* (Chicago: Univ. of Chicago Press, 1974), p. 204.

6. Chambers, *The Mediaeval Stage*, II, 345. See also the more recent research of Giles Dawson, *Records of Plays and Players in Kent, 1450–1642*, Malone Society Collections, 7 (Oxford, 1965), pp. 188–98, and also the survey in Clifford Davidson, "The Middle English Saint Play and Its Iconography," in *The Saint Play in Medieval Europe*, ed. Clifford Davidson, Early Drama, Art, and Music, Monograph Ser., 8 (Kalamazoo: Medieval Institute Publications, 1986), pp. 52–58.

7. *Records of Plays and Players in Norfolk and Suffolk, 1330–1642*, ed. John Wasson and David Galloway, Malone Society Collections, 11 (Oxford, 1980–81), p. 190.

8. *A Calendar of Dramatic Records in the Books of the Livery Companies of London, 1485–1640*, ed. Jean Robertson and D. J. Gordon, Malone Society Collections, 3 (Oxford, 1954), pp. 3–4.

9. Browne, *The Making of T. S. Eliot's Plays*, p. 55. In December 1934, when he was working on *Murder in the Cathedral*, Eliot saw two medieval plays, an Annunciation from the N-town cycle and a continental Nativity, produced by E. Martin Browne and his wife at a parish church in Sussex.

10. Pollard's anthology, which attracted considerable interest in the United States, was an important school text that had already gone through five editions by 1909; see also the discussion by David Bevington, "Drama Editing and Its Relation to Recent Trends in Literary Criticism," in *Editing Early English Drama: Special Problems and New Procedures*, ed. A. F. Johnston (New York: AMS Press, 1987), pp. 19–22.

218

11. T. S. Eliot, "Poetry and Drama," in *Selected Prose*, ed. John Hayward (Harmondsworth: Penguin, 1953), p. 77. Very likely Eliot would also have been familiar with John M. Manly's edition of *Pre-Shaksperean Drama* (1897), of which the first volume includes examples of early drama ranging from tropes to the allegorical moralities. The tempting of a hero who is also a Mankind figure does not take place in *Everyman*, but seems otherwise fairly characteristic of the morality genre, if we can judge from *Mankind* and *The Castle of Perseverance*. The influence of *Everyman* on the structure and theme of *Murder in the Cathedral* is overestimated by Martin L. Kornbluth, "A Twentieth-Century *Everyman*," *College English*, 21 (1959), 26–29. See the more balanced assessment by Grover Smith, Jr., *T. S. Eliot's Poetry and Plays* (Chicago: Univ. of Chicago Press, 1956), p. 192.

12. Herbert Howarth, *Notes on Some Figures Behind T. S. Eliot* (Boston: Houghton Mifflin, 1964), p. 147.

13. Joseph Wood Krutch, "The Holy Blissful Martyr," *Nation*, 142 (1936), 460.

14. Lionel J. Pike, "Liturgy and Time in Counterpoint: A View of T. S. Eliot's *Murder in the Cathedral*," *Modern Drama*, 23 (1980), 277.

15. David E. Jones, *The Plays of T. S. Eliot* (Toronto: Univ. of Toronto Press, 1960), p. 51.

16. See *Christian Rite and Christian Drama in the Middle Ages*, pp. 18–25.

17. *Of the Laws of Ecclesiastical Polity* V.lvii.3; quoted in *Anglicanism*, ed. More and Cross, p. 408.

18. For an earlier reading of this passage, see the 1935 acting edition, as cited by Pickering, *Drama in the Cathedral*, p. 184.

19. T. S. Eliot, *The Complete Poems and Plays, 1909–1950* (London: Faber and Faber, 1971), p. 198. On the theology of the Mass as sacrifice, see for convenience *The Oxford Dictionary of the Christian Church*, 2nd ed., ed. F. L. Cross (Oxford: Oxford Univ. Press, 1974), p. 1221.

20. Harrison, *Ancient Art and Ritual*, p. 26.

21. Ibid., p. 127.

22. Ibid., p. 126.

23. T. S. Eliot, "Dramatis Personae," *Criterion*, 1 (1923), 305–06.

24. See Margolis, *T. S. Eliot's Intellectual Development*, p. 182.

25. T. S. Eliot, "Dialogue on Dramatic Poetry," in *Selected Essays* (New York: Harcourt Brace, 1950), p. 35.

26. T. S. Eliot, "Religious Drama: Medieval and Modern," *University of Edinburgh Review*, 9, No. 1 (Autumn 1937), 10.

27. See Jones, *The Plays of T. S. Eliot*, p. 79, and also Helen Gardner, *The Art of T. S. Eliot* (1949; rpt. London: Faber and Faber, 1969), p. 138.

28. Owen Barfield, *Saving the Appearances* (London: Faber and Faber, 1957).

29. Eliot, "Poetry and Drama," p. 78.

30. Robert Speaight, "With Becket in *Murder in the Cathedral*," in *T. S. Eliot: The Man and His Work*, ed. Allen Tate (New York: Delacorte Press, 1966), p. 187.

31. See Edna G. Sharoni, "'Peace' and 'Unbar the Door': T. S. Eliot's *Murder in the Cathedral*," *Comparative Drama*, 6 (1972), 135–53.

32. Eliot, "Poetry and Drama," pp. 78–79. Eliot's actual statement is that he "may, for aught I know, have been slightly under the influence of *St. Joan.*"

33. W. H. Auden, "The Martyr as Dramatic Hero," *Listener*, 4 Jan. 1968, p. 2.

34. Cf. William V. Spanos, *The Christian Tradition in Modern British Verse* (New Brunswick, N.J.: Rutgers Univ. Press, 1967), pp. 93–104; Michael T. Beehler, "*Murder in the Cathedral*: The Countersacramental Play of Signs," *Genre*, 10 (1977), 329–30.

35. Eliot, *Complete Poems and Plays*, p. 186.

36. Ibid., p. 211.

37. Browne, *The Making of T. S. Eliot's Plays*, p. 43.

38. Cf. Spanos, *The Christian Tradition*, p. 89. For a further echo of the Crucifixion in this play, see John P. Cutts, "Evidence for Ambivalence of Motives in *Murder in the Cathedral*," *Comparative Drama*, 8 (1974), 202, 209. Cutts suggests echoes of the *Stabat Mater*.

39. Eliot, *Complete Poems and Plays*, p. 202.

40. See, for example, the illumination in the *Très Riches Heures* of the Duke of Berry; see Erwin Panofsky, *Early Netherlandish Painting* (1953; rpt. New York: Harper and Row, 1971), II, fig. 90. Eliot may further have known that one March day, the twenty-fifth, was reputed according to tradition to have been not only the day of the Annunciation to Mary but also the original day of the Crucifixion.

41. Cf. William J. McGill, "Voices in the Cathedral: The Chorus in Eliot's *Murder in the Cathedral*," *Modern Drama*, 23 (1980), 295, and see also Karl P. Wentersdorf, "The Symbolic Significance of *Figurae Scatologicae* in Gothic Manuscripts," in *Word, Picture, and Spectacle*, ed. Clifford Davidson, Early Drama, Art, and Music, Monograph Ser., 5 (Kalamazoo: Medieval Institute Publications, 1984), pp. 1–19.

42. Eliot, *Complete Poems and Plays*, p. 214.

43. A facsimile, prepared by Bernhard Bischoff under the title *Carmina Burana*, was published by the Institute of Medieval Music in 1967; the figure of Fortune and her wheel appears on fol. 1. There is a possibility that Eliot would have known the *Carmina Burana* through the edition of J. A. Schmeller (3rd ed., Breslau, 1897), recommended by Haskins in his Bibliographic Note appended to the chapter on Latin poetry in his *Renaissance of the Twelfth Century*, p. 192.

44. See Eliot's anonymous review of Haskins' *Renaissance of the Twelfth Century* in the *Times Literary Supplement*, 11 Aug. 1927, p. 542.

45. Howarth, *Notes on Some Figures*, pp. 199–200.

46. Eliot, *Complete Poems and Plays*, p. 184.

47. See especially Louis L. Martz, "The Wheel and the Point: Aspects of Imagery and Theme in Eliot's Later Poetry," in *T. S. Eliot: A Selected Critique*, ed.

Leonard Unger (New York: Rinehart, 1948), pp. 444–62; Donna Gerstenberger, "The Saint and the Circle: The Dramatic Potential of an Image," *Criticism*, 2 (1960), 336–41.

48. See Shapiro, "The Medievalism of T. S. Eliot," pp. 205–06.

49. Eliot, *Complete Poems and Plays*, p. 67.

50. Eliot, "Poetry and Drama," p. 78.

51. See J. T. Boulton, "The Use of Original Sources for the Development of a Theme: Eliot in *Murder in the Cathedral*," *English*, 11 (1956), 3–8. The sources surveyed are those printed in translation in *English Historical Documents*, II: *1142–1189*, ed. David C. Douglas and George W. Greenway (New York: Oxford Univ. Press, 1953), pp. 698–769.

52. Browne, *The Making of T. S. Eliot's Plays*, p. 41.

53. Boulton, "The Use of Original Sources," pp. 3–8.

54. Eliot, "Poetry and Drama," p. 78.

55. *Criterion*, 12 (1932–33), 142–44. See also Howarth, *Notes on Some Figures*, pp. 267–68, for further comment and for notice of an anonymous review of Herbert Read's *English Stained Glass* in the *Criterion*, 6 (1927), 474–75, and of Sidney Dark's spiky *St. Thomas of Canterbury* (London: Macmillan, 1927).

56. *South English Legendary*, as quoted by Borenius, *St. Thomas Becket in Art*, p. 8; cf. *The South English Legendary*, Pt. 2, ed. Charlotte d'Evelyn and Anna J. Mill, EETS, o.s. 236 (London, 1956), pp. 671–72.

57. *South English Legendary*, p. 671.

58. The Christmas sermon, which in Eliot's play emphasizes not only the Incarnation but also the Crucifixion, was historically delivered on a Friday (see Stanley, *Historical Memorials*, p. 68), the day of the week on which Christmas fell in 1170; Friday was, as everyone knows, the day of the Crucifixion.

59. Wormald, p. 143. Except for an experimental attempt, after the transfer of the play to the theater, to place Becket in Eucharistic garb for the sermon—an

attempt that was judged unsatisfactory—the protagonist of *Murder in the Cathedral* wore Benedictine garments, to which he added a cloak for travel; see Browne, *The Making of T. S. Eliot's Plays*, p. 62.

60. *Liber Usualis* (Tournai: Desclée, 1961), pp. 437–38.

61. Browne, *The Making of T. S. Eliot's Plays*, p. 48.

62. *Legenda aurea*, trans. William Caxton (London, 1483), fol. lxvi^v.

63. Speaight, "With Becket in *Murder in the Cathedral*," p. 184.

64. Clifford Davidson, "Types of Despair in 'Ash Wednesday'," *Renascence*, 18 (1966), 216–18.

65. Eliot's verse and plays have, of course, proved to be more personal than was previously thought. See especially the biography by Lyndall Gordon, *Eliot's New Life* (New York: Farrar, Straus, Giroux, 1988), *passim*.

66. *The Life of Saint Meriasek*, ed. and trans. Whitley Stokes (London: Trübner, 1872), p. 265.

67. Eliot, *Complete Poems and Plays*, p. 213.

68. Boulton, "The Use of Original Sources," p. 5.

69. *The Late Medieval Religious Plays of Bodleian MSS Digby 133 and e museo 160*, ed. Donald C. Baker, John L. Murphy, and Louis B. Hall, EETS, 283 (London, 1983), p. 94; translation of this passage is from David Bevington, *Medieval Drama* (Boston: Houghton Mifflin, 1975), p. 752.

70. Eliot, "Poetry and Drama," p. 79.

Chapter 10
Modern and Medieval

1. Interview on National Public Radio, 1 Nov. 1990.

2. The Museum's brochure, written by Deni McIntosh McHenry, also notes Dine's untypical "willingness to confront art from the past, to deal directly with

tradition," in this case the classical tradition observed in examples of the art of antiquity at the Glyptothek in Munich. Dine, who received early attention for his untraditional role in "Happenings," is usually thought of as a representative of Pop Art.

3. On Isidore's influence, see especially Joseph R. Jones, "Isidore and the Theater," *Comparative Drama*, 16 (1982), 26–48.

4. See Hardison, *Christian Rite and Christian Drama in the Middle Ages*, pp. 1-34, for the classic refutation of the biological-evolutionary model.

5. Text in Young, *The Drama of the Medieval Church*, I, 249-50; see also Sheingorn, *The Easter Sepulchre in England*, p. 20, and facsimiles in figs. 3-4.

6. See especially David Bevington, "Discontinuity in Medieval Acting Traditions," *The Elizabethan Theatre, V*, ed. G. R. Hibbard (New York: Archon, 1975), pp. 1-16.

7. While careful examination of the conditions of staging medieval drama may be said to date from Thomas Sharp's *Dissertation on the Mysteries* (1825), Glynne Wickham's *Early English Stages*, Vol. I (London: Routledge and Kegan Paul, 1959), must be given credit for stirring renewed interest in such study. The use of pageant wagons seems to have been a regional practice in England, for they were hardly universal even there in spite of the fame of such staging in various municipalities. The Lille plays, which are being edited by Alan E. Knight, appear to be unique among continental dramas in that they were presented on wagons rather than on fixed stages; see Knight's "Manuscript Painting and Play Production: Evidence from the Processional Plays of Lille," *EDAM Newsletter*, 9 (1986), 1–7.

8. Clifford Davidson, "Positional Symbolism and Medieval English Drama," *Comparative Drama*, 25 (1991), 66–76.

9. Mary Douglas, *Natural Symbols: Explorations in Cosmology* (New York: Pantheon, 1982), p. 51.

10. Davidson, "Positional Symbolism," p. 69.

11. See Darryll Grantley, "The National Theatre's Production of *The Mysteries*: Some Observations," *Theatre Notebook*, 40 (1986), 70-73.

12. Stanton B. Garner, Jr., "Visual Field in Beckett's Late Plays," *Comparative Drama*, 21 (1987-88), 349–73.

13. Martin Esslin, *The Field of Drama* (London: Methuen, 1987), p. 42.

14. Pamela Sheingorn, "The Visual Language of Drama: Principles of Composition," in *Contexts for Early English Drama*, ed. Marianne Briscoe and John C. Coldewey (Bloomington: Indiana Univ. Press, 1989), p. 173.

15. See Harrison, *Ancient Art and Ritual*, pp. 26, 37–48.

16. Furnivall, *Digby Plays*, p. xiii.

17. *The Staging of Religious Drama*, ed. Meredith and Tailby, p. 107.

18. Pamela M. King and Asuncion Salvador-Rabaza, "La Festa d'Elx: The Assumption of the Virgin, Elche (Alicante)," *Medieval English Theatre*, 8 (1986), 21-50.

19. *The Staging of Religious Drama*, ed. Meredith and Tailby, pp. 95-96.

20. Text by T. S. Eliot; for the music, see Andrew Lloyd Webber, *Cats: The Songs from the Musical* (London: Faber Music, n.d.), p. 106.

21. See Meyer Schapiro, "The Image of the Disappearing Christ," *Late Antique, Early Christian and Mediaeval Art* (New York: George Braziller, 1979), pp. 266-87.

22. *A Middle English Treatise on the Playing of Miracles*, ed. Davidson, p. 40.

23. Ibid., pp. 35, 60-61.

24. T. Northcote Toller, *An Anglo-Saxon Dictionary: Supplement* (1921; rpt. London: Oxford Univ. Press, 1955), p. 708, *s.v. spilere*.

25. Jocelyn Price, "Theatrical Vocabulary in Old English: A Preliminary Survey," *Medieval English Theatre*, 5 (1983), 62.

26. *OED*, *s.v. player* (I.4); the word also, of course, designated one who performs music on an instrument (I.5).

27. Hildegard of Bingen, *Ordo Virtutum*, ed. Audrey Ekdahl Davidson (Kalamazoo: Medieval Institute Publications, 1985).

28. "'Sponsus' at Kalamazoo," *Medieval Music-Drama News*, 6 (Summer 1987), 6.

29. *The Wakefield Pageants in the Towneley Cycle*, ed. Cawley, pp. 1-13; on the date of the manuscript, see especially Alexandra F. Johnston's review of the facsimile edition of the Towneley manuscript in *Renaissance and Reformation*, n.s. 1 (1977), 167-68.

30. *The Holkham Bible Picture Book*, ed. W. O. Hassall (London: Dropmore Press, 1954), fol. 5.

31. Text by Alain Robbe-Grillet, trans. Richard Howard (New York: Grove Press, 1962).

32. Transcription by Angelo Raine, as quoted by Barbara Palmer, "'Towneley Plays' or 'Wakefield Plays' Revisited," *Comparative Drama*, 21 (1987-88), 342.

33. Pär Lagerkvist, *The Eternal Smile and Other Stories*, trans. Alan Blair *et al.* (New York: Random House, 1954), pp. 55ff.

34. Bergman, *A Film Trilogy*, pp. 57–59. Karin's report of her experience is as follows: "The door opened. But the god who came out was a spider. He had six legs and moved very fast across the floor. . . . He came up to me and I saw his face, a loathsome, evil face. And he clambered up onto me and tried to force himself into me. But I protected myself. All the time I saw his eyes. They were cold and calm. When he couldn't force himself into me, he climbed quickly up onto my breast and went on up the wall. . . . I've seen God."

35. Ibid., pp. 99-104.

36. Following the traditional liturgy in the *Ordning för den Allmanna Gudstjänsten*; see above, chap. 1.

37. For a survey of the current state of knowlege about the texts and records of English medieval drama, see Ian Lancashire, *Dramatic Texts and Records of Britain: A Chronological Topography to 1558* (Toronto: Univ. of Toronto Press, 1984).

226

38. Ingram, ed., *Coventry*, p. xix.

39. John R. Elliot, Jr., *Playing God: Medieval Mysteries on the Modern Stage* (Toronto: Univ. of Toronto Press, 1989), p. 47.

40. E. Martin Browne and Henzie Browne, *Two in One* (Cambridge: Cambridge Univ. Press, 1981), p. 65.

41. Ibid., p. 72.

42. Ibid., pp. 65–66; see also Elliott, *Playing God*, pp. 46–54.

43. *The English Churchman*, 2 April 1931, as quoted in Browne and Browne, *Two in One*, p. 64.

44. See Robinson, *Studies in Fifteenth-Century Stagecraft*, pp. 1–15, and Elliott, *Playing God*, pp. 44–70.

45. The film was *One Summer of Happiness*, directed by Arne Mattson and in Swedish; see the *Minneapolis Star*, 27 Feb. 1953; for a review, see the (London) *Times*, 5 Mar. 1953, p. 10.

46. Tony Harrison, *The Mysteries* (London: Faber and Faber, 1985).

47. See Elliott, *Playing God*, pp. 25–40.

48. See especially the discussion in Barish, *The Anti-Theatrical Prejudice*, pp. 45–47.

49. Canon 5; quoted by Christine Catharina Schnusenberg, *The Relationship between the Church and the Theatre, Exemplified by Selected Writings of the Church Fathers and by Liturgical Texts until Amalarius of Metz* (Lanham, Maryland: Univ. Press of America, 1988), p. 36.

50. J. A. A. Ogilvy, "*Mimi, Scurrae, Histriones*: Entertainers of the Early Middle Ages," *Speculum*, 38 (1963), 608-12; Richard Axton, *European Drama of the Early Middle Ages* (London: Hutchinson, 1974), p. 19; Chambers, *The Mediaeval Stage*, I, 32n.

51. John of Salisbury, *Frivolities of Courtiers and Footprints of Philosophers*, trans. Joseph B. Pike (Minneapolis: Univ. of Minnesota Press, 1938), p. 39.

52. *Summa Theologica*, II, ii, Q. 168, Art. 3, Reply Obj. 3; I quote from the translation by the Fathers of the English Dominican Province (New York: Benziger, 1947) (italics mine).

53. In Robert of Brunne's *Handlyng Synne*, miracle plays, presumably in the open air, are condemned, but not the playing of the Resurrection and Nativity "in the cherche": "That is to seye, how God ros/ . . . with flesshe and blode;/ And he may pleye withoutyn plight/ howe God was bore in yole night" (ed. F. J. Furnivall, EETS, o.s., 119 [1901], p. 155). Such Resurrection and Nativity dramas would probably be liturgical plays.

54. For the texts of this more elaborate type of *Visitatio Sepulchri*—a type which includes the race of Peter and John to the sepulcher and additionally Christ's appearance to Mary Magdalene, scenes which were absent in the earliest and most rudimentary forms of the play," see Lipphardt, ed., *Lateinische Osterfeiern und Osterspiele*, V, 1455-1607.

55. See especially Sheingorn, *The Easter Sepulchre in England*, pp. 33-45.

56. Young, *The Drama of the Medieval Church*, I, 112-48.

57. *Summa Theologica* II, ii, Q. 13, Art. 1.

58. Ibid., II, ii, Q. 13, Art. 3, Reply Obj. 1.

59. John Webster Melody, "Blasphemy," *Catholic Encyclopedia*, II (1913), 595.

60. *Kalamazoo Gazette*, 14 Sept. 1988.

61. Hardison, *Christian Rite and Christian Drama in the Middle Ages*, pp. 56-59; Schnusenberg, *The Relationship between the Church and the Theatre*, pp. 278-81.

62. Lynette Muir, *Liturgy and Drama in the Anglo-Norman Adam*, Medium Aevum Monographs, 3 (Oxford: Blackwell, 1973), p. 15.

63. *York*, ed. Johnston and Rogerson, I, 43; trans. ibid., II, 728.

64. Ibid., I, 158.

65. Ibid., I, 109.

66. *Coventry*, ed. Ingram, p. 264.

67. *York*, ed. Johnston and Rogerson, I, 55.

68. *The Staging of Religious Drama*, ed. Meredith and Tailby, p. 144.

69. See especially the review by Grantley, "The National Theatre's Production of the *Mysteries*," pp. 70–73; see also my "Positional Symbolism and English Medieval Drama," pp. 66–76.

70. *York*, ed. Johnston and Rogerson, I, 47-48.

71. *A Middle English Treatise on the Playing of Miracles*, ed. Davidson, pp. 40-41, 46.

72. *York*, ed. Johnston and Rogerson, I, 352–53 (italics mine).

73. Ibid., I, 353.

74. *Tudor Royal Proclamations*, ed. Paul L. Hughes and James F. Larkin (New Haven: Yale Univ. Press, 1964), II, 123.

75. *Chester*, ed. Lawrence Clopper, Records of Early English Drama (Toronto: Univ. of Toronto Press, 1979), pp. 248, 252.

76. *Cumberland, Westmorland, Gloucestershire*, ed. Audrey Douglas and Peter Greenfield, Records of Early English Drama (Toronto: Univ. of Toronto Press, 1986), pp. 168ff, 219.

77. See Nichols, "Books–for–Laymen: The Demise of a Commonplace," pp. 457–73.

78. *Cumberland, Westmorland, Gloucestershire*, p. 219.

79. William Lambarde, *A Perambulation in Kent*, revised ed. (London, 1826), p. 205.

80. Lambarde, *Dictionarium Angliae Topographicum et Historicum*, pp. 459–60.

81. Ibid., p. 460.

82. See Elliott, *Playing God*, pp. 17–24.

83. See Robert Speaight, *William Poel and the Elizabethan Revival* (London: William Heinemann, 1954), Pl. facing p. 224. Only through a technicality was Poel's production of *Everyman* declared to be not covered by the Blasphemy Act, since the play had been written before the passage of this specific legislation; see Robert Potter, *The English Morality Play* (London: Routledge and Kegan Paul, 1975), p. 246.

84. Browne and Browne, *Two in One*, pp. 191-94. For a survey of modern productions of English medieval drama, see Elliott, *Playing God*, and also Robinson, *Fifteenth-Century Stagecraft*, pp. 1–15. These sources need to be supplemented for the period since c.1980.

85. Harrison, *The Mysteries*, p. 38.

86. See the program notes in the booklet entitled *The Making of the Mysteries* (1985).

87. Davidson and Nichols, eds., *Iconoclasm vs. Art and Drama*, pp. xxii–xiv.

88. Published at London in 1697.

Index

231

AMS Studies in the Middle Ages. No. 20
ISSN: 0270-6261

Other titles in this series:

1. Josiah C. Russell. *Twelfth Century Studies,* 1978.

2. Joachim Bumke. *The Concept of Knighthood in the Middle Ages.* Trans. W.T.H. Jackson and Erika Jackson. 1982.

3. Donald K. Fry. *Norse Sagas Translated into English: A Bibliography.* 1980.

4. Clifford Davidson, C.J. Gianakaris, and John Stroupe, eds. *Drama in the Middle Ages,* 1982.

5. Clifford Davidson. *From Creation to Doom: The York Cycle of Mystery Plays* 1984.

6. Edith Yenal. *Charles d'Orléans: A Bibliography of Primary and Secondary Sources.* 1984.

7. Joel T. Rosenthal. *Anglo-Saxon History: An Annotated Bibliography, 450-1066.* 1985.

8. Theodore John Rivers. *Laws of Salian and Ripuarian Franks.* 1988.

9. R.C. Famiglietti. *Royal Intrigue: Crisis at the Court of Charles VI, 1392-1420.* 1986.

10. Barry Gaines. Sir Thomas Malory: *An Anecdotal Bibliography of Editions, 1485-1985.* 1990.

11. Milla Cozart Riggio, ed. *The Wisdom Symposium.* 1986.

12. Josiah Cox Russell. *Medieval Demography.* 1988.

13. J. Bard McNulty. *The Narrative Art of the Bayeux Tapestry Master.* 1989.

15. Donald Gilman, ed. *Everyman and Company: Essays on the Theme and Structure of the European Moral Play.* 1989.

16. Clifford Davidson. *Visualizing the Moral Life: Medieval Iconography and the Macro Moralities.* 1989.

17. Deborah M. Sinnreich-Levi and Gale Sigal, eds. *Voices in Translation: The Authority of "Olde Bookes" in Medieval Literature.* 1992.

18. Clifford Davidson and John H. Stroupe, eds. *Drama in the Middle Ages.* Second Series. 1991.

19. D. Thomas Hanks, ed. *Sir Thomas Malory: Views and Re-Views.* 1992.